Published in 2014 by aspye
Printed by Lavenham Press Ltd
ISBN 978-0-9558797-8-4

Churchill's

"MOST SECRET"

Special Duties Branch

Limited Edition

Acknowledgements

We drew regularly on the advice of David Hunt whom we wish to thank most profoundly for generously sharing his expert knowledge as a retired senior Army officer, together with his World War 2 and Aux Units research. We are indebted to Brian Drury for his kind permission to use some of his photographs and for finding the charging instructions for a 6-volt 72 AH battery, as well as the explanation for Freddie's shoulder flash. Our heartfelt thanks must also go to Colin Anderson, Katie Hart and Harry Townsend for their kind permission to use some of their photographs. We would also like to offer our grateful thanks to the farmers, landowners, gamekeepers and estate managers for kindly permitting access onto their land; to Mrs Jill Monk and Ms Barbara Culleton for so generously sharing their memories with us; to Mr GW Hammond for taking us to the message drop locations he used as a runner, aged only 15; to Mr F Greengrass for keeping safe for 25 years some artefacts rescued from an IN Station; to Mr R Howard for keeping vandals at bay; to Mr and Mrs Fidgem for kindly permitting access into their loft; and to the Appell family for kindly sharing copies of all the papers given by Arthur Gabbitas to their predecessors at Bachelor's Hall in Hundon. A big thank you must also go to George Brown, curator, and to the Trustees of the British Resistance Organisation Museum (BROM) in Parham, Suffolk, for generously permitting access to their archive; and to the friendly and helpful staff at the National Archives (TNA) and the Imperial War Museum (IWM). Our special thanks go to the many people we have met in the course of our research, who readily and courteously offered information and advice. To list them all by name would go beyond the scope of this book.

Every effort has been made to trace the ownership of the illustrative material reproduced in this book, and written material quoted. If any copyright holders have been inadvertently overlooked the publishers will be pleased to make the necessary arrangements at the first opportunity.

Relevant contemporary terms rather than modern substitutes were used throughout the text. Thus reinforced underground shelters are not referred to as bunkers (a relatively recent addition to the English language derived from the German word 'Bunker') but dugouts and the term 'wireless' was given preference over 'radio', as in the UK in the 1940s (radio) receivers or transceivers were commonly called wireless sets.

Please note that almost all the locations mentioned in this book are situated on private land and must not be accessed without the owner/s' permission. No liability can be accepted for any loss or damage caused by attempts to reach or by visiting the locations described.

Contents:

Pencilled annotations on generator room wall at Halstead IN Station (Essex)

Preface

A number of books have already been written about the history of the operational patrols of the British Resistance Organisation, the Auxiliary Units (AU), which were made up almost entirely of stay-behind civilians trained to sabotage and harass the enemy in the event of an invasion. At the same time a network of civilian observers and spies was set up whose task it was to also stay behind, but rather than to sabotage they were to observe enemy troops and their movements, and to pass on any information and all of their observations to secret wireless stations, the so-called OUT Stations. These stations were operated by civilians who had a legitimate reason to be seen out and about, such as doctors, postmen and women, milk roundsmen, school teachers, midwives, vicars and of course farmers. The civilian spy network is said to have consisted of about 3250 men and women. They all had to sign the Official Secrets Act, and, like the men who were part of the sabotage branch of Auxiliary Units, only very few ever talked about their experience, and when some finally broke their silence it was decades after the event.

Because of the great secrecy involved, information about the secret wireless networks, set up by and run by AU Signals in cooperation with the AU Auxiliary Territorial Service (ATS), is scarce. The unit was officially referred to as the Special Duties Branch of GHQ Home Forces Aux Units. Not only did everybody involved have to sign the Official Secrets Act; they were also forbidden to mention their activities even to close family members. Furthermore, the sophisticated technology of the wireless networks - including the wireless sets used, of which no trace remains, and the fact that the various 'players' were kept in small, self-contained groups or cells, that they were deliberately not informed about what exactly they were doing, and that they had little personal contact with each other for the duration of the war, had the desired effect: the eyewitnesses who talked about their experiences decades later, knew next to nothing. It was also common practice to move the ATS subalterns, the signallers and even the Intelligence Officers (IOs) to new locations every so often. Kitty Hills, one of the longest-serving AU ATS subalterns, for instance, is known to have worked in at least five different IN Stations, and Lieutenant Frank Oakey (Royal Signals) appears to have served as the Intelligence officer (IO) for at least three different regions in three years.

The authors have tried, to the best of their knowledge, to shed some light onto how the Special Duties Branch of the Auxiliary Units worked and who was involved. Not many of the secret files and documents have survived and those that have are now available to the public, provided they can be found and identified in the vast archives of the Imperial War Museum and the National Archives. Interviews and eyewitness accounts, based on the recollections of events which happened 70 years ago, are also available. However, as all good historians (and interrogators) know, "if there is a delay, the memory stops recollecting what happened and begins to rationalise how it happened" (Peter Wright, former assistant director of MI5 in *Spycatcher*). For this reason information based on memory is more often than not confused and unreliable.

How it all began

After the surrender of France on 22 June 1940 and with German forces now occupying the French coast, the Prime Minister, Sir Winston Churchill, called for highly secret units - officially they were to be known by the nondescript name of "Auxiliary Units" - to be created with the aim of resisting the threat of invasion and occupation of the United Kingdom by Nazi Germany.

The key figure in establishing this resistance organisation was Colonel (later Major General) Sir Colin McVean Gubbins KCMG, DSO, MC - a Special Operations Executive (SOE) officer in the employ of Military Intelligence (Research) [MI(R)]. Gubbins was born in Tokyo and educated at Cheltenham College and at the Royal Military Academy in Woolwich. Commissioned into the Royal Field Artillery in 1914 he served as an officer in a battery on the Western Front, where he was wounded and later awarded the Military Cross. In 1919, he joined the staff of General Sir Edmund Ironside in the North Russia Campaign. After a period spent in Signals Intelligence at the General Headquarters (GHQ) India, Gubbins graduated from the Staff College at Quetta in 1928, and in 1931 was appointed as a General Staff Officer (GSO) in the Russian Section of the War Office. His posting in April 1933, as a Brigade Major RA of 4th Division HQ East Anglian District at Colchester, where one of his tasks was to organise the Territorial Army (TA) annual camps and field firing exercises, for the first time brought Colin Gubbins into contact with a great many enthusiastic part-time soldiers. After his promotion to Brevet Major in 1935 he joined MI1. In October 1938, in the aftermath of the Munich Agreement, he was sent to the Sudetenland as a military member of the International Commission. After his promotion to Brevet Lieutenant-Colonel, he, in April 1939, joined the General Staff (Research) branch [GS(R)] in the War Office, which was later to become MI(R), where he wrote training manuals on irregular warfare including *The Partisan Leader's Handbook, The Art of Guerrilla Warfare* and *How To Use High Explosives* - the latter was co-authored by Millis Jefferis (Major-General Sir Millis Rowland Jefferis, KBE, MC), a MI(R) explosives expert.

On 2 June 1940, Colonel Gubbins was tasked with raising the Auxiliary Units, which he briefly commanded. On 20 October of the same year he joined the SOE as the Director of Operations.

In a taped interview conducted after the war and broadcast, in 1998, in the BBC Radio programme "Secret Army", Sir Colin was asked if he really believed that the secret resistance organisation set up by him would have had any impact, had the Germans invaded. His reply was as follows:

> "We British are not really conspiratorial. It would have taken us some time in Britain before we could have made a really valid contribution, I think, to a serious resistance."

As already mentioned, the resistance organisation consisted of two distinct parts, one for guerrilla activities by small groups (called operational patrols) of stay-behind civilians, trained to operate from underground hides, and the other for intelligence work. Both were to operate in areas occupied by the Germans in the event of an invasion. The role of the operational patrols was to disrupt communications, destroy fuel and ammunition dumps and to harass and inconvenience the enemy in any way possible, but not to damage the essential infrastructure of the country. Bridges, rail and road links, canals and waterways, telephone lines and other existing lines of communications were to be left intact and in working order, as the Army's counter-attacks to push out the invaders would be made so much easier if it did not have to contend with blown bridges and destroyed roads. The first of these patrols were organised in Kent and by the end of the year there were about 300 of them in various counties along the coast. Their members wore Home Guard uniforms, but kept themselves very much to themselves.

At about the same time, a second but completely separate part of the organisation, the Special Duties Branch (SD), was set up and selected civilian volunteers in the most threatened coastal areas of Britain who were trained to, in the event of German occupation, act as observers (spies) and report on German military activities from within the occupied area. Observers were soon to deposit their reports in dead letter drops, to be collected by runners, who would then have delivered them to secret wireless stations (called OUT Stations), where civilian operators transmitted the reports to military manned IN Stations outside the occupied area. The IN Station then delivered the reports, sometimes by dispatch rider or, more commonly, by telephone to the appropriate Army HQ. David Hunt has established that typically, IN-Stations were some 25 or more kilometres (15 miles) inland; while OUT Stations might be up to 15 kilometres (10 miles) inland with the majority being located within about 8 kilometres (5 miles) of the coast (personal communication). The majority of IN Stations consisted of a purpose-built hut. During 1942 concealed dugouts were also constructed. If the enemy occupied the area, these IN Station dugouts could operate closed down for up to 21 days. Researcher David Hunt believes that in case the HQ the station served had to withdraw, wireless links to other, more rearward stations, called the Inner Network, would enable incoming intelligence reports to be re-routed to a new HQ site. GHQ Home Forces Aux Units controlled both the AU operational patrols and the work of the Special Duties Branch but although the patrols and the SD spy networks often worked in the same areas, neither was aware of the existence or roles of the other.

On 29 August 1941, Field Marshal Lord Alanbrooke (then General Sir Alan Brooke) - the Commander in Chief Home Forces - wrote in his *War Diary*:

> "Left at 8.30am to spend a day with the auxiliary units in Kent and Sussex. These units comprise two main elements – one an information one equipped with wireless, and another a sabotage one equipped with explosive and weapons. Both are intended to work behind the enemy in the event of an invasion."

The Special Duties Branch

It is documented in the notes on the approved Army Establishment dating from July 1940 that the Headquarters of the Special Duties Branch (HQ SD), which was already in existence, was attached to the HQ of GHQ Home Forces Auxiliary Units on 22 July 1940 - three weeks after it had been established. (TNA, WO 199/738)

In a "Top Secret" memorandum dating from the summer of 1944, General Sir Harold Edmund Franklyn, the then Commander in Chief of Home Forces in Britain, wrote:

> "There are 10 Areas covering the coastal belt from the North of Scotland down to, but excluding, Devon and Cornwall and including parts of South Wales. Each area is under an IO (Intelligence Officer).
>
> In each area an organisation has been built up of civilians able to transmit accurate information about the enemy in event of raids or invasion.
>
> There are well above 200 R/T (Radio/Telephony) stations situated throughout the coastal areas – mostly concealed underground in dugouts capable of holding three men. These stations are known as OUT Stations and are manned entirely by civilians.
>
> These OUT Stations – which are 'fed' by SUBOUT Stations in many cases – communicate with IN Stations which are manned by Royal Signals personnel and ATS officers.
>
> IN Stations are sited in depth with an inner system established at HQs of Commands.
>
> In order to run the area organisation, the War Establishment allows a total of 14 officers and 15 other ranks (ORs), making a total of 32 (sic). To install, service and generally maintain the RT net, Auxiliary Units Signals requires a total of 152 made up of 75 officers and 69 ORs (which are employed on purely signal maintenance in addition to watch-keeping and assisting in training of civilian personnel) and 57 officers and 3 ORs ATS personnel whose job is watch-keeping, training and assisting in general duties." (The National Archives (TNA, WO 199/738)

In a document dated 28 June 1944, Major RMA Jones, Officer Commanding AU Signals, describes the task of the Special Duties Branch:

> "The Special Duties Branch of Auxiliary Units is organised to provide information for military formations in the event of enemy invasion or raids in Great Britain, from areas temporarily or permanently in enemy control. All this information would be collected as a result of direct observation by specially recruited and trained civilians who would remain in an enemy occupied area. Auxiliary Units Signals are responsible for providing the communications to enable the civilian observers to pass their information to a military HQ. All traffic is by wireless (R/T), using very high frequency sets. Information is

collected at IN Stations (manned by Royal Signals or ATS officers) and is passed from there to mil fmn (military formations). IN Stations have concealed dugouts in which station crew can, if necessary, live without coming above ground at all for three weeks at a time. This includes provision for battery charging, feeding etc." (TNA, WO 199/1194)

The original HQ SD comprised 27 all ranks, two staff officers, 11 Intelligence officers (IOs), each with his own 4-seater car and driver, and a couple of clerks. The 11 IOs were to set up the civilian spy network; signallers had as yet to be taken on board. Six months later (Establishment dated 20 Feb 1941), the SD Branch included from Royal Signals an instrument mechanic and four operators wireless and line (OWLs). All OWLs came from the Royal Corps of Signals (RCS). There is also the following note:

> "The following additional Royal Signals personnel will be allowed for the Special Duties Branch to be filled as and when required: Maj x 1; Capt x 1; Lt x 2; Sgt x 1; Cpl x 2, L/Cpl x 15; Signalmen x 26; Drivers (RASC = *Royal Army Service Corps*) x 6; ATS x 40." (TNA, WO 199/1194)

The first phase of setting up the organisation consisted of establishing a network of civilian spies who would report enemy sightings, activities, and troop movements. They would write their observations on a piece of paper, which was then deposited in one of the network's pre-arranged dead letter drops. Other members of the network, commonly referred to as runners, would collect these messages, hide them in slit tennis balls and deposit these in another dead letter drop or take them direct to an OUT Station once these were established. The designs of dead letter drops varied, with some seemingly having been buried tin cans or lengths of drainage pipes.

Mrs Ursula M Pennell, a civilian observer for the SD Branch, lived near the village of Cley on the North Norfolk coast. She has described how one day she was approached by "a charming young officer", who explained to her that his organisation was in the process of setting up a network of people, three miles apart and about three miles from the coast, who would "stay put" if the Germans came. Would she be interested?

> "The officer explained what I had to do and he told me the names of my contacts. It was a schoolmaster, at the village school in Weybourne, to the east (his name was Edgar Coe and he was the school's headmaster). He was my contact there. The other was a retired schoolmistress at Blakeney that I vaguely knew. If the Germans came I had to gather all, every information I possibly could. I was given leaflets with the badges and uniforms and those things I had to learn and was told that I must never lose them. I kept them in one of my purses or stuck them in my bra wherever I went. I had instructions to destroy them when the Germans came.
>
> I was the only one and I don't know who went inland. I know they did go inland because they did explain to me there were quite a lot of doctors in this, a few doctors anyhow. They were ideal because they had every excuse for going about the countryside and also for communicating with each other. The officer said there were two he knew in my area.

He had a map of our area and something like the X-ray of a person and he put this on top of the map and then they would discuss some medical detail about Mrs so-and-so, something to do with her white lung or what have you, and that would perhaps be North Walsham or something like that, where the Germans had arrived. It was about explaining without mentioning the place; they would use this part of the human body they would speak about. The one doctor came to see me, Ingram, yes, his name was Ingram, I think. I can't be sure." (BBC Radio interview, "Secret Army" 1998)

If the "doctor's" name was indeed Ingram *(sic)* he can only have been Captain Douglas Ingrams, the SD IO who in 1944 co-ordinated the Norfolk spy network. (More about Captain Ingrams on page 140 – Bewley Down OUT Station)

Aux researcher David Hunt believes that initially there were no wireless communications and assumes that runners would have had to cross the "front line" to deliver their reports (pers comm). The Auxiliary Units Signals were subsequently formed, within SD, to take responsibility for providing the communications, which would enable the passing on of information to a military HQ by means of radio/telephony. Captain Ken Ward has confirmed that when he was posted to this newly formed unit – based at Bachelor's Hall in Hundon, Suffolk, in January 1941, its name was "Auxiliary Units Signals". At the time of his arrival a trial wireless network had already been set up and was operating in Kent.

The signallers were soon to be joined by officers from the Auxiliary Territorial Service (ATS), referred to as "Auxiliary Units ATS", with the first volunteers having been hand-picked from among their ranks by the then Chief Controller, Lady Carlisle. The ATS was the women's branch of the British Army in WW2. It was formed in September 1938, initially as a voluntary non-combatant service, acquiring military status in 1941. (In February 1949 it was merged into the Women's Royal Army Corps (WRAC)). The ATS was organised in groups comprising companies and platoons, which were commanded by ATS officers.

During the early phase of the war, ATS personnel were used in support roles only, but due to the great shortage of men, the possible use of women in operational roles was investigated and duly implemented. On 9 May 1941, the ATS was finally given full military status, followed by a Charter allowing for mixed batteries to be formed. Anti-Aircraft Command (Ack-Ack) was the first command to have mixed units.

ATS personnel serving in these mixed batteries were permitted to wear the cap badge of the Regiment or Corps they were attached to – a tradition that was continued until the disbandment of the WRAC in 1990. The ATS officers who were recruited into the Special Duties Branch formed part of AU Signals and it has been documented that at least some of the subalterns wore the Royal Signals badge. All Auxiliary Units (AU operational patrols, AU Signals and AU ATS) were controlled from their HQ based at Coleshill House, a country estate with a large manor house near Swindon on the Berkshire-Wiltshire border.

In early 1942, the Special Duties Branch comprised 135 ATS and 63 officers and other ranks (ORs) from the Royal Signals. Following a revised Establishment, numbers were then reversed in that the strength of ATS officers was reduced to 31 and the number of AU signallers increased to 114 (including ORs and drivers), with effect from May 1942.

On 8 June 1942, Beatrice Temple, then Senior Commander of AU ATS, received instructions to stop recruiting and on 19 June authority was given to her to enrol the last three civilians. By this time the networks covered ten designated regions along the coastal belt, reaching from the north of Scotland to (but excluding) Devon and Cornwall, and including parts of South Wales. Each area was controlled by an IO.

In pre-invasion exercises, OUT Station operators coded and transmitted all the information they received from their observers, via runners, to their local IN Stations, sited according to a system established at Army HQs and Commands. Furthermore, some OUT Station operators would seem to also have acted as the 'Key men' of the local networks. Part of their responsibility was the establishing and maintaining of their networks of observers, the allocation of specific tasks and probably also the vetting of their spies' reports before passing them on to the IN Station. They also liaised between Operational and SD IOs. All the civilian wireless operators, as well as their helpers, the observers and runners, were approved only after detailed background checks had been conducted "by people to whom security was their business" (MI5), recalled Captain (later Colonel) Noel Andrew Cotton Croft DSO, OBE, when referring to the vetting of AU patrol and group leaders.

Some of the AU signallers referred to the OUT Stations as "Coast Stations" because they were commonly situated much closer to the coast than the IN Stations. As General Sir Franklyn explained in his memorandum (see page 6), many of the OUT Stations were 'fed' by SUBOUT Stations and OUT Stations in turn communicated with IN-Stations. David Hunt believes that SUBOUT Stations provided links forward of OUT Stations, often towards the coast, to speed up the passage of information to OUT Stations (pers comm). Ken Ward, however, has caused some confusion by asserting that in his and his colleagues' terminology SUBOUT Stations were referred to as unmanned relay stations or repeaters.

> "At times we had to receive and send from an intermediate area because we could not get the pass. It was a purely hidden device, often up a tree. A chap on a motorbike would go there once a week to change batteries." (Ken Ward in interview conducted by J Warwicker, 10 August 1999; IWM ref: 29472)

The IN Stations (some of the AU signallers referred to them as "Base Stations") were manned by either AU Signals or ATS officers. All IN Stations were sited at locations suitable for wireless transmission, ie on high ground that ideally provided a line of sight path. The information received from their network of OUT Stations was then to be passed on to the Intelligence branch of the Army HQ the IN Station was attached to. ATS officer Dorothy Rainey confirms that their responsibility was the collating of information from OUT Stations which was then passed on to Army HQ. (Letter to Mr Sealy, BROM Archive)

The everyday wireless traffic was conducted from purpose-built huts, but from mid-1942 onwards concealed dugouts containing food rations for 21 days, toilet facilities and provisions for battery charging were built near the majority of these huts. It is of interest to note that on 12 June 1942, Beatrice Temple had a long discussion with Major Charles Randell (the then commander of the AU Special Duties Branch), trying to persuade him that ATS could not be allotted to such stations, apparently to no avail. As her AU ATS subalterns had already been working at many IN Station huts, she can only have been referring to the dugouts which were about to be built.

A number of IN Stations, and in particular those situated further inland, would appear to have served as Relays in that the messages they received came directly from IN Stations and was passed on to the higher levels of Army command rather than to divisional headquarters. Characteristically, these stations were not served by a network of OUT Stations. These sites are referred to by the authors as Inner Network or IN/Relay Stations so as to differentiate them from IN Stations that received their information from their own networks of OUT Stations.

IN/Relay Stations should not be confused with repeater stations, sometimes also referred to by some as relay stations. Roy Russel would seem to be talking about relay stations whereas Stan Judson is talking about repeater stations:

> "Buildings or hills and mountains would prevent reception. The solution was to pick up the signal where it could be received, transfer it by wire to a new transmitter sited beyond the obstruction, and send it on its way towards its objective from there. This might be repeated if there were further sight-line obstructions, manned or unmanned and visited for maintenance. It was an imperfect system but the best we had." (Roy Russell, undated letter)

> "We tried once in Scotland. We tried to put some aerials up; you could have your aerial with a director, and a reflector behind that. We tried to put some wires up between the OUT and the Main (IN) Station, to see if it would be effective and it had no effect at all." (Stan Judson interview, IWM ref: 29468)

Intelligence gathered at the Army HQ from a variety of sources was passed on to the Command HQ in form of Intelligence Summaries (INTSUMs). Combined with intelligence gathered by the Command HQs' own sources, the total of information concerning the area of responsibility, including the information gathered by the SD Branch, eventually reached the General Staff Intelligence Branch (GS Int) at GHQ Home Forces as the final destination for all Intelligence. In May 1940, GHQ Home Forces were based at Kneller Hall in Twickenham, West London. Presently, Kneller Hall is home to the Royal School of Military Music and the largest employer of musicians in the United Kingdom. By July, the main component of the GHQ Home Forces had moved to St Paul's School in Hammersmith and the Advanced HQ had been allotted several rooms in the Central War Room which was located in the basement under the western side of the new public offices facing Great George Road.

In his stand-down letter (dated 4 July 1944), distributed to every member of the Auxiliary Units Special Duties Branch, General Sir Harold E Franklyn, the then Commander in Chief of GHQ Home Forces, specifically refers to the importance attributed to SD's intelligence reports: "The security reports regularly provided by Special Duties have proved of invaluable assistance to our security staffs."

What exactly these security reports entailed is a matter of interpretation. It has been suggested that the reports contained information provided by civilian spies tasked with monitoring and reporting "careless talk" and suspicious activities of their neighbours. Major Jones however, makes no mention of this. According to Jones, "the Special Duties Branch of AU is organised to provide information for military formations in the event of enemy invasion or raids". Perhaps Sir Harold referred to the new role given to the OUT Stations in mid 1943, which was to report rumours regarding the concentrations of troops for the D-Day invasion circulating from East Anglia and all along the South Coast that the War Office was very keen to learn about. Major Peter Forbes believes that this was the probably most important task assigned to the SD Branch during the four years of its existence.

The following list of destinations (Army HQs) the IN Stations' reports were to be sent to in 1944 was produced by Major Jones. (TNA, WO 199/1194)

Caithness	North Highland District HQ
Sutherland	North Highland District HQ
Angus	North Highland District HQ
Fife	Scottish Command HQ
East Lothian	Scottish Command HQ
Berwickshire	Scottish Command HQ
Northumberland	Northumbrian District HQ
Durham	Northumbrian District HQ
Yorkshire North Riding	North Riding District
Yorkshire East Riding	East Riding & Lincolnshire District HQ
Lincolnshire	East Riding & Lincolnshire District HQ
Norfolk	Norfolk & Cambridgeshire District HQ
Suffolk	Essex & Suffolk District HQ
Essex	Essex & Suffolk District HQ
Kent	East Kent District HQ + SE Command HQ
Sussex	Sussex District HQ
Hampshire	Hants Sub Dist HQ + Hants & Dorset Dist HQ
Dorset	Dorset Sub Dist HQ + Southern Command HQ
Somerset	South Western District HQ
East Devon	South Western District HQ
Pembrokeshire	South Wales District HQ
Carmarthenshire	South Wales District HQ
Glamorgan	South Wales District HQ
Monmouthshire	South Wales District HQ

In Eastern Command, together with Northern and South-Eastern Command and Western Command (Wales), all IN Stations passed their information to their District HQs. In South-Eastern Command (East Kent District and Sussex District), the Command HQ was also a recipient. Dorset and Hampshire appear to have been special cases as information was passed to the Dorset Sub-District HQ or Hampshire Sub-District HQ, respectively, plus to Hampshire and Dorset District HQ and to Southern Command HQ. In Scotland, in all but one county the IN Stations reported to Scottish Command HQ. The Caithness IN Station, however, passed its information to Highland District HQ.

During the four years of the organisation's existence, altogether 30 IN Stations, also referred to as Base stations or as Control stations (because they controlled the wireless traffic within their area network), 125 OUT Stations and 78 SUBOUT Stations had been constructed and equipped with wireless sets and aerials by the summer of 1944. All stations were sited at strategic locations in coastal areas, covering the east coast of Scotland, Northumberland, Lincolnshire and East Anglia and the south coast from Kent, Sussex, Hampshire (including the Isle of Wight), Somerset, Dorset and East Devon. By the end of November 1943, 700 aerials had been installed and approximately 500 wireless sets (including a number of WS17 ie No.17 wireless sets) were in use. (SDS/3/3064, 15 November 1943; TNA, WO 199/1194).

Two networks had also been established on the South Wales coast. A map produced by Major Jones, showing the locations of all the IN Stations, and the wireless paths linking them with their OUT Stations, provides a good overview of the scale of the operation at the time it was closed down at the end of June 1944. This map does, however, not show any of a number of changes implemented during previous years, ie since the start of the operation.

Considering that the closing down involved more than 900 operational bases (OBs) used by the operational patrols, as well as a great many SD IN and OUT Station dugouts, scattered over 44,000 square miles, and most of them well away from roads, the actual labour and transport involved in collecting stores and equipment was enormous. Some of the heavier items used by the SD Branch included all the wireless sets, generators and about 1,500 accumulator batteries together with multitudinous stores and equipment. It was estimated that two months at least would be required to complete this task.

Another important factor was, of course, security. Were OBs and SD dugouts allowed to remain intact, empty and thrown open to the public? The authorities had considered it desirable that the whole of the organisation, its functions, role and methods should remain secret and pigeonholed in the War Office, just in case. If OBs and SD dugouts with their ingenious doors and camouflaged entrances were to become local sights, security would certainly be gone for good. On the other hand, if the entrances were filled in or blown up, security would not suffer and there would be the additional advantage that however much one of the involved wanted to talk about their adventures, they would not be believed unless they could show something, and a heap of earth was deemed to be most unconvincing. Whereas most of the operational patrols were left to deal with the tasks involved themselves, regular personnel were ordered to deal with the SD dugouts.

The IN Station huts were dismantled and most of the dugouts were cleared of furniture and stripped of the wiring before the entrance and exit openings were capped. On 18 October 1943, Beatrice Temple had noted in her diary that all recruiting had already been stopped, although several more ATS subalterns were recruited after this date, probably to fill vacancies. All wireless sets were returned to the Army depots: the WS17 and WS36 sets were sent to the depot at Woolwich and all 'special sets' (the TRDs, TRMs and TRFs) were taken to No.1 Special Communications Unit (SCU) at Whaddon Hall in the Aylesbury Vale district, Buckinghamshire, where extreme care appears to have been taken to completely destroy every single one of them. Captain Ward recalls that the sets were collected at closedown and discarded. How he would have known and why he would have been involved is not clear, as by then he had long since left SD for the Inter Services Research Bureau (ISRB)/SOE. Deemed to be of no further use, the special sets are said to have been disposed of in one of the disused mine shafts used by the MoD for redundant equipment. Concrete is believed to have then been poured over them.

> "All Stations dismantled and closed down. All dugouts have been blocked as ordered by GHQ HF Auxiliary Units. All huts have been cleared and handed over to local QSs and GEs. Special Duties Branch, GHQ Auxiliary Units have been advised of clearance and de-requisitioning of land is now in progress. All documents in respect of personnel have been checked and accounted for.
>
> All documents of a security nature have been checked and orders for disposal are awaited. All vehicles have been concentrated at this HQ and will be retained for approximately ten days.
>
> The completion of all closing down at HQ will be effected approximately 14 September 1944." (TNA, WO 199/1194)

The AU signallers were returned to Catterick Camp in Yorkshire for retraining to enable them to be posted to normal Signals units. The Signal Training Centre retained some of them as instructors. Most of the AU ATS officers were discharged from the Army and moved on to civilian jobs. Everybody else soon returned to his or her ordinary lives.

Most of the people who were involved never talked about their wartime activities, and had it not been for Captain Ken Ward, Sergeants Alf Ellis, Frank Hewitt, Les Parnell, Stanley Judson, 2nd Lieutenant Roy Russell and Arthur Gabbitas (AU Signals), and a handful of ATS subalterns including Sally Waterhouse-Brown (whose sketches have not only provided many invaluable clues but almost certainly also the only existing depictions of a TRD wireless set), Barbara Culleton, Yolande Bromley, Marina Bloxam, Winifred Read, Dorothy Monck-Mason and others - but not Senior Commander Beatrice Temple, so it seems - who many years later shared at least some of their experiences, nothing would today be known about the secret wireless networks of the AU Special Duties Branch. Many questions, however, remain as yet unresolved.

Auxiliary Units Signals HQ at Bachelor's Hall, Hundon

In early 1941, Captain (later Major) John Hills, the Officer Commanding AU Signals, assisted by Captain Ken Ward and his team, started to recruit radio "hams" who were given the task of designing and manufacturing a small radio-telephony set that would be simple to use and could withstand damp conditions. The unit was based at Bachelor's Hall at Hundon (south Suffolk). When Major Hills left AU Signals in autumn 1941, Major Thomas "Hugh" Winterborn took over and Major RMA Jones, who used to be employed by WG Pye Radio Ltd (owned by Charles Orr Stanley) before he came into the Army, replaced him in summer 1942. Major Green commanded the unit at stand-down.

Bachelor's Hall in 2012

The first HQ of the Auxiliary Units Signals were set up at a fine manorial house located on the outskirts of the village of Hundon in south Suffolk. Bachelor's Hall is set back from the road and surrounded by an extensive garden, which at the time included an orchard. A number of outbuildings, a large barn amongst them, adjoin the house, now a family home.

Captain Ken Ward recalled that Major John Hills met him around Christmas 1940, and asked if he would be interested to join a new project as his staff captain, adjutant and workshop officer. The major pointed out that the men should bring along their wives because female wireless operators were required. Subsequently, Thea Ward became one of the first wireless operators at the Halstead (Essex) IN Station. Captain Ward reported to Major John Hills at The Bull public house in Long Melford where he not only found the major with his wife and two children but also Captain Freddie Childe (from the Intelligence Corps, the IO for Suffolk and Essex) as well as Corporals Chalk and Crawley, both RASC already settled at the Bull. Asked if the pay books of the first signallers who were posted in were stamped "Auxiliary Units (Signals)", Captain Ward replied:

> "Oh yes, we were called that before we existed and it is what I was posted to".

> "So I arrived at Long Melford. John was living in the Bull with his wife and two kids and Freddie Childe, who was the IO, was living there as well.... anyway, so I was taken upstairs to a bedroom which they had converted into an office and Freddie Childe read the riot act to me and made me swear *(sic – the OSA was signed, not sworn)* to the Official Secrets Act."

Soon it was decided to find a suitable location for setting up HQ in East Anglia:

> "Because that (East Anglia) was the next area to be dealt with and it was fairly central to the whole of the coast. So we scoured around and we eventually discovered that Bachelor's Hall had been vacated by the Manchester Regiment, who had been accommodated there, and was empty. So we went and had a look at it and decided that it had what we needed. Well it hadn't got electricity, but you had a big house here with hot and cold water, oil lamps, Tilley lanterns, you know, and a range of outbuildings. At the back there was a large farmhouse kitchen which was capable of feeding the troops and plumbing, two septic tanks and that sort of thing, with main drainage. There was also a large barn, which was ideal for working."

> "In Kent, a pilot scheme with a few civilian-operated coast stations (OUT Stations) working to a Base Station (IN Station) at the static division, working with the county IO Peter Fleming, was already in place. Our brief was to establish similar networks along the coast from Berwick on Tweed to the Devon border. Close liaison with the county IOs was necessary to ensure that locations were suitable for siting concealed sets and aerials."

Initially, the unit consisted of only a handful of men: Tom Higgins and Ron Dabbs designed the receiver, Bill Bartholomew and Jack Millie the transmitter; Les Parnell, Jimmy McNab and John Mackie were in charge of designing the power supply and metalwork, with Bill Air completing the team. One man (George Spencer) was allocated the task of choosing suitable IN Station sites, which, for obvious reasons, needed to be concealed from the public. Suitable trees for the erection of aerials and providing good wireless reception was essential. All the stations required copper-wire dipole aerials. Where possible, the aerials were strung in high trees, with the aerial feeder cables being hidden in V-shaped grooves that had been cut out of the tree bark. After placing the copper wire in the groove it was covered by the previously removed strip of bark. The normal working range of the sets was up to about 30 miles, but according to Major Jones by 1944 the longest range achieved was 64 miles (100 kilometres). The team was under the command of Captain Shanks. For administrative purposes the team was attached to a unit at nearby Clare from where they drew their rations.

After Bachelor's Hall had been chosen and approved of, personnel and transport had also to be found.

> "So we went beating around the bush with not much success and the first thing that we got was a bunch of RASC (*Royal Army Service Corps*) drivers, I think there were about nine of them, and they had been in the Army for a week, so they weren't exactly military but they were all trained drivers, except one who was a chap from Glasgow, and he came into the office and I said 'have you got a clean driving licence?' They had all got clean driving licences, and he said, yes, he had a clean license. 'Can you manage a Ford V8 Staff Car?' He said 'I don't know sir, I've never driven a car, I was 2nd hand on a steam wagon'. He was a great bloke."

Asked if there was one set of IOs for the Auxiliary Units patrols and another for the spy networks, Captain Ward said that he didn't know. All he knew was that Captain Fred Childe was the IO for East Anglia, Captain Fleming covered the South, Captain Owen Hall-Hall was based in Dorset and Major John Collings in Norfolk. Unlike the AU operational patrols and the Scout Sections attached to them, who knew of each others' existence and often worked together, the men and women of the Special Duties Branch, be they Army or civilian, had no contact with the operational branch, which in turn, at least officially, knew about the existence of a secret wireless network operating in their areas only at the highest level on a need to know basis. Intelligence officers would have had a need to know and hence were aware of, although perhaps not fully informed about Special Duties Branch operations in their respective counties. There are some indications however that at least some of the AU patrols operating near a wireless station did know about its existence, albeit purely through observation.

An AU Signals officer was sent out to liaise with the AU operational patrols' IOs, acting as the only link between the two. Captain Ward thought that although there was this tenuous link, they never officially knew that the AU patrols existed. He also made clear that his team was not manufacturing sets for the AU patrols. Asked if he knew anything about AU patrols having been issued with standard domestic Murphy receivers in 1943, and which purpose these might have served, Ken Ward replied: "Probably for socialising to stop the guys getting bored, I can't think of any other reason." Captain (later Lieutenant Colonel) Norman JL Field confirmed that from November 1940 to August 1941, during his time as IO in Kent, certainly no wireless sets were used for communications either within or between patrols. (Letter to Arthur Gabbitas, dated December 1998)

Ken Ward confirmed that all the sets they built were to be used at civilian locations, by civilians who would remain in enemy occupied territory.

> "Farmers, vicars, bakers, butchers, candlestick makers, bar maids, all sorts of strange people and each of them had a wireless station somewhere near the coast where they could know what was happening. And they had a network

of reporters working to them, people just wandering around the countryside who had put a message in a tennis ball and roll it down a chute into the station or whatever."

Ken Ward recalls that the transport used for maintaining the OUT Stations were often old motorcycles with sidecars, of which they had 24.

"So 24 motorbikes arrived with another bunch of men, who had to be trained to ride motorbikes with side cars on them, well it's one thing riding a motorbike without a side car but it's quite a different thing, we made an awful mess of the fences and ditches around Hundon, most of them succeeded in the end. So these teams of 2 would go out from wherever they were based and visit the stations, change the batteries, charge the batteries, they were responsible for battery charging at the "Met" huts (see pages 88 and 142), normally they worked from a "Met" hut out to the area, but they had to be very careful not to be seen when they went near to the station and that sort of thing. In some areas we actually sent them in civilian vehicles. So that was all part of the Hundon operation."

The first wireless sets were designed by Major John Hills and manufactured by W Bryan Savage Ltd at Kingsbury (later Watford). According to Captain Ward, the Savage sets had the size of a shoebox. They were quench-operated, with the transmitter/receiver positioned in one box and the power unit in another, and the controls on top. About 50 of these sets would seem to have been produced. At some stage, however, the men were getting increasingly frustrated with the Savage sets, which (according to Ken Ward) were difficult to open, difficult to repair and not very well built. Consequently, they decided to develop their own and within about three weeks, says Ken Ward, they had produced what became known as the TRD. Major Jones makes a short mention of the sets in his report and Ken Ward has provided a more detailed description:

"The initial sets were VHF Quench-type duplex telephony units designed by John Hills. The quench is in fact a duplex telephone transmission being voice-switched, using a 4-metre spectrum. The original John Hills sets and the TRDs could work to each other. Both were Quench sets, a principle developed before the war by the Signals Experimental Unit of the Cambridge University. *(Sic - Superregenerative quench operation was patented by Edwin Armstrong in 1922.)* It was a double-frequency system such that an ordinary receiver would only hear 'mush' so that no codes were needed. The TRD developed by Ron Dabbs was a great improvement on the original sets, easier to use and to service. Both used 6V accumulators as the power source, converted to AC at suitable voltage by means of a Mallory vibrator power pack sourced from Masterradio Ltd of Watford. In general, no mains electricity was used. Batteries were recharged by small Army-issue petrol generator sets."

Captain Ward and his team not only built the sets and installed them in the Coast stations, as he referred to the OUT Stations run by civilians, they also instructed the operators in how to use them. The unit's own test station was at Bachelor's Hall, housed in one of the upstairs bedrooms, where all their sets were tested working to 'Buttercup', the IN Station at Halstead (Essex), where the operators were Mickey Brown and Thea Ward (Captain Ken Ward's wife). The test station was also used for conducting voice tests.

"We immediately took over the manufacture of the sets and their installation in the "Met" huts (IN Stations, see also pages 88 and 142) and the coastal, concealed OUT Stations. Corporal Chalk and his mate were the experts in installing the aerials in trees, lofts, barns etc. The first areas to be equipped after Kent were Norfolk, Suffolk and Essex, with their "Met" huts at static Divisional HQ near Norwich, Halstead and Hatfield Peverel. The IOs concerned with finding and briefing the civilian operators of Coast stations (OUT Stations) were Major John Collings in Norfolk and Captain Freddie Childe. The latter had his billet in Great Yeldham (see page 48). (The interview with Ken Ward, excerpts of which have been quoted above, was conducted by John Warwicker in 1999; IWM ref: 29472)

Captain Ken Ward and his wife Thea *(BROM Archive)*

The Radio Communications Division of ISRB (Inter Service Research Bureau, a branch of the SOE) agreed to take over the manufacture of the TRD sets needed for replacements or extensions. In January 1942, Captain Ward was posted to them and he later arranged a contract for the manufacture of TRDs with Peto Scott Ltd.

Much of the information currently known originates from the recollections of men like Arthur Gabbitas, young non-commissioned officers (NCOs) who did not know the command structure. Some of their memories may give the impression that AU Signals ran the show, but this was not so. "The Royal Signals were and are a Service Corps", writes Major Forbes. "They take their instructions from the Operational Branch, and in this particular case their instructions came from the GSO2 at HQ AU at Coleshill. It had always been the tradition from the beginning that the G2 ran SD." (Major Peter Forbes to John Warwicker, 31 January 2002; BROM Archive)

The TRD

In view of the highly specialised nature of the TRD set and the most secret nature of the task on hand, it was strongly recommended that personnel be carefully selected, with an officer of the AU Signals branch taking part when new recruits were to be interviewed. Only men of responsible character and discretion were to be entertained. Their medical category, however, needed not to be high except that their speech and hearing had to be of a standard suited for R/T transmission. (Memorandum dated 4 April 1942, TNA)

In addition to the TRD, WS17 may have been required, by OUT Stations and the SUBOUT Stations serving them, for communicating with each other. The WS17 was a portable transceiver commonly used in WW2 for communications between searchlight Section HQ and detachments and Anti-Aircraft batteries. During 1943, however, the SD headquarters ordered at least 200 of these sets, considerably more than would appear to have been needed for this task.

> "A further 100 WS17 sets have been applied for." (Monthly notes to IOs, No 5, July 1943)

> "Receipt of a further 100 WS17 sets. Fresh sites will not be submitted before completion of the present programme which calls for at least some 170 more of these sets. IOs will be asked for recommendations for further sites at a later date and consideration will be given to their installation in areas which at present are without them." (Monthly notes to IOs, No 6, August 1943)

It would therefore seem that the requests for WS17 as well as for new TRD sets were made because of a change of plan which included the manning of IN Stations by night as well as by day, in all raid areas. By August 1943, SD HQ were, inexplicably, also organising tests of a warning system which had been set up - at a time when the threat of an invasion had almost disappeared.

For the first time the Monthly notes reveal that during 1943 newer models replaced old TRD sets:

> "Several IOs have enquired about a replacement of old TRDs for new ones. However, TRDs are coming through very slowly indeed from the manufacturers but eventually all old sets will be replaced – the old ones being held as a reserve, after reconditioning. No new ones are as yet in stock. Replacements will be made according to plans already made, starting with Eastern Command." (Monthly notes to IOs, No 5, July 1943)

As is evident from a recall notice, WS36 sets were also issued. WS36 sets were contained in two wooden boxes for the transmitter, with each box measuring about 55 cm (width) by 40 cm (height) and 40 cm (depth) (22 x 17 x 17 inches), and a receiver (Model R208) that was slightly larger than one of the transmitter boxes. The WS36 sets took up a lot of space and because they required an AC mains power supply they were not suitable for use in all of the IN Stations.

Furthermore, in autumn 1943, 30 Murphy B81 and B93 wireless receivers were requested by and issued to the Signals Section Auxiliary Units (TNA, WO

199/936). It would appear that these civilian sets were intended for use by the IN Station operators (according to Major Jones there were 30 IN Stations) to maintain a listening watch for Beetle warning messages (the Beetle Organisation also used these sets). Both were portables running on batteries and designed by Ewan Minns. The B81 had an "all-weather" finish of black rexine, piped with green leather, and green plastic knobs; the B93 also had a black rexine finish, with a white rubber "grommet", and black plastic knobs. Two R308 VHF intercept receivers (working on mains or 12V batteries) were also requested.

The Beetle WT Organisation's special wireless links allowed for messages warning of impending raids to be passed immediately to five Army Commands (Scottish, Northern, Eastern, Western and HQ Western Area). These headquarters broadcast in plain language, with only the location in code, to all other HQs and units that had been issued with Murphy wireless receivers.

> "The ability to repel and attack depends largely on immediate and accurate warning being passed to such local defence formations as are in a position to take immediate offensive action. A variety of means exist for the collection of such information, but the most extensively organised systems of observation are the Observer Corps and the Coastguard and the Coast Watching Services. At present the main Naval and Air Force centres obtaining this information are HQs, Fighter, Bomber and coastal Commands, and the three Area Combined HQs. It is necessary to pass this information to military formations; primarily Army Command HQs. To be effective it is essential that the collection and dissemination of the information be extremely rapid and independent of landline. The "BEETLE" system is supplementing to, and will operate concurrently with, the landline systems." (TNA, WO 199/955)

The equipment used by the summer of 1944 in the various IN, OUT and SUBOUT Stations consisted of 250 TRD sets, specially built either in the HQ workshop or by contract; 28 TRM sets; 36 TRF sets and 200 WS17 sets (see Appendix D). The frequencies allotted ranged between 48 and 65 mcs (megacycles/second). (Major RMA Jones, TNA, WO 199/1194)

When Barbara Culleton arrived at SD HQ at Bachelor's Hall she was shown how the various wireless sets were assembled. She remembers that the original TRDs were contained in two wooden boxes and that later two green metal sets were used. Sergeant Jack Millie too recalls that "the earlier models were two-box efforts and rather cumbersome; they gave considerable trouble and were not too well received by the operators". Ken Ward has confirmed that the equipment went through several stages of development, and it would seem that the two-box sets recalled by Barbara Culleton were indeed the prototype TRDs designed by W Bryan Savage (see page 17). The later model is described as having been contained within a single box.

The TRD used 6-volt, 85 AH accumulator batteries and the set was based on three separate chassis comprising transmitter, receiver and a power unit. Descriptions vary and indeed, Ken Ward, when asked about this, has said, "we used whatever we could get hold of", indicating that not all the sets looked exactly the same. He describes them as having had two large tuning knobs on the front panel for separately adjusting the transmitter and receiver frequency but it appears, because the frequencies were fixed, that the operators could make only minor adjustments. The same knobs and dials can be found on many homemade 1940s radios as they were readily available and could be bought in any radio shop.

"The output of the transmitter was checkable by the simple means of placing an ordinary flash lamp bulb across the two terminals on the front panel and it used to vary in brightness with the modulation." (Undated letter from Bill Bartholomew to Arthur Gabbitas, BROM Archive)

TRD BUILT LATE 41-42

TRANSMITTER	SWITCHING POWER SUPPLY. 6 V. INPUT.	RECEIVER
RK34	◯ VIBRATOR	◯ EF50
◯ 6V6 OR 6F6	REC ◯ 0Z4	◯ EF39
◯ 6C5	[TRANS]	◯ 6C5

Drawing by Jack Millie of a 1941/1942 model TRD *(BROM Archive)*

"The original John Hills sets and the TRD could work to each other. Both were quench sets, a principle developed before the war by the Signals Experimental Unit of the Cambridge University STC to provide non-interceptible R/T communication for RA observation posts back to guns. Non-technically it was a double frequency system such that an ordinary receiver would only hear 'mush' so that no codes were needed. The TRD developed by Ron Dabbs and his team was a great improvement on the original sets, easier to use and to service. Both used six-volt accumulators as the power source converted to AC or suitable voltage by means of a Mallory Vibrator power pack sourced from Master Radio Ltd of Watford. The WS17 set was an Army issue set. In general no mains electricity was used. Batteries were recharged by small Army issue petrol generator sets. The reason no signals were intercepted was twofold: first the quench system and secondly the very limited and directional range of the sets. In some areas we had to establish concealed repeater stations between particular Coast stations and the "Met" hut. We had initially quite a problem to get good signals from the Isle of Whight stations to Winchester, as an example. The aerials were horizontal dipoles, I can't remember precise operational frequency; wave lengths around 4.7 meters with a range of about 25 to 30 miles depending on aerial siting and intervening terrain." (Ken Ward in letter to J Warwicker, 24 April 1999; BROM Archive)

Jill Monk, whose father, Dr Alec Holman, had an OUT Station in his home at Aylsham (Norfolk), received some training in operating the wireless set. Mrs Monk provided the following information (interview on 10 April 2012):

Was the information flow one-way (from OUT Station to IN Station) only?

"The only reply we received after transmitting messages was 'Message received'. We had to be on tap at certain hours to receive messages. There were certain set hours when to broadcast and when to listen."

How did the wireless set operate and how were the controls used?

"We had to switch two and fro, depending on whether we were transmitting or receiving." The set was a rectangular box with switches and black knobs and I seem to recall that these knobs were set into something of half-moon shape."

How was the wireless set operated regarding the main dials?

"We switched it on, adjusted the frequency until connected, then passed on our messages. The "Message received" reply confirmed that the messages had got through. Sometimes we had to make several attempts before getting through."

What kind of information did the secret messages contain and what sort of code was used?

"We collected information by observations made on the ground such as bombing squad movements, troop assemblages, movements and numbers, vehicle movements, identification of battalions and regiments, anything else unusual. The information was coded before being passed on."

"It was some sort of letter code but I can't remember how it worked. The coding was done by my mother."

Was one of your tasks the scanning of the airwaves for spy transmissions?

"We were operating on a set frequency and there was no way to listen to anything else except to whomever it was we were connected with (we did not know who it was we were transmitting to)".

Curiously, Barbara Culleton has said that one of her duties was to listen out for enemy agents broadcasting to Berlin.

"We were to note times, voice, the language, if possible, and where it was on the range. I heard an agent broadcasting nearly every time." (Owen Sheers, Guerillas in waiting, The Guardian, 20 October 2007)

David Hunt points out that most agents used Morse code, not voice, and that in order to communicate with Berlin an HF set was required (pers comm). TRDs used VHF which has a very short range, making the use of sky wave (a radio wave reflected back by the ionosphere, permitting transmission around the curved surface of the earth) impossible. Furthermore, the Radio Security Service, not Special Duties, was responsible for keeping a wireless watch for such transmissions.

In his report, Major Jones describes the transmitter power output as having been approximately 1½ watt, and the dimensions of the case as 41 x 24 x 23 centimetres (15½ x 9³/₈ x 9¼ inches). The controls consisted of an on/off switch, a send/receive switch, a receiver tuning dial and a volume control knob. The transmitter had a speech amplifier, modulator and push-pull oscillator; the receiver comprised an RF stage, super-regenerative detector and an output stage. (TNA, WO 199/1194)

The reproduction version of a TRD as it might have looked can be seen on display at the British Resistance Organisation Museum at Parham (Suffolk). All attempts to create a fully operational TRD set have to date failed and descriptions of how it looked vary. Amongst the private papers of an ATS subaltern, the authors have however found what would seem to be the only surviving contemporary illustrations of a TRD wireless set (see page 101). Sally Waterhouse-Brown who operated one of the sets and who was a gifted artist, made the drawings in 1943. Since new TRDs would seem to have replaced the old ones during 1943 it is not clear which version is depicted. Wireless sets of that time were commonly painted, usually black or drab olive or dark green, and occasionally brown whereas the drawing shows what looks like an unpainted metal case. It is difficult to estimate the size of the set, which was contained within what seems to be a light grey aluminium body (either plain or anodised) that would appear to roughly fit the measurements given by Major Jones. It fitted into a drawer-like case made from the same material.

At least some of the IN Station operators wore so-called head and breast sets, a combination of headphone and a microphone/speaker, with the microphone requiring a canvas strap around the neck to support its weight, leaving the hands free for other tasks.

> "The output could be via a loudspeaker or headphones. This was contained in a case similar to the power unit." (Undated letter from Bill Bartholomew to Arthur Gabbitas, BROM Archive)

The normal range of the TRD was up to 30 miles but depended greatly on the nature of the terrain. The longest operational link in use in June 1944 was 64 miles, which is approximately 100 kilometres (Major Jones). Field trials were necessary in order to find the ideal location for IN Station sites and the placement of their aerials. Besides finding suitable locations for the IN Stations and the setting of the RF (Radio Frequency, ie radio signals coming inbound to a receiver or outbound from a transmitter) of the IN Station transceivers, the quench frequency (ie the lower frequency signal, used to quench intermittently a high-frequency oscillator in a super-regenerative receiver) also required adjustment, as each of the networks also had their own quench frequency. The quench frequency was adjustable by inserting a screwdriver into a slot in the front panel, the idea being that it was only adjusted very rarely, once it had been set. (Ken Ward).

Aerials had to be placed as high as possible above ground level and they had to be kept clear of surrounding objects. High elevations between stations had to be avoided wherever possible, because ideally the sending and receiving aerials had to be able to "see" each other. This form of transmission is known as space wave (line of sight) and it was the form most commonly used at the time. The maximum line of sight distance between two aerials depended on the height of each aerial. In some areas so-called repeater stations had to be established between particular locations. There was also initially a problem getting good signals from the Isle of Wight OUT stations to their IN Station at Winchester (see also Ken Ward's letter, page 21).

IN-Stations were for this reason frequently sited on high ground that afforded uninterrupted views over the area where the OUT Stations were situated. The aerial feeder cables, commonly 30 to 40 feet (9 to 12 metres) long, were hidden under the bark of nearby trees and the horizontal dipole aerials were strung out along the branches.

AU Signals officer Stan Judson has provided some interesting details:

> "The aerial would be up a tree, a selected tree which often was most difficult to climb so what we had, we usually got a hammer, tied a string to it and threw it (over the branch they wanted to reach). Pick a tree with a fairly few branches lower down, and if you study trees you'll find that they have a black line coming down, because they get dust on them and the rain, the water, finds its path and it doesn't make a channel but usually a black line which is ideal for concealing the black cable up to the aerial."

Corporal Arthur Gabbitas
(Source: A Gabbitas)

The aerial feeder cable was commonly concealed in a V-shaped groove cut into the tree bark where it was held in place by steel clips. After the cable was in place the bark was replaced over it. 30,000 yards of feeder cable of the type B.A.3.A.P were ordered, and presumably used, for the setting up of approximately 700 aerials during the course of the operation. (Major Jones) Bert Davis, one of the AU Signals maintenance men, recalls that beech trees were preferred because it was easy to sink cables into their bark and camouflage them with putty filler and paint. (*The Mercian Maquis*, page 122)

Aerial trees (clockwise starting at top left): Thornham Magna, Alnwick *(Photo: Colin Anderson)*, Norwich and Ardingly *(Photo: Brian Drury)* IN Stations.

Auxiliary Units Signals in the Field

The following is an excerpt from the 1942 diary kept by Alfred "Alf" N Ellis, an AU Signals officer who helped setting up the wireless networks in Hampshire (including the Isle of Wight), Somerset, Dorset and Devon. His tasks were to collect batteries requiring recharging from IN and OUT Stations, testing and installing aerials and wireless sets, as well as to set up new stations and wireless links. His diary entries show that the signallers were very busy and regularly travelled vast distances.

27 May	08:20
	Omagh – tested aerials. X and
	Major called
	Pay
	R8-9 received
	Byfield - Southampton
28 May	Byfield – aerial + reflector for
	Gory/Gony?
	5 – R7-8 R9
	6 – R8-9 both ways
	Wire for 6
	Be at Hut for 9. Phone X 3/-
29 May	Omagh for phone from X. Not to go
	upland. Took remainder of day at
	Lost Pay. Rest Day
30 May	Byfield – replaced wire
	Gory/Gony? aerial for rod +
	reflector aerial
31 May	Omagh – West Moors – Byfield
	R7 - R8-9
	Osterley R5 - R7
	Batteries 101.72.116
1 June	07:30-22:10
	07:30 – Isle of Wight. Put set in
	dugout.
	Changed set @ 4 recam? Aerial
	(117.284.122)
	Byfield R8 T6
	Omagh R9 – put new aerial @ 3
	area
	Left batteries 268.277.229

Arthur Gabbitas has provided a detailed description concerning his recruitment to AU Signals, and of his tasks as one of the members of a three-man crew responsible for the maintenance of a wireless network comprising an IN Station and its associated OUT Stations.

"I was called up in 1940 to Catterick (Catterick Infantry Training Centre in North Yorkshire) and trained as a wireless operator. At the end of our training we were chosen for varying theatres, five of us were designated to go to Auxiliary Units, although we weren't aware of what it was all about. We went down to Coleshill, where we spent several weeks whilst they were assembling the Signals side of things. Then we went to Hundon, in Suffolk, to the Signals HQ where they were building the sets, and trained in the use of these sets. I was then sent to Winchester where I spent some time and was then moved to Buckland St Mary near Taunton (Somerset), and then later on up to Lincoln and that is where I continued until we were disbanded in 1944.

We were in civilian billets and had to start work at eight o'clock in the morning. There were three of us: two wireless operators and an instrument mechanic. While one operator was at the Base station the other operator and the mechanic went out to the OUT Stations to take their batteries and change them so they always had fully charged batteries; if necessary, to check hidden aerials in the trees that they were still firm after the winds and that the down leads (feeder cables) were still hidden under the bark. Of course, if there had been any operational requirements we would have left our civilian billets and gone to our stations." (Interview by Stephen Sutton, IWM, Ref: 14819/2).

Another account comes from Stanley Judson, who, although he too spent some of his time in Lincolnshire, met Arthur Gabbitas for the first time 70 years after the event:

"In May 1941 I was posted with three others from the Royal Signals Training Battalion in Harrogate to Auxiliary Units at Sudbury, where no one had heard of this Unit and we were forced to spend the night on the floor of an empty shop in town. The next day we were driven to a house in the country called Bachelor's Hall, where we did very little apart from climbing trees and sign the Official Secrets Act. I was then sent to Lincolnshire, accompanied by two other NCOs (non-commissioned officers) under the command of a captain. We were all billeted in a vicarage (Canwick House) and from that base we set up a series of secret wireless stations throughout Lincolnshire and South Yorkshire, to be used by civilian operators who were selected and trained by Army Intelligence. The wireless sets and batteries were concealed in boxes with detachable lids, sunk in the ground and camouflaged. This method of concealment had its drawbacks as the operators were open to discovery and when the local village coal merchant and his companion at Donington on Bain were overheard operating the set the person listening was able to summon a nearby Army unit who surrounded the wood and captured the operatives before they could make their getaway. After this incident all stations were converted to purpose-made dugouts equipped with bunks and stocked with Army K-rations, paraffin heaters etc. During 1944 I was moved to Edinburgh as Area Sergeant under the command of a Signals officer in charge of all the Special Duties operations from Alnwick to John O'Groats." (Letter dated 25 October 1991, BROM Archive)

Back row: J Hemstock, R Cain, Ellison, Bevan, Clowes, McLeavey, Leaverland, Pettitt, Harvey, Sims, Casey, Bayldon
4th row: Gilbert, Shipley, Prior, Ferguson, David, F Hewitt, Larkin, Greening, J Mackie, Caldow, Foard, A Gabbitas, Winsbury, Crawley
3rd row: T Higgins, Harvey, Nicholson, Dudding, Greay, Escott, Furmston, Eagleton, Brown, Montgomerie, Dodds, Murrow, Duffell, Wright, Marshall, Baker, Davey
2nd row: B Bartholomew, Gambles, Ferguson, Dunford, Orr, Cash, Allen, Morris, Shooter, B Davis, Dallimore, Martin, Healey, Lindeman, Cropper, MacKender
Front row: Joan Hayman, S Judson, A Ellis, G Spencer, Moriarty, Weatherhead, Capt T Shanks, Maj Green, Lt Thimont, J Fletcher, R Dabbs, Chalk, Millie, Air, Parnell

Auxiliary Units Signals at Coleshill House in 1944
(Photographer unknown, BROM Archive)

A list compiled from information contained in a contemporary manuscript (written by Adrian Monck-Mason) gives a fairly accurate picture as to which items would have been found in an IN Station at the time it was in use. Although referring to a handful of networks in the south only (Omagh, Golding, Chirnside, Byfield and Osterley), it may reasonably be assumed that the same would have applied, with perhaps minor variations, to all existing IN Stations.

The original manuscript covers two pages and includes items that IN Stations were supplied with, such as:

> 1 Charging set 550W (Lyons) complete with (charging) panel etc
> 2 Aerials made up spare complete
> 6 Batteries 85 AH
> 1 Table barrack folding
> 1 TRD complete station
> 1 TRD spare
> 1 Lamp electric No.1 (the old bicycle lamp torch)
> Electric light wiring, switches, plugs
> Sockets, lamp holders, shades
> Lamp electric 6V 6W (presumably bulbs for the DC lights)
> Lamp electric 230V 40W
> Field telephone
> 1 or 2 Telephones, spare

Sergeant Frank Hewitt and 2nd Lieutenant Roy Russell *(right)* of Auxiliary Unit Signals *(Photo dates and sources unknown)*

The ATS come on Board

ATS cap badge

A.T.S.: South-Eastern Command Officers
Chief Commandant the Countess of Carlisle (right) is Assistant Director, A.T.S., South-Eastern Command. On the staff is Company Commander Cynthia Charrington, daughter of Brigadier Charrington

(Photo source and date unknown)

Parallel with the building of wireless sets and the setting up of wireless networks, operators were required for manning the IN Stations. Presumably to save military manpower, the authorities decided that these should be recruited from the ATS. The first ATS wireless operators were chosen by the then Chief Controller of ATS, Lady Bridget Helen "Biddy" Monckton (Service number: 192026), otherwise known as the Countess of Carlisle. They helped setting up the Kent IN Station at Hollingbourne which formed part of the original pilot scheme. Kitty Hills, the wife of Major John Hills (SD HQ Bachelor's Hall) and Thea Ward, the wife of Captain Ken Ward, were amongst the first SD wireless operators in East Anglia. In November 1941, Beatrice Temple, fondly referred to as "Belinda Blue-Eyes" by many of her ATS subalterns, joined the staff at Hannington Hall.

The ATS and AU Signals officers working in the field were commonly accommodated, with board, in civilian billets, which at least in some instances appear to have been arranged by the local police. For administrative purposes, the signallers were attached to the nearest Army HQ. Before they were issued bicycles, the ATS subalterns frequently depended on AU Signals soldiers for transport.

In a document dated 1 February 1943 and marked "Most Secret", Colonel Lord Glanusk (the then Commander of Auxiliary Units), makes some interesting comparisons between the circumstances of detachments manned by men and those crewed by ATS, and also highlights the differences between ATS officers and ORs and the difficulties involved:

> "The men on these detachments always have a car, as this is essential for their work. Billets therefore do not necessarily have to be within walking or cycling distance. The men are attached for pay etc to the nearest military unit and can use the car to attend pay parades.
>
> ATS detachments however are not provided with a car. Billets must therefore be within walking or cycling distance, which very greatly limits the choice of accommodation. The Officer of any unit to which the auxiliaries were attached for pay would have to make a special journey to pay them.
>
> Accommodation is extremely difficult to find and if the only suitable billet is a large house with no staff, arrangements are made for the ATS officers to become members of the local male Officers' Mess but it is obviously undesirable that three ATS ORs alone should be fed in a soldiers' dining room.
>
> ATS ORs would have to be attached to the nearest ATS unit, meaning that an ATS Officer had to make a journey of sometimes 15 to 20 miles (25 to 30 kilometres) every week to pay three ATS ORs. For reasons of security, the Officer could not go to the place of duty; she would therefore have to be at the billet at a time when all three ORs were off-duty (ie before 9am), during the lunch hour or after 6pm. The average ATS company officer had neither the time nor the transport for this duty.
>
> The supervision of ATS ORs on these isolated detachments could not be adequately carried out by the Senior Commander, who is unable to visit more than once a month, owing to the distance. Nor could it be adequately carried out by the nearest ATS Officer, who for reasons of security would have no access to the place of duty of the ORs and no control over their hours of work."

Lord Glanusk was well aware of and acknowledged the fact that some of the conditions required to resolve all these issues were contrary to ATS policy. He therefore concluded that it was impractical to overcome the difficulty of combining suitable accommodation and adequate administration of ATS ORs with any degree of security. As security was the over-ruling and vital factor, he came to the decision that the employment of ATS officers was therefore essential. (TNA, WO 199/378)

After the move of SD HQ from Bachelor's Hall to Coleshill House in the winter of 1941, staff accommodation and a number of offices for administrative purposes was found at Hannington Hall, a 17th century manor house owned by the Fry family (the Quakers and chocolate makers), located only a short distance from Coleshill. Hannington Hall changed its role three times: from billet to requisitioned quarters (supplied with Army furnishings and rations) and finally, on 25 June 1942 it was agreed that the Hall should become an 'Attery' (ATS term for an ATS training centre) for officers (Barbara Culleton).

A small administrative staff and a workshop, where major repairs and special work was carried out, were located in the grounds of Coleshill House, HQ of the Auxiliary Units. Barbara Marion Culleton recalls that she worked both at Hannington Hall and at Coleshill House when she was Beatrice Temple's assistant.

Shortly before the AU Signals HQ had left Bachelor's Hall for Coleshill House, Major Thomas "Hugh" Winterborn had succeeded Major John Hills as the OC. (He was replaced by Major RMA Jones, Royal Signals, in March 1942.) Major Winterborn (Service number: 44188) had served with the Army in China and Japan, in Ceylon and in Burma, before joining MI5. He spoke Chinese and Japanese fluently. Holding the rank of a lieutenant he was restored to the Establishment on 15 March 1939 (London Gazette).

With the rank of a captain, he was then employed at the War Office in 1940; working for the MI2(c) (Military Intelligence) section (TNA, WO 208/1219A) and from 1941 to 1942 he was the commanding officer of the Special Duties Branch. There is a record that in 1945 he sought employment with the SIS (Letter from Major General Sir William Ronald Campbell Penney KBE, CB, DSO, ML, dated 30 September 1945). In 1946, Major Winterborn was promoted to (temporary) lieutenant colonel and received an OBE, and on 1 January 1950 he retired.

According to Peter Wright, (Assistant Director of MI5) who worked with Winterborn after the latter had just successfully completed "Operation Party Piece" (which in 1955 gave MI5 total access to the Communist Party of Great Britain), "his operations were always beautifully planned right down to the last detail, and although often complex, were invariably executed with military precision". In Wright's own words: "For five years we bugged and burgled our way across London at the State's behest, while pompous bowler-hatted civil servants in Whitehall pretended to look the other way." (Peter Wright, "Spy Catcher", page 54)

One of the staff officers based at Hannington Hall was Major Petherick, who was in charge of setting up the Special Duties Branch spy network. Beatrice Temple described him in her diary as "not prepossessing". Major Maurice Petherick (1894-1985) was a Conservative Party politician and served as the Member of Parliament (MP) for Penryn & Falmouth from 1931 to 1945. Captain Charles E Randell ("pleasant but pompous") who later replaced Major Petherick, was also based at the Hall (from November 1941 to December 1942). He took some of the ATS training courses.

These courses usually lasted four days and included practical map reading, taken by Major Nigel Oxenden, then a HQ staff officer. Signals and cipher training took up one or two days and was held at Coleshill House whereas all other courses for the subalterns, who arrived in small groups, took place at Hannington Hall. The first of these courses was scheduled for 17 March 1942, and Waddy Cole, Elizabeth Stronach and Dorothy Monck-Mason were the first to attend, with Nina Clifford, Doris Adams-Beck and Phyllis Britton to follow a week later. Alma Hildyard took the course during April, followed by a group comprising Sarah Curtis, Eleanor Norman-Butler, Enid Thompson and Mickey Browne in early May, and Joan Paget, Mary Ronald and Peggy Brown in mid-June. However, a number of subalterns were soon to be made redundant.

The May 1942 War Establishment documents that the strength of AU ATS, which until then had amounted to 135, was to be decreased to 31. From the same date onwards however, the numbers of Royal Signals OWLs were to be increased. On 24 March the then Commander in Chief of GHQ Home Forces, General Sir Bernard Charles Tolver Paget, GCB, DSO, MC, had already advised Lieutenant Colonel Beyts of AU HQ of his decision that in the future, IN Stations serving Divisional HQs were to be manned by AU Signals personnel instead of ATS officers.

Major Winterborn had first mentioned to Beatrice Temple the possibility of ATS numbers being cut down to 31 on the occasion of a visit to Hannington Hall, only days before he was replaced by Major RMA Jones. Beatrice Temple was horrified but two days later Major Winterborn and Major Petherick had nevertheless already agreed to a reduction. Of interest in this context is a note mentioning, for the first time in an Establishment, a "Senior Commander, ATS". This was, of course, to be the then Junior Commander Beatrice Temple.

Urgent arrangements had subsequently to be made and in mid-May Beatrice Temple visited the ATS HQ in Cheltenham to offer a number of her now surplus officers for transferral to other duties. Several others, including Doris White and Mary Shaw, were posted to SD HQ where they served as Beatrice Temple's new administrative assistants. Hilary Graham, Margaret Whiting, Wendy Kaines, Joan Fox and one of the Hackwood sisters were retained as Stores officers.

Not quite a year later, Colonel Lord Glanusk, who by then had succeeded Lieutenant Colonel Bill Beyts as Commander of Auxiliary Units, realised that decreasing the strength of ATS had been a mistake. In a document marked "Most Secret", dated 1 February 1943, he writes:

> "Experience has proved that a mistake was made in reducing the number of ATS Officers from 135 to 31, as Royal Signals, while technically desirable, are not necessarily a satisfactory substitute." (TNA, WO 199/738)

"Belinda Blue-Eyes"

Beatrice Temple (1907 - 1982), the niece of William Temple (the then Archbishop of Canterbury) had already served several years with the ATS although she had initially intended to join the Women's Royal Naval Service (WRNS), because she wanted to stay in Scotland, where she lived at the time, and be able to travel about. She wanted to drive lorries too, but seemingly she never did. Instead, in 1938, she joined the ATS, recalling later that she would have volunteered for any organisation that wouldn't tell her beforehand what it was all about. Beatrice Temple's service number was 192882.

According to a long-term friend, Beatrice Temple was very adept at organising things. The authorities would seem to have agreed, in that they promoted her to the rank of captain almost straight away, and gave her the job of company commander.

> "I had only five days to become an officer. I learned to drill with sergeants in the Guards and studied military law but my job consisted mainly of doing administrative work."

No details are known regarding Beatrice Temple's activities until 30 May 1941, which the London Gazette records as the date of her promotion to 2nd subaltern, and then an entry in her diary, dated 10 November 1941, when she was interviewed by Colonel CR Major (whom she describes as "delightful") at the War Office. The colonel advised that her posting would be imminent. It took ten more days though, for the posting telegram to arrive - the newly appointed Junior Commander was to report to Highworth. The diary entry, dated Thursday, 20 November 1941, reads "Posting telegram arrived, Subaltern Temple – Junior Commander". On her arrival on 24 November she was met by "charming" Colonel GHB Beyts (Coleshill staff officer) and taken to Hannington Hall by Colonel CR Major, who had taken over the command of AU from Colonel Gubbins in December 1940. On her arrival, a butler opened the door and a maid asked if she could unpack her cases. (Barbara Culleton recalls that at that time the Fry family still had 14 servants.)

As it was customary for local ATS company or platoon officers to visit the places of work and the billets their subalterns lived in, and to liaise with their local IOs, it was essential for maintaining security to put one commander in charge of the whole AU ATS group despite the work places of individual group members being widely dispersed. The date of Beatrice Temple's appointment to Senior Commander can be found in an amendment to the March 1942 War Establishment (WE No. VIII/203/1, Amendment No. 11), dated 30 May, which allows the addition of "1 Senior Commander, ATS" as well as a driver, a clerk and a 4-seater car, with effect from 4 May 1942. From the day of her appointment as Senior Commander, Beatrice Temple was officially in charge of the group of ATS within AU Signals (controlled by GHQ Home Forces Aux Units). The entries in her diary are, however, proof of her having visited the AU

ATS operators at their IN Station sites as well as in their billets many months before she was given the powers of a Group Commander.

Beatrice Temple's duties as Senior Commander of AU ATS included the organisation and staffing of the secret wireless stations and the welfare of her officers. Initial visits had to be made to IN Stations to ensure that sufficient security was in place for the ATS wireless operators. For instance, before Major Jones' instructions, according to which (from July 1943 onwards) an ATS officer was required to sleep at her place of duty could be put into practice, ATS policy first had to be revised. As a result it was then decided that not one but two ATS subalterns were to sleep at their workstation.

Beatrice Temple was also responsible for finding suitable accommodation (billets) for the subalterns who worked at the various IN Stations; transport to and from the place of duty had to be arranged; access to medical and dental facilities, to shops and banks etc also had to be considered in the planning. It would appear that decisions made by her as the Senior Commander of the ATS were frequently made in collaboration with Major Jones, the OC of AU Signals, with whom she was equal in rank.

This photograph depicting a group of AU ATS subalterns was taken in the autumn of 1941 on the occasion of a training course at No.1 Officer Cadet Training Unit (OCTU) at Craigmillar, Edinburgh. Beatrice Temple (centre front row) is wearing her Tartan skirt. The lady at far left is believed to be Thea Ward. *(Source: Winifred Read, pictured at far right)*

Apart from paying regular visits to the ATS officers at IN Stations and billets, and taking part in many training exercises, Beatrice Temple regularly attended the monthly conferences for senior ATS officers held at Salisbury and at the Group HQs at Cheltenham and Oxford. It is of interest to note that, according to Barbara Culleton, she also made regular visits to Camp 020 (although only one such visit is recorded in her diary - an overnight stay on Saturday, 4 September 1943) and its reserve camp, Camp 020R (opened in January 1943), but not apparently to the Combined Services Detailed Interrogation Centre (CSDIC) at Beaconsfield (run by MI19). Camp 020 was an MI5 interrogation centre based at Latchmere House, a former lunatic asylum on Ham Common in Middlesex. Run by Lieutenant-Colonel Robert "Tin Eye" Stephens (so called because he wore a monocle), the camp held German agents and many members of the British Union of Fascists (BUF), to be interrogated and "broken". The spies imprisoned there were essentially placed in a legal vacuum, outside of both national and international law; they were not classified as combatant prisoners and therefore the Geneva Convention and other international military regulations did not apply to them. Neither was the camp listed or inspected by the International Red Cross. Colonel Stephens has always denied claims that torture had been used at his camp but in 2012 the journalist Ian Cobain revealed that documents obtained at the National Archives would seem to prove that torture methods had been used after all. Interrogators used decrypted German intercepts (received from the code-breakers at Bletchley Park) to convince the prisoners that British Intelligence knew everything about their missions. The prisoners could either work for the British or be hanged. Latchmere House continued to be used as a prison until 2013 when it was sold to a private developer. A reserve Camp, Camp 020R, located at Huntercombe near Nuffield in Oxfordshire, was used mainly for long-term detention. It is currently known as HM Prison Huntercombe.

Another one of Beatrice Temple's duties was to recruit AU ATS officers so that the requirements of the ever-changing policy could be met. Potential candidates were frequently interviewed at the Ladies' Carlton Club or in the tearoom at Harrods, both in London, but also at other locations. Beatrice Temple is said to have interviewed more than 100 women.

When an interview was successful, the candidate was then required to pass a voice test. The voice tests at Bachelor's Hall, the first SD HQ, were conducted at the AU Signals' own test station which was housed in one of the bedrooms, and they involved the Halstead IN Station where Captain Ken Ward's wife, Thea, was one of the operators. After the move of SD HQ to Coleshill House the voice tests continued from there.

As many of the candidates to be recruited were civilians who joined the ATS as a cover, they first required some basic military training, and because ATS regulations did not allow ATS ORs to serve in isolated detachments or to live in civilian billets, the AU ATS recruits who were chosen to work at IN Stations had to be made officers (see also page 31). And so, after having passed their voice test, the successful candidates were sent on a shortened training course which frequently took place at No.1 ATS OCTU at Carlisle House, Craigmillar, in

Edinburgh. Once passed out and commissioned as 2nd subalterns, they were ready to be sent off to work at an IN Station, although some, at least, appear to have received some further training. The recruitment of civilians was stopped during 1942, with the last three civilians being enrolled in July 1942.

Dorothy Monck-Mason (nee Rainey) recalls:

> "After initial training in Scotland (No.1 OCTU), we were posted in units of three to live in billets, after receiving further training by a special Signals unit and directed by the IO of the district we were stationed. Our training was in collating information from OUT Stations and we practised coding and decoding of messages posted to Army HQ." (Letter to Mr Sealy, 24 December 1996; BROM Archive).

Barbara Culleton remembers having spent some time at "a secret location in Essex" (Great Yeldham); Yolande Bromley recalls having trained at Tunbridge Wells (ATS HQ), and Wynne Read remembers being instructed in wireless telegraphy at Challock Lees, north of Ashford. Sally Waterhouse-Brown, who like most others was sent to the ATS OCTU in Edinburgh for initial training - which she finished as the best cadet – received further training at Tunbridge Wells and at Camberley (Surrey), a British Army staff college.

And, of course, all throughout 1942 and 1943 small groups of AU ATS subalterns were invited to attend the courses held at Hannington Hall. Practical training was also continued on site in the form of exercises, which would last from several days to a whole week. Exercises were held regularly every month throughout the four years the organisation existed and once the dugouts had been constructed, the operators would work and live in them for the duration of the exercise.

Instructions on how to conduct these exercises were issued to all SD IOs:

> "We consider that any group which practices fifteen times in the two months period is good."

> "It will, we think, be a stimulus to the maintenance of enthusiasm if members realise that by being a trained body in the defence of the country, they are actively assisting in providing reinforcements for theatres of war. A greater than ever responsibility will be laid on us as new offensives become developed." (Monthly notes to IOs, No 5, July 1943)

> "The best effect of these periods is NOT being experienced by all IOs, owing to lack of previous thought and preparation for them. Although there are many experiments for creating interest and providing useful training in these group practices, the IO should always send out to Group Leaders a general situation of raid or invasion conditions upon which messages should be originated. Much real value is to be gained by careful preparation, and by the introduction of "novelties" of a competitive character." (Monthly notes to IOs, No 6, August 1943)

Barbara Culleton

Barbara Culleton, whose nickname was "The Battling Bantam" (Bantam because of her small size) first met Beatrice Temple at Hickleton Hall, where she and Margery Pye had been manning the IN Station. Although Barbara Culleton worked with Beatrice Temple for only eight months, she clearly remembers her fondly:

"Beatrice Temple was responsible for the administrative matters of all ranks in AU ATS. Duties included interviewing and selection of candidates; registering and inspecting of billets; occasional collection and distribution of supplies, equipment and welfare items; visiting R/T stations and personal contact with ATS branches of the War Office, London District HQ, District and Group HQ throughout the country.

She interviewed candidates at the OCTUs (Edinburgh, Egham and later Windsor) and at the Harrods store in Knightsbridge, London, until the end of September 1943. Personnel required for non-commissioned vacancies were interviewed at their units or came to Hannington Hall.

IN Stations manned by ATS officers were visited regularly, often covering great distances. Service transport was not always available and either she had to go by train or use her own car. Usually overnight accommodation at her destination would be arranged in advance. If none was available, she would sleep in the vehicle or go in search for a barn, haystack or even a field. Breakfast the next morning would be cooked on the spot. Beatrice Temple was hardworking and very thorough in all she undertook.

She was a very kind person with a great sense of humour. In her spare time she would indulge in cycling, horse riding, walking, tennis, dancing and picking wild mushrooms. Although she enjoyed occasional visits to the theatre, she was an avid cinemagoer and took every opportunity to visit one. In addition she was an accomplished needlewoman and knitter and had great expertise in a range of handicrafts.

After being discharged from the ATS, Beatrice Temple was appointed Secretary of the Women's Land Army for London and Middlesex and then Medical Records Officer at the (Royal) London Hospital.

On returning to Sussex, she took up several civil appointments connected with housing associations and schools and she was particularly interested in the welfare of crippled and other disabled people. Her father, who had been a County Councillor for Lewes, died in March 1957 and Beatrice was persuaded to stand for the vacancy. She was Mayoress twice before finally, in 1972, becoming Mayor of Lewes. She continued to serve on the council until her retirement in 1976.

Even in these busy years she added to her leisure pursuits with the design and working of tapestries and papermaking, colourful sheets of notepaper with matching envelopes being her speciality. She also had a wonderful collection of seashells, many from the Seychelles.

Invited to give talks to local associations, she would take a drawer or two with her but relied more on the numerous colour slides which she took to illustrate the full collection. Her other favourite pursuits were bell ringing and gardening.

Beatrice Temple died on 26 September 1982."

That the feeling was reciprocal is evident in Beatrice Temple's diary entry detailing their first meeting, which reads: "Quite taken by little Culleton - cheerful, seems pleasant and willing". During the following days it was arranged that Barbara Culleton should work as Beatrice's assistant and a week later Beatrice Temple herself picked her up at Swindon station. Barbara Culleton recalls:

> "When I arrived at Hannington Hall it was as a 'billettee'. We shared the Fry's accommodation and food. They still had 14 servants. Mr and Mrs Fry sat at opposite ends of an enormously long table and they always dressed for dinner and so we felt we should also make an effort. Normally the four of us, including Major Petherick, were spread out down each side of the dining table but as soon as Army rations appeared we were bunched together in the centre. Then one wing of the Hall was requisitioned by the Area Quartering Commandant and all the comfortable furniture was soon replaced with iron bedsteads and Army-issue mattresses."

> "Welfare was of prime importance and that included also provision to be made for recreational facilities. A few were available locally but in order to have a wider choice, authority was obtained for 'recreational' transport to be provided, within limits, for such as ENSA entertainments (Entertainments National Service Association – set up in 1939 to provide entertainment for British armed forces personnel during WW2) and the cinema. Invitations from regimental units to their social events usually came with the offer to send transport."

Barbara Culleton's time in SD was to last for only eight months, because a few months after she was posted in, the authorities decided to decrease the strength of the AU ATS, and despite a strong plea made by Colonel Beyts -"Not only do we want a Senior Commander, we want this Senior Commander!" - the War Office had even questioned the necessity of having a Senior Commander (see also page 33).

The SD IOs discussed the weeding-out process, each attempting to keep their best officers, and when it was decided to move a handful of ATS subalterns to other duties at HQ, at least some of the IOs would appear to have requested for certain subalterns to be retained at the IN Stations they worked. Major Winterborn, for instance, had agreed for Joan Boitel-Gill to be moved to HQ but Captain Oakey pointed out that Mickey Brown was far too valuable to be moved, and Major Crawley tried to persuade Beatrice Temple not to move Eleanor Norman-Butler.

Colonel Beyts at least did get what he had wished for when Beatrice Temple was eventually installed as Senior Commander on 4 May 1942. One year later the policy would seem to again have been reversed when an increase of 25 ATS was requested and agreed upon (in January 1943), as is documented in the Establishment passed on 30 April – one year too late for Barbara Culleton, who was one of the subalterns to be affected by the May 1942 cull (see also page 33).

Barbara Culleton's farewell party was held on 3 May 1942 at Hannington Hall. Colonel and Lady Glanusk, Mr Fry, Major and Mrs Wilfred W Harston, Captain and Mrs Nigel Oxenden, Captain BH Tracey, Captain Tallant, Joan Boitel-Gill and Mary Burton, Major Charles Randell's secretary and sister of Edwina Caroline Gearey Burton, an AU ATS wireless operator, all attended. "BC departed (with some difficulty) at 09.30" reads Beatrice Temple's diary entry for the following day. Barbara Culleton's military service record shows that she was posted to Combined Operations. She retired in 1957 holding the honorary rank of Junior Commander.

Barbara Culleton is presently living in a care home in East Sussex.

Barbara Marion Culleton
(Source: BROM Archive)

View into the main chamber of the Alnwick (Northumberland) IN Station dugout. Remains of shelves and the openings of the two large ventilation ducts can be seen on the dividing wall, with the exit tunnel opening in the generator room visible in the background. *(Photo: Colin Anderson)*

A similar view of the Halstead (Essex) IN Station.

The IN Station at Heathfield Park (East Sussex) with many of its original features still in place and in good condition. *(This drawing is based on a photograph taken in 2010)*

The IN Station at Norwich (Norfolk) is in an equally well-preserved condition.

The IN Stations at Hollingbourne, Kent (above) and at Shipley, West Sussex (below) are less well preserved. *(Photos: Brian Drury)*

The collapsed IN Station site on the Blorenge near Abergavenny, Wales.
(Photo: 'gubbins', 2011)

The site of the IN/Relay Station at Ousden (Suffolk) of which only the concrete hut platforms remain. The station never had a dugout.

View into the main chamber of the IN/Relay Station at Ardingly (West Sussex) *(Photographer unknown)*

Two views of the Winchester (Hampshire) IN Station, one showing a view into the main chamber with the exit tunnel opening seen in the background (right) and one of the large glazed ceramic ventilation ducts traversing the generator room. *(Photographer unknown)*

The wartime Diaries

The ATS subalterns Doris White and later also Mary Shaw, former AU ATS wireless operators, replaced Barbara Culleton. It took three more years before Beatrice Temple too left Hannington Hall for good, on 13 March 1944 "with own car loaded to the brim". She was posted to Greenford COD Group as 2nd in command and on the occasion of a visit from "Oxo" (Captain NV Oxenden, AU HQ staff officer based at Coleshill House) she learnt that "Aux Units SD is packing up – very sad." She also received a visit from Major John Hills (the former CO of AU Signals), asking for assistance for his wife Kitty, one of the first AU ATS wireless operators in East Anglia, who was stuck in one of the transit camps waiting for a new posting. This apparently never came through because Kitty Hills left the ATS on 25 July 1944, a fate that she shared with most of her AU ATS colleagues who, because of the specialised nature of their duties and their lack of experience in the ATS proper, were virtually unemployable. The passing-out parade was held at OCTU No.2 (Windsor) on 30 August 1944, where Beatrice Temple was reunited, albeit only for the day, with 23 of her former officers. The rest of the war was spent in 'unexciting' jobs (her own words) in ATS administration, where she eventually reached the rank of Chief Commander, the equivalent of a lieutenant colonel in the Army.

After the closedown of the Special Duties Branch, Beatrice's diary entries soon become sporadic and then cease altogether. Her diaries covered the period from her posting to SD, including the arrival at Highworth on 24 November 1941, until closedown in summer 1944. Sadly, the original diaries – many pages of handwritten notes chronicling daily events; duties and chores; visits to IN Station sites and to ATS offices and HQs; names of people met in the course of her duties; discussions with HQ staff officers and ATS subalterns - were destroyed about ten years ago. A transcript made by Barbara Culleton shortly before the originals were destroyed fills 63 pages. The following random excerpts, dating from 20 and 21 January 1943, are typical examples illustrating just how busy her days were.

> "Morpeth. Saw G1 – said he would ask but not force OC Unit to have ATS in Mess. Spent ages with Colonel Leethbridge – offered several suggestions but said he would do his best with OC Unit. On to Alnwick – Pamela there – lunch in hut. After lunch met Colonel Villiers – willing to have them. Back to hut – picked up Pamela – introduced to Anderson, then tea in Mess. At 5.0 lifted Colonel Villiers, batman and luggage. Dinner at Hotel with Colonel Villiers and Colonel Grant. Returned to Newcastle. Overnight stay.

> Scotch Corner – lunch with Whiting, Filer and Read - Filer and Read feel far from home! South Dalton – got bogged and had to be extracted by farm cart – cost 5/- ! Britton very disgruntled. Beverley. Overnight stay."

The following excerpts are based on a much abridged typescript version created by Barbara Culleton and published here by her kind permission. Additional information regarding the AU ATS officers and the dates of their commissions was taken from the London Gazette and its Supplements.

Mar. 1   Col. Beyts at HH — entirely new arrangement made for Grey.

2   Maj. Winterbourn at HH. going almost at once — Possibility that number of ATS may be cut down to 30. Thinks we should get Boitee - Gee.

3   Maj. W & Maj. P. have agreed on only 30 ATS.

4   Reigate — (Lady Carlisle Sick) — said Sub. helped CSO's office "you're the Queen - bee of the hush - hush Party"! Worked at Swindon for Col. Beyts and discussed possible change of policy.

7   Blandford — looked in at billet, then Hut (lunch) then again and to billet hunt — mostly fruitless. Home via Salisbury & Marlborough (Capt. R. at Salisbury all day)

8   HQ Party — first discussed Syllabus for Courses with Maj. Part Col. Maj., Maj. P., Col. Beyts, Anty, new Col., Capts. Warston, Randell & Mike Henderson + Capt. Tracey.

10   Shrivenham — (Called in Barrack Warden) + chairs, rugs + wpbs delivered HH late.

11   Grey arrived HH + furniture.

13   HH with Grey. Maj. P. — new OC, Sigs. Capt. Ince, new MTO — Capt. Crawley. Maj. Winterbourn + Ione at HH — told of awful version of GHQ decision??? Horrified.
... of protest to Col. Beyts?? (Any connection e previous remark?) Maj. P. leave 17th. Brief Gill arrived at HH.

16   R.6 to Hell — interviewed by 2 Cols ... Bolt... C.O. wants Course made to last a week. Capt. ...list Farrer, Tracey + Maj. Winterbourn. Successful billet hunt for R.6 with Capt. Crawley.

28 Nov 1941
HUNDON: Maj Winterborn and Capt Ward

Captain Ken Ward joined the unit in January 1941 with the rank of staff captain. A trial network in Kent consisting of an IN Station and five OUT Stations was already operational.

29 Nov 1941
NORWICH: Eleanor Norman-Butler, Capt Shanks
Ely: Interview with Joan Boitel-Gill

Eleanor Mary Norman-Butler was commissioned as a 2nd subaltern on 7 September 1941. She was amongst the last to leave at closedown in July 1944 when she (like all her remaining colleagues) was posted to No.1 War Office Holding Unit and struck off the strength of Auxiliary Units. Her last posting appears to have been to the Ousden IN/Relay Station. She had been attached to HQ West Suffolk District when she was posted out.

Joan Ursula Boitel Gill was commissioned as a 2nd subaltern on 21 September 1941. "Sombre woman, imagine very efficient – candidate for HQ", noted Beatrice Temple.

Captain Tom Shanks was part of the AU Signals HQ staff at Bachelor's Hall.

The Norwich IN Station (call-sign "Bowling") was initially a hut situated within the grounds of Sprowston Hall, the then Forward HQ of the Norfolk (later 76th) Division. The new location, operational from sometime in 1942 onwards, had a dugout, which, in 2012, was discovered in very good condition. The every-day workstation at this new location was housed not in a hut but in a nearby folly tower.

1 Dec 1941
Gt Yeldham: Pye and Culleton interviewed
DONCASTER: Maj Winterborn

Great Yeldham is a village in north-east Essex. When the first AU Signals HQ was established at Bachelor's Hall, Hundon, Captain John Hills had brought ATS subaltern Mickey Browne up from Kent because of her secretarial experience. She soon took over the trainee ATS wireless operators, who stayed in one of a pair of requisitioned semi-detached cottages at Great Yeldham. Captain Freddie Childe and his family lived in the other. The cottages were built by the Land Settlement Association (a country-wide scheme set up in about 1934 under the Benevolent Societies Act by the Carnegie UK Trust) to provide accommodation and smallholdings of four to seven acres for unemployed miners.

"To Swindon to pick up 'little Culleton'", commented Beatrice Temple. Barbara Marion Culleton (205716) was commissioned as a 2nd subaltern on 7 September 1941 in an Emergency Commission. On 18 September, her military service record shows her as having been posted to Hundon in Suffolk, where she spent some time at the AU Signals HQ, then based at Bachelor's Hall. On 9 October she moved to 1st Corps HQ, which at the time was based at Hickleton Hall, in the West Riding district of Yorkshire. As of 8 December 1941, Barbara Culleton was attached to the HQ of the Auxiliary Units (at Coleshill House). In May 1942, when the number of AU Signals was increased by 70 whilst the number of AU ATS was decreased by 104, ie from 135 to 31, Barbara Culleton was amongst the officers affected by this policy, and the posting to Combined Operations on 4 May 1942 - on the same date that Beatrice Temple was appointed Senior Commander ATS – effectively ended her career in AU ATS. Barbara Culleton remained with the ATS for many years longer; she retired from the Royal Women's Army Corps on 7 August 1957, retaining her rank as captain.

Margery Anne Pye was commissioned as a 2nd subaltern on 20 July 1941. She relinquished her commission on 1 January 1943 on ceasing to be employed.

Doncaster refers to Hickleton Hall, then owned by Lord Halifax, in the West Riding district of Yorkshire. The IN Station served the HQ of 1st Corps, which was stationed there. From 1961 until 2012 the Hall was a Sue Ryder care centre.

9 Dec 1941
London: Interview with Pte Dray at CRO Office

12 Dec 1941
CANTERBURY: Hilary Paddock and Hilary Graham
REIGATE: Doris White and Thompson
HEATHFIELD: Wynne Read and MN Filer on leave

The Canterbury (Kent) IN Station is believed to have been located near the barracks (see also page 116). It had no OUT Stations of its own and would seem to have served as an outpost of Harrietsham (Hollingbourne) IN Station.

Hilary Joan Paddock was commissioned as a 2nd subaltern on 3 August 1941, with seniority and precedence 20 July 1941, next below Mrs DM Baily.

Hilary Graham (married name Gordon) was promoted to 2nd Subaltern on 7 September 1941. She was later sent to work at the IN/Relay Station at Ousden in West Suffolk (call-sign "Gorey").

The Reigate (Surrey) IN Station is believed to have been situated on Reigate Hill but its exact location has as yet to be found. Reigate Hill was also the location of the HQ of South Eastern Command (see also page 154).

Enid Mary Thompson was commissioned as a 2nd subaltern on 21 September 1941 in an Emergency Commission. Isobel Doris White was commissioned on 7 September 1941. She remained in the ATS until 29 October 1944 by which time she held the rank of Junior Commander. The work of both appears to have been confined to the Reigate IN Station. In early January 1943, Doris White was moved to HQ where she took over Barbara Culleton's role as Beatrice Temple's administrative assistant.

Heathfield Park (East Sussex) was the HQ of the 55th (Lancashire) Division. The IN Station was located near the folly tower at the north-western end of Heathfield Park. It consisted of a hut equipped with wireless sets and a dugout nearby. Access to the dugout was gained by pulling back a loose piece of bark on a tree, and pressing the switch that was concealed under it. A trap door located about 50 yards away slowly lifted, giving access to a ladder leading down into a small room. The walls of this room had shelves holding boxes of explosives and ammunition, but under one of the shelves there was a hidden catch that gave access to the wireless room, equipped with wireless sets, food, clothing and bunks. Adjoining this room was another one which had a chemical toilet and an emergency exit. (Winifred Read in: *Heathfield Park*, Roy Pryce, 1996). The station was closed in November 1943 (see also page 158).

Winifred Audrey "Wynne" Read was commissioned as a 2nd subaltern on 3 August 1941, with seniority and precedence 20 July 1941, next below Mrs DM Baily (196756). In a letter (in BROM Archive, dated 5 July 1994) she wrote that besides Heathfield Park she also worked at several other locations (in January 1943 she was at the Scotch Corner IN Station. Miss Read worked as a private in the Pay Corps near Sidcup when she was recruited and then trained in wireless telegraphy at Challock Lees near Ashford. She was among the last to leave when on 25 July 1944, she was posted to No.1 War Office Holding Unit and struck off the strength of Auxiliary Units.

At closedown in July 1944, her former colleague, Marjorie Filer, had been attached to "F" Coy East Riding & Lincolnshire District Group ATS. Marjorie Nora Filer was commissioned on 3 August 1941, with seniority next below Mrs DM Baily.

The role of Mrs Doris Margaret Baily (196756) is not clear. She was promoted 2nd subaltern on 20 July 1942, with seniority next below Mrs B.M.E.S.M.G. Bonaparte-Wyse (196530).

13 Dec 1941
TUNBRIDGE WELLS: Marjorie Barden
EAST GRINSTEAD: Curtis alone
WEST GRINSTEAD: Richardson and Trevakis
WINCHESTER: Vaile and Dicken
SALISBURY: Holmes alone

12th (XII) Corps District HQ was based at 16 Broadwater Down, Tunbridge Wells (Kent). No details are currently known regarding the exact location of an IN Station, which might have served these headquarters. Tunbridge Wells was also the location of an ATS HQ.

Marjorie Lilian Barden was commissioned as a 2nd subaltern on 29 June 1941. She is known to also have worked at Heathfield Park (East Sussex) IN Station for some time. Marjorie Barden appears to have been one of the first women to be recruited and she was one of the last AU ATS to leave, working until closedown on 25 July 1944, when she was posted to No.1 War Office Holding Unit and struck off the strength of Auxiliary Units.

Two Army HQs were situated near East Grinstead (West Sussex): 4th Corps Advanced HQ was based at Paddockhurst (the manor house presently forms part of Worth School) and the Rear HQ was at Turners Hill. In the summer of 1941 the Canadian Corps took over the responsibility for the defence of the district. The IN Station was situated in the grounds of Wakehurst Place, Ardingly, currently owned by the National Trust. Discovered in 2008 by estate workers, the dugout, which is in fair condition (the exit end has collapsed but much of the original wiring is still in situ) has been recorded and then sealed (see also page 157).

Sarah Henrietta Curtis was commissioned as a 2nd subaltern on 29 June 1941. After she married her surname changed to Olesinka. She stayed in the ATS after closedown and was granted the honorary rank of Junior Commander in June 1947.

Sybil Hazel Richardson was commissioned in Emergency Commissions on 21 Sept 1941, together with a batch of 15 other women, who all worked as wireless operators at various IN Stations.

Winifred Eve Trevaskis too was amongst the large batch of altogether 16 AU ATS subalterns to be commissioned on 21 September 1941. She later worked at the Scotch Corner (East Riding of Yorkshire) IN Station for some time. Sybil Hazel Richardson who also worked at Challock (Kent) and Hatfield Peverel (Essex) IN Stations had been attached to the HQ of East Riding & Lincolnshire District at closedown in July 1944.

West Grinstead refers to the IN Station near Shipley (West Sussex, see also page 155), sometimes also referred to as Knepp Castle, a 12th century motte and bailey fortress in the vicinity, of which only a short section of wall remains. West Grinstead Manor was the base of the 47th (London) Division HQ. In November 1941, after the Canadian Corps had taken over from 4th Corps, the 1st Canadian Division had their Advanced HQ there. Their Rear HQ was at Woodgaters. The IN Station had the call-sign "Harston" and its location has been found and recorded. The manor house, designed to look like a medieval castle, was demolished in the 1960s due to damage suffered during the requisition.

The Winchester (Hampshire) network (call-sign "Omagh") was set up by Alf Ellis and his team of AU signallers. The IN Station (in good condition but inaccessible) is located in the garden of Pitt Manor. It served the HQ of 4th Division, based at Winchester (see also page 112).

Whereas Marjorie Vaile appears to only have worked at Winchester, Betty B Dicken is known to also have worked at South Dalton (East Riding) IN Station. The third in this team, Bettine Mary Holmes, was commissioned as a

2nd subaltern on 21 Sept 1941 and later worked at the Blandford (Dorset) IN Station.

Mrs Betty Berkeley Dicken was commissioned as a 2nd subaltern on 7 September 1941. Marjorie Muriel Berkeley Vaile was commissioned on the same date. *(Betty Dicken's maiden name was Vaile and she was Marjorie's sister.)* Sadly, Betty Berkeley Dicken, then 27-years old, committed suicide on 8 November 1943 (at Heathfield Park) by deliberately inhaling the poisonous carbon monoxide gasses generated by the battery-charging engine.

Several Army HQs were situated in the vicinity of Salisbury (Wiltshire): 5th Corps HQ was at Alderbury, Southern Command HQ at Wilton and 43rd (Wessex) Division HQ in Salisbury. Major Peter Forbes, who in late 1943 visited all the IN Stations, recalls that the Salisbury IN/Relay Station was near Wilton House (letter to Arthur Gabbitas, 1 Feb 1998; BROM Archive). Southern Command HQ was based at Wilton House. Beatrice Temple met the "new very young Major Forbes at hut" on Friday, 3 September 1943 (see also page 165). During 1941 and 1942 the IN Station was located near the rectory in Alderbury before it was moved to a new location near Wilton.

15 Dec 1941
HALSTEAD: *Thea Ward and Mickey Browne*
HATFIELD PEVEREL: *Kitty Hills*
THORNHAM MAGNA: *Margaret Whiting and Yolande Bromley*

The Halstead (Essex) IN Station (call-sign "Buttercup") consisted of a hut and a dugout. The latter was located in the grounds of Dynes Hall which was the HQ of the 42nd Division. The dugout is in good condition and has been recorded (see also page 152).

The Hatfield Peverel (Essex) IN Station passed on its information to the Essex Division HQ which was located in its vicinity, at Berwick Place, Hatfield Peverel. General Frederik E Morgan visited the site on 4 February 1943. He is perhaps best known as the Chief of Staff to the Supreme Allied Commander (COSSAC), the original planner of Operation Overlord. The exact location of the IN Station has as yet to be found.

The Thornham Magna (Suffolk) IN Station (call-sign "Chariot") was situated within the perimeter of the 15th (Scottish) Division HQ at Thornham Magna Hall but moved to a nearby wood in the autumn of 1942 when AU signallers took over its operation (see also page 145).

Thea Ward, Kitty Hills were among the first wireless operators who worked at IN Stations in East Anglia; Mickey Browne helped setting up the network in Kent. Amy Dorothea Ward was commissioned as a 2nd subaltern on 3 August 1941, next below Winifred A Read. She relinquished her command on 23 March 1942, when her husband, Captain Ken Ward, left AU Signals for the IRSB/SOE.

Kathleen Marie "Kitty" Hills was the wife of Major John Hills, who at the time was with AU Signals HQ at Bachelor's Hall, Hundon. She was commissioned as a 2nd subaltern on 20 July 1941. Kitty Hills later also worked at Hatfield Peverel (Essex), Buckland St Mary (Somerset) and Thornham Magna (Suffolk) IN Stations. At closedown in July 1944, she had been attached to HQ South Western District.

Margaret Esme Whiting was commissioned as a 2nd subaltern on 29 June 1941 and remained in the ATS until 15 December 1944. She and Yolande Bromley formed a team, first at Thornham Magna and later at the Bury St Edmunds IN Station (both in Suffolk). Margaret Whiting also worked at Halstead, Lincomb (Worcs) and Doncaster (West Riding).

Yolande Audrey Yvette Bromley (married name Alston) was commissioned as a 2nd subaltern, with seniority and precedence 29 June 1941, next below Mrs B.M.E.S.M.G. Bonaparte-Wyse (196530). She married on 7 July 1942 and relinquished her commission on 20 April 1943.

Phyllis Michelle "Mickey" Browne was also commissioned on 29 June 1941. She was moved from Kent to Essex, where she helped to train novice AU ATS wireless operators at a requisitioned cottage in the village of Great Yeldham. For some time she also worked as a Stores Officer. Mickey Browne's married name was Trant. She relinquished her commission on 27 June 1948 and was granted the honorary rank of subaltern.

16 Dec 1941
LINCOLN: Mary Alexander and Ann Gunter

Canwick Hall (see also page 119) was the seat of the Sibthorp family, with the present house dating from 1810. During WW2 it was the home of Arthur William de Brito Savile Foljambe, 2nd Earl of Liverpool from 1939 to his death there in May 1941. His half-brother, Gerald Foljambe, succeeded him in his titles. Both the 1st and the Lincolnshire Divisions were stationed at Canwick Hall (the latter was disbanded in autumn 1941). There also used to be a Royal Signals centre (presumably unconnected) which operated from a concrete bunker situated in a former quarry near the village centre. The main Signals camp, originally occupied by the staff, later became a POW camp (Camp no. 1012 - referred to as Canwick Camp).

Mary Alexander was commissioned on 21 Sept 1941. At closedown on 25 July 1944 she had been attached to the HQ of West Essex Sub District. Ann Lettice Valborg Gunter was commissioned on 21 Sept 1941, together with a number of other AU ATS. Her surname changed to Dielman after her marriage, and she is remembered by Stanley Judson as a talented sculptress, a career she appears to have pursued after the war. She stayed in the ATS and later in the WRAC, where she was promoted to lieutenant in May 1952. Ann Dielman died on 31 May 1998 in the Victoria Nursing Home in Hove, East Sussex. In the death notice, "Sculptress" was given as her profession.

The 2nd subalterns Mary Alexander and Ann Gunter later also worked together as a team at Cheddon Fitzpaine (near Taunton in Somerset, call-sign "Golding"), and at Norwich, Halstead and Tunbridge Wells IN Stations.

After lunch, returned to Bachelor's Hall and then Hotel (White Hart) in Great Yeldham. Met Thea Ward and Mickey Brown – am amazed at Mrs Ward, so nice marrying Capt. W!

22 Dec 1941 – Miss Hilliers and Pte Brown for tests (at Hannington Hall)

1 Jan 1942
CANTERBURY: Wendy Kaines, Hilary Graham and Hilary Paddock

> Wendy Monica Pax Kaines was commissioned as a 2nd subaltern on 20 July 1941. She relinquished her commission on 15 December 1944.

2 Jan 1942
REIGATE: Doris White and Thompson
TUNBRIDGE WELLS: Marjorie Barden
HEATHFIELD: Wynne Read and Filer

3 Jan 1942
TUNBRIDGE WELLS: Marjorie Barden found hut open
EAST GRINSTEAD: Curtis
Tea with Seaver

10 Jan 1942
WINCHESTER: Davis

> Margaret Eileen Davis was commissioned on 2 February 1942. Her name appears in context with the IN Station at Winchester (Hampshire) only. On the occasion of her visit, Beatrice Temple found two men at the hut, complaining about wireless interference. She did not note how the issue was resolved.

13 Jan 1942
London: Interviews with Waddy Cole, Mrs Phyllis Britten and Miss Ronald at Major Petherick's house

> Phyllis Marion Britten was commissioned as a 2nd subaltern on 11 March 1942, relinquishing her commission on 8 November 1944. She worked at Tunbridge Wells, Canterbury and Blandford IN Stations.

Mary Patience Ronald (married name Whigham) was commissioned on 11 March 1942 and based at Canterbury; she left ATS on 24 October 1943.

Florence Margaret "Waddy" Cole too was commissioned on 11 March 1942. She worked at the Norwich and later at the Bury St Edmunds IN Stations and relinquished her commission on 20 December 1944.

14 Jan 1942
London: Interviews with Mann and Carver at Ladies Carlton Club

24 Jan 1942
Aldershot: Interviews with Sgt Hackwood, Pte Hackwood and Pte Stronach at ATS Coy

Muriel Helen Hackwood worked at the Winchester and Edinburgh (call-sign "Barnack") IN Stations. She was one of the last to leave when she was posted to No.1 War Office Holding Unit and struck off the strength of Auxiliary Units at closedown in July 1944. She relinquished her commission on 30 November 1944.

Her sister, Edith Margaret Hackwood was also in AU ATS. The sisters were commissioned as 2nd subalterns on 27 June 1942 but whereas Muriel worked as a wireless operator, Margaret later became a Stores Officer, remembered by Stanley Judson for painting the doors and shutters in the AU Signals officers' quarters because she had so little else to do. (Letter to Arthur Gabbitas, dated 11 February 1995; BROM Archive)

Elisabeth Templer Stronach was commissioned on 11 March 1942 and later worked at the Winchester IN Station.

27 Jan 1942
Sevenhampton: Interview with Dodo Campbell

Evelyn Doriel Mary "Dodo" Campbell was commissioned as a 2nd subaltern on 30 May 1941. She worked at the Lincoln and Doncaster IN Stations and was remembered by Stanley Judson as having been one of the IO's lady friends. (Letter to Arthur Gabbitas, dated 11 February 1995; BROM Archive)

31 Jan 1942
Norwich: Interview with Joan Boitel-Gill – stayed overnight at Cole's house

1 Feb 1942
LINCOLN: Joan Fox and Hildyard

Joan Marion Fox later also worked at Salisbury (Wiltshire), Lincomb (Worcester) and Doncaster (South Yorkshire) IN Stations.

Alma Vernon Hildyard was commissioned on 15 January 1942 and after the war pursued a successful career with the ATS: in December 1945 she was appointed temporary Junior Commander; in December 1946 she received an MBE and was granted the honorary rank of Junior Commander; in December 1950 she was granted the honorary rank of Captain and promoted to Lieutenant.

2 Feb 1942
DONCASTER: Pye, Hay and Whiting

4 Feb 1942
HATFIELD PEVEREL: MA Lloyd, Burbage and Richardson

Marion Avis Lloyd was commissioned as a 2nd subaltern on 15 January 1942. She appears to only have worked at Hatfield Peverel, whereas her colleague, Marguerite Burbage (223872), who was commissioned on the same date, later moved on to work at Norwich IN Station. Miss Burbage was granted the rank of Honorary Junior Commander in October 1948.

At closedown of the Special Duties Branch in July 1944, her colleague Marion Lloyd had been attached to HQ South Eastern Command.

5 Feb 1942
London: Interviews with Badgerow and Wood at Ladies Carlton Club

Priscilla Mary Badgerow was commissioned in February 1942. She later worked at Tunbridge Wells.

Millicent Mary Magdalene Wood was commissioned on 11 March 1942; her name does not appear again on the diary pages. Beatrice Temple describes her as "vivacious".

6 Feb 1942
London: Interviews with Dodo Campbell, Miss Lawrence, Miss Bird, and Mrs McDonnell at Ladies Carlton Club

Airlie Abinda Campbell was commissioned as a 2nd subaltern on 15 April 1942. She is known to also have worked at Thornham Magna (Suffolk) and Hollingbourne (Kent) IN Stations. At some time between the date of her commissioning and the date she relinquished it on 15 May 1944, she married Clive Gascoyne, a member of the Sittingbourne Auxiliary Units operational patrol. In an interview her son, James Campbell Gascoyne, recalls that his mother never spoke about her wartime activities but that his father once took him to the site of the Harrietsham (Hollingbourne) IN-Station after the war (British Resistance Archive). Beatrice Temple describes her as "delightful".

Mrs Margaret Mary Lawrence was commissioned on 27 November 1941; her name does not appear again in the diary.

16 Feb 1942
BLANDFORD: Ann Ellis-Hughes and two others

The Blandford (Dorset) IN Station was situated in Buzbury Wood, near where 3rd Division was stationed at Langton House (see also page 107).

Mrs Anne Ellis-Hughes was commissioned as a 2nd subaltern on 7 September 1941. She later worked at the Ousden IN/Relay Station in West Suffolk.

18 Feb 1942
London: Interview with Pte Dray at CRO Office

23 Feb 1942
CANTERBURY: Graham in hut, Paddock and Davis in billet
– had them to dinner

24 Feb 1942
CHALLOCK
TUNBRIDGE WELLS: Maj Dawnay G2I
HEATHFIELD

Challock was the location of an IN Station in Kent, which is reported to have been situated on White Hill (Adrian Westwood, Kent Auxiliary Units website). Captain Norman Field recalls that the station was one of the first to have been set up and presumably it formed part of the trial network because it seems to already have been in place when Captain (later Lt Colonel) Norman Field took over from Captain Peter Fleming in autumn 1940 (see also page 116).

25 Feb 1942
EAST GRINSTEAD: Pam Irving and Richardson
WEST GRINSTEAD: Janet Purves-Smith and Richards

Myfanwy Janet Purves-Smith, whose married name was Wise, was commissioned on 15 March 1942 and relinquished her commission on 29 September 1944. She is known to have worked at the Halstead (Essex) and Alnwick (Northumberland) IN Stations. In July 1944 she was attached to HQ Alnwick Sub-District. Rosemary Beatrice Richards was commissioned on 15 March 1942; she relinquished her commission on 12 May 1942.

7 Mar 1942
BLANDFORD: Billet, hut, and billet hunting

23 Mar 1942
SALISBURY: Hut and billet
BLANDFORD: Kaines and D Monck-Mason, and Capts Jones and Hall-Hall

> Two ATS "Meteorological officers" are said to have been billeted on a property called "Swinfen" in Light's Lane, Alderbury.
>
> Dorothy Eileen Monck-Mason, nee Rainey, was commissioned as a 2nd subaltern on 11 March 1942. She worked at Salisbury (Wiltshire) and Reigate (Surrey) IN Stations.
>
> Captain (sic) Jones was Major RMA "Spud" Jones, mentioned by Major Peter Forbes in a letter to Arthur Gabbitas (dated 1 Feb 1998, BROM Archive), the officer commanding AU Signals. Captain Owen B Hall-Hall was the IO for the Winchester-Salisbury area. The diary of Alf Ellis (dated 1942) reveals that his codename was "Chaney".

Maj Winterborn, Maj Jones, Capt Hall-Hall, Mr Monck-Mason & wife and Kaines. Very glad I went down to Blandford today – a psychological moment to arrive at Hut!

25 Mar 1942
London: three interviews at Harrods, one Duthie

30 Mar 1942
REIGATE: White and Thompson, supply of equipment
CHALLOCK: Hut closed, Pamela Adams-Beck seen in billet

> Doris Elsie "Pamela" Adams-Beck was commissioned on 20 February 1942. She would appear to have worked only at the Challock (Kent) IN Station and her name does not appear again in the diary. The London Gazette records the date she relinquished her commission as 30 March 1944.

31 Mar 1942
CANTERBURY: Hilary Paddock, equipment; Graham in hospital
HATFIELD PEVEREL: Lloyd and Richardson (Burbage had left)

1 Apr 1942
HALSTEAD: Margaret Whiting and Clifford
THORNHAM MAGNA: Kitty Hills and Yolande Bromley; supplies
NORWICH: Burbage - Talked about lack of Security.

> Nina Clifford was commissioned on 11 March 1942; she relinquished her commission on 15 December 1944.

2 April 1942 - Major Collings has further proof of Burbage's lack of Security.

14 Apr 1942

Driven to WINCHESTER - but full of workmen. Billet reported all gone to Southampton. Misdirected to Salisbury.

SALISBURY: Rosemary Astley-Cooper and Bettine Holmes both wish to be platoon officers.

BLANDFORD: Ann Ellis-Hughes and Dorothy Monck-Mason
BARNSLEY (Glos): Pye and Hay-Whiting at hut
LINCOMB (Worcs): Margaret Whiting and Joan Fox

> Rosemary Ann Astley-Cooper was commissioned as a 2nd subaltern in an Emergency Commission on 21 Sept 1941, together with a batch of other AU ATS, including Bettine Mary Holmes, who was the daughter of a Quarter Master General.

> Pamela Hay-Whiting (married name Goodman) was commissioned on 15 January 1942 and remained in the ATS until 5 November 1945.

> Barnsley and Lincomb appear to have been the locations of temporary IN Stations. The locations do not feature again in Beatrice Temple's diary nor are they marked on Major Jones' map.

17 Apr 1942
Shrivenham - Capt Boydon refused to hand over any equipment

20 Apr 1942
London: Interviews with Sgt Thomas and Pte Mary Shaw

Mary Frances Shaw was commissioned on 27 June 1942 and later worked at the Bury St Edmunds (Suffolk) IN Station until in October 1942, when she was knocked down by a car and sustained serious head injuries (from which she fully recovered). She was later moved to HQ and Rosemary Astley-Cooper took her place at the Bury St Edmunds IN Station. In December 1943 Mary Shaw was typing letters for the OC (Officer Commanding) ATS Auxiliary Units at HQ at Coleshill House.

21 Apr 1942
REIGATE: All well
EAST GRINSTEAD: Curtis and Seaver have had a row
WEST GRINSTEAD: Purves-Smith only
HEATHFIELD: All well
TUNBRIDGE WELLS: Alexander alone

Hope Leslie Seaver was commissioned as a 2nd subaltern on 7 September 1941; she relinquished her commission on 24 March 1944.

CHALLOCK: Richardson and Hilliers

Constance Mary Caroline Hilliers was commissioned on 11 March 1942 and stayed in the ATS until 1949.

22 Apr 1942
CANTERBURY: Wendy Kaines and Hilary Graham
Did Cipher with Alexander (Tunbridge Wells), explained new policy (decrease of ATS numbers) to Richardson (Challock); Hilliers asked about change to Ack-Ack

29 Apr 1942
WINCHESTER: Hut empty. Dicken and Vaile in billet. Back to hut- waited until Stronach appeared.

1 May 1942
REDHILL/REIGATE: White. Monck-Mason arrived

6 May 1942
TUNBRIDGE WELLS: Gunter

EAST GRINSTEAD: *Maj Unwin Canadian Unit*

The Canadian Corps formed part of South-Eastern Command. Having taken over from 4th Corps in November 1941, the 1st Canadian Corps Advanced HQ was located at Wakehurst Place, with the Rear HQ at Worth Priory. Major Unwin was the CO of the Canadian Divisional HQ at Tunbridge Wells.

7 May 1942
HATFIELD PEVEREL/HALSTEAD
THORNHAM MAGNA: *Capt Oakey*

Captain (later Lieutenant) Frank D Oakey was the SD IO for the Norwich area in spring 1942. By the autumn of 1943 he was billeted at an address in Sevenoaks as the IO for Kent and he was later moved to Somerset.

8 May 1942
NORWICH: *Found all three. Capt Knight G31*
LINCOLN: *Pye and Dodo Campbell*
DONCASTER: *Whiting and Airlie*

13 May 1942
YORK/S DALTON: *Capt Shanks*

18 May 1942
LONDON: *GHQ Maj Feeney*

19 May 1942
WINCHESTER: *Hut empty, three in billet*
BLANDFORD: *Ann Ellis-Hughes and Phyllis Britten*

20 May 1942
WEST GRINSTEAD: *Janet Purves-Smith and Hazel*

25 May 1942
REIGATE: *Thompson*

26 May 1942
HEATHFIELD: Majs Randell and Jones and Capt Fraser at hut
TUNBRIDGE WELLS/CHALLOCK/CANTERBURY

EAST GRINSTEAD: Canadian Corps gone, British to take over

Captain (later Major) Robert Fraser from the Intelligence Corps was the SD
IO for the South Eastern district. Major RMA Jones was the commander of
AU Signals from March 1942. He was based at Coleshill House.

27 May 1942
CANTERBURY: Wendy Kaines and Graham; Paget off duty

28 May 1942
London: Interviews with Sgt Ellis and Evans

No information has been found about Evans and Sergeant Ellis. The latter
could not have been Sergeant Alf N Ellis of AU Signals, who, according to his
diary, spent the day setting up an aerial with reflector at the Salisbury IN
Station.

1 June 1942
CANTERBURY: Bomb damage to billet. Graham and Paget. Rations and
bedding etc taken over.

4 June 1942
DONCASTER: No ATS at hut, equipment left at "B" Mess

5 June 1942
SOUTH DALTON: Col Devereux

Market Weighton: Capt Shanks; "visited" S Dalton via radio call. Up a little
hill to broadcast back to Doncaster – surprised as "Belinda calling"

Dalton Hall in South Dalton (East Riding), near Beverley, was the HQ of the
Yorkshire Division. This division was directly under the command of
Northern Command and later came under 1st Corps. The site was found and
recorded by Alan Williamson (see page 169).

9 June 1942
NORWICH: Waddy Cole only

10 June 1942
All night exercise, participated until 4.30am

12 June 1942
Long session with Maj Randell at HQ – tried to pin him down to circular letter saying ATS can't be allotted to Stations. No good!

18 June 1942
London: Interviews at Harrods, one failed to arrive (McGarry), remainder unsuitable

20 June 1942
REIGATE: Thompson, Doris White and Lady Carlisle
EAST GRINSTEAD: Seaver alone

> Bridget Helen "Biddy" Monckton, 11th Lady Ruthven of Freeland, CBE (27 July 1896–17 April 1982), known as The Countess of Carlisle between 1918 and 1947, as Lady Monckton between 1947 and 1957, as The Viscountess Monckton of Brenchley between 1957 and 1965 and as The Dowager Viscountess Monckton of Brenchley between 1965 and 1982, was a British peeress and Conservative member of the House of Lords. She is reported to have recruited the first handful of ATS wireless operators who helped setting up the trial network in Kent.

26 June 1942
HEATHFIELD: Only Marjorie Barden
TUNBRIDGE WELLS: Mary Alexander and Priscilla Badgerow

27 June 1942
WEST GRINSTEAD: Hazel

30 June 1942
TAUNTON: Visited hut. Capt Coxwell-Rogers and Mr Monck-Mason

The IN Station (call-sign "Golding") was situated near Volis Farm in the parish of Kingston St Mary and consisted of a hut and a nearby dugout which appears to still be in place, albeit inaccessible. The HQ of 8th Corps was at Hestercombe House (see also page 139).

Captain Coxwell-Rogers was the SD IO for South and Southwest.

Adrian Monck-Mason was the husband of Subaltern Dorothy Monck-Mason (nee Rainey), one of the ATS wireless operators. Adrian Monck-Mason was the operator of an OUT Station located on his chicken farm near Charing in Kent (see also page 118).

1 July 1942
London: Interview with Cpl Norris

Elizabeth Janette Norris was commissioned on 21 August 1942 and stayed with the ATS until 3 March 1948, when she relinquished her commission on account of disability. She was granted the honorary rank of Junior Commander.

2 July 1942
EDINBURGH: Mr Ross, Capt Hally and Mr Thimont. Searched for billets

Lieutenant Bernard Maurice Thimont from the Royal Corps of Signals had previously been the IO for Lincolnshire.

The Edinburgh IN Station (call-sign "Barnack") was situated on Braids Hill on the south-western fringe of the city in an area that was back then and still is a golf course. The Advanced HQ of Scottish Command was at Riccarton House in Currie, Edinburgh.

Captain John Hally (from the Intelligence Corps) was the IO for Scotland.

8 July 1942
HQ Coleshill House: Moss

Silvia Joan Moss was commissioned as a 2nd subaltern on 28 August 1942. She worked at the Scotch Corner (North Yorkshire) IN Station. By closedown in July 1944 she had been attached to HQ East Kent District.

10 July 1942
NORWICH: New site. Ann Gunter interviewed
THORNHAM MAGNA: Seaver and Clifford

HATFIELD PEVEREL: *Capt Childe and Mr Bradley*
HALSTEAD: *Saw site, picked up Mickey and found billet*

Captain (later Major) Wilf Bradley was the SD IO for Suffolk, Norfolk, Essex and Lincolnshire, with HQ in Bury St Edmunds, and from summer 1943 onwards from Newcastle to John O'Groats, with HQ in Edinburgh.

Presumably the new sites referred to were the newly constructed dugouts at Norwich/Thorpe St Andrew (Norfolk) and at Halstead/Dynes Hall (Essex). Mickey was Subaltern Mickey Browne (nee Trant).

12 July 1942
REIGATE: *Thompson*

14 July 1942
HQ Hannington Hall: *Interviewed June Pearce, Joan Pratten and Fiddes-Watt*

June I Pearce worked at the Alnwick (Northumberland) IN Station. At closedown in July 1944 she had been attached to "F" Company East Riding & Lincolnshire District Group ATS; she relinquished her commission on 17 March 1945.

Joan Priestley Pratten at some time also worked at the Canterbury (Kent) IN Station. She was one of the last to leave when at closedown on 25 July 1944 she was posted to No.1 War Office Holding Unit and struck off the strength of Auxiliary Units. The London Gazette records that she relinquished her commission on 29 Sept 1944.

Captain AG Fiddes-Watt was an Intelligence officer who helped setting up AU operational patrols in Scotland, first in the Aberdeen area and later in the Outer Hebrides. He was also a trained artist and a talented painter, working in London as a picture restorer after the war.

15 July 1942
LINCOLN: *Pye and Campbell in hut with three operators*
Exercise participation until 4.30am

16 July 1942
DONCASTER: *Investigating complaint about Cole with IO in charge of ATS Coy*

17 July 1942
SCOTCH CORNER: *With Capt Farrer.*

Investigation carried out with two G2s and one G3.1 of alleged breaches of security by Tom Shanks. Going direct to ATS about billets. Capt Brodie

The Scotch Corner Hotel served as the HQ of 10th Corps and the IN Station was located in the near vicinity but its exact location has as yet to be found.

Captain Michael Farrer was the SD IO for Yorkshire and he also occasionally lectured at Coleshill House.

26 July 1942
REIGATE/EAST GRINSTEAD

27 July 1942
SEVENOAKS/HEATHFIELD/TUNBRIDGE WELLS: Capt Fraser
CHALLOCK: New hut

28 July 1942
TUNBRIDGE WELLS/WEST GRINSTEAD

2 Aug 1942
WINCHESTER: Sports Day, one of the Hackwoods seen

5 Aug 1942
ALNWICK: With Capt Grover and Lady Milward. DCRE site – Div HQ

The Alnwick (Northumberland) IN Station (call-sign "Otley") was located near the village of Heiferlaw and consisted of a hut and a dugout. The latter has been found in a fairly good condition (see also page 137). The Alnwick Sub-District HQ was in nearby Alnwick. The 54th (East Anglian) Division was at Leamington House and the Northumberland Division in Newgate Street, both at Morpeth. Captain Eric Cyril Grover was the SD IO for Northumberland and at another time the IO in South and Southwest.

6 Aug 1942
EDINBURGH: With Capt Hally to see Irving. Interviewed Dallimore at OCTU

Edith Mary Dallimore was commissioned as a 2nd subaltern on 21 August 1942. She had been attached to Sussex District Signals at closedown in July 1944. The London Gazette records that she relinquished her commission on 25 July 1944.

12 Aug 1942
TAUNTON: With Capt Coxwell-Rogers to site and farm. Capt Tracey and Mr Lloyd

> Captain BH Tracey spent at week at Coleshill at the end of April 1942. Mr Lloyd appears to have been the GOC-in-C Southern Command, Lt-General Sir Henry Lloyd, who seems to have paid an incognito visit to the IN Station site.

13 Aug 1942
BUCKLAND ST MARY: Capt Coxwell-Rogers and Kitty Hills
BLANDFORD: Dorothy and Ann
Dorchester: Capt Hall-Hall and Monck-Mason

> The IN Station at Buckland St Mary in Somerset (call-sign "Chirnside) was located at the site of Castle Neroche and consisted of a hut and a dugout. The dugout is believed to still be intact but inaccessible. The location of the hut is known but the Nissen-type hut has been removed (see also page 141).

> The ATS subalterns referred to as Dorothy and Ann were Dorothy Monck-Mason and Ann Ellis-Hughes.

> Captain Owen B Hall-Hall was the SD IO for Hampshire and Dorset.

14 Aug 1942
Winchester: Records Office
SALISBURY: Bettine Holmes

15 Aug 1942
TAUNTON: Orderly to be attached. Brown (billet)

19 Aug 1942
Short lecture to officers at hut

23 Aug 1942
REIGATE: Thompson for the last time. Olga [Jensen]
HATFIELD PEVEREL: Lloyd
Colchester: Capt Childe

24 Aug 1942
BURY ST EDMUNDS: *Mickey, Shaw and Freddie Childe*
THORNHAM MAGNA

> This is the first mention of the IN Station at Bury St Edmunds (West Suffolk), which appears to have been added to the network in autumn 1942. Several days before Beatrice Temple's visit to the IN Station, an ATS orderly had died there in suspicious circumstances but no further mention is made in the diary concerning this incident (see also page 147).

29 Aug 1942
Aldermaston: Choose three orderlies. Subaltern Rush

> Elizabeth Rush was commissioned on 11 November 1941 and was soon to start work as a wireless operator at the Harrietsham (Hollingbourne) IN Station and in March 1943 she was one of three wireless operators to have worked at the East Grinstead (Ardingly) IN Station in West Sussex. Subaltern Rush left the ATS on 28 October 1946.

31 Aug 1942
LINCOLN: *Dodo Campbell alone*
DONCASTER: *Hilary and Airlie*

1 Sept 1942
SCOTCH CORNER: *Capt Shanks and Capt Farrer*

2 Sept 1942
Newcastle: Capt Grover
ALNWICK: *Hopette [Hope Leslie Seaver] and Capt Shanks*
EDINBURGH: *Rosemary Astley-Cooper (in red belt)*

3 Sept 1942
SOUTH DALTON: *Dicken alone*
9 Sept 1942
WEST GRINSTEAD: *Janet alone. Canadian Commandant re transport*

18 Sept 1942
HEATHFIELD: *Barden beginning sad business of handing over*

CANTERBURY: Ronald in hut. Benjie and Hilliers in mess
TUNBRIDGE WELLS: All three there (one Britten)

19 Sept 1942
EAST GRINSTEAD: Hilary there
REIGATE: Doris White

23 Sept. 1942
WINCHESTER: Hackwood
SALISBURY: Joan Paget

4 Oct 1942
REIGATE: Doris White and company
EAST GRINSTEAD: Paddock alone
HEATHFIELD: Last time. Marjorie Barden alone

5 Oct 1942
TUNBRIDGE WELLS: Eleanor

Eleanor refers to subaltern Eleanor Norman-Butler

6 Oct 1942
HATFIELD PEVEREL: All three there
HALSTEAD: Banjy, Nina and Capt Childe
BURY ST EDMUNDS: Mickey Browne
THORNHAM MAGNA: Last time. Airlie alone

10 Oct 1942
Newcastle: Capt Grover

11 Oct 1942
Morpeth: With Capt Shanks re ATS local leave and allowances

13 Oct 1942
SALISBURY: *Paget and Fox*

> Joan Marion Fox was commissioned on 15 Jan 1942; she had been attached to HQ Southern Command at closedown in July 1944.

BLANDFORD: *Monck-Mason alone*
TAUNTON: *Capt Coxwell-Rogers*

14 Oct 1942
BUCKLAND ST MARY: *Kitty Hills*
CHEDDON FITZPAINE: *Mary Alexander, Priscilla Badgerow and Ralph (sic)*

> Margaret Relph was commissioned on 29 August 1942.

19 Oct 1942
DONCASTER: *Eleanor and Dodo Campbell*

20 Oct 1942
SCOTCH CORNER: *Moss, Colson, Margaret and Capt Shanks*

> Thora Margaret Colson was commissioned as a 2nd subaltern on 26 February 1942.

21 Oct 1942
ALNWICK: *Troops all round but with radio. Ann, Pearce and Jensen*

> Olga Elizabeth Jensen was commissioned on 27 June 1942. She had been attached to HQ South Eastern Command at closedown in July 1944. Her colleagues at Alnwick were Ann Gunter and June Pearce.

30 Oct 1942
SALISBURY: *Dorothy Monck-Mason and Joan Paget*

3 Nov 1942
REIGATE: *Eve and Hilary*

4 Nov 1942
CANTERBURY: *Phyllis Britten, Joan Pratten. (Patience away)*

5 Nov 1942
HARRIETSHAM: *Elizabeth Rush and Peggy*

> The Harrietsham IN Station was located near the village of Hollingbourne (Kent). It consisted of a hut and a dugout. The latter has been found and recorded (see also page 116). The (12th Corps) Maidstone Sub-Area HQ was based at nearby Aylesford. General Eric G Miles - the General Officer Commanding-in-Chief South-Eastern Command - is known to have visited the site on 26 January 1944.

> Subaltern Vivien Aline Deirdre McKerral "Peggy" Brown worked for AU ATS from her commission on 28 August 1942 until 22 March 1943. Her colleagues at Harrietsham were Elizabeth Rush and Rosemary Beatrice Richards, who was commissioned on 15 January 1942 and left ATS after only a few months, on 12 May of the same year.

12 Nov 1942
SALISBURY: *Found hut with windows open, light and heater on – no one there*

13 Nov 1942 - *Priscilla and Airlie at hut (Mary on leave)*
15 Nov 1942 – *Maj Jones at HQ*

18 Nov 1942
DONCASTER: *Eleanor and Joan Fox*
SOUTH DALTON: *All three well and happy. Capt Farrer*

19 Nov 1942
ALNWICK: *Ann*

20 Nov 1942
SCOTCH CORNER: *"The Three"*
DONCASTER: *Eleanor*

24 Nov 1942
BURY ST EDMUNDS: *Mickey, Yolande and Margaret*

25 Nov 1942
HALSTEAD: Ann Gunter. Billet hunting all day

26 Nov 1942
HATFIELD PEVEREL: Cicely
* "OTHER PLACE": Avis and Pamela*

27 Nov 1942
Tunbridge Wells
REIGATE: Doris

30 Nov 1942
SALISBURY: Bettine Holmes. DAQMG re possible billet

1 Dec 1942
HATFIELD PEVEREL: Cicely Hopkins. Three bicycles
HALSTEAD: Three bicycles
BURY ST EDMUNDS: Last three bicycles. Mary Shaw

The diary entries continue on an almost daily basis until 13 March 1944, the day when Beatrice Temple left Hannington Hall for Haywards Heath in Sussex, her next posting.

Some of the IN Station dugouts would seem to still have been in the process of being improved as late as mid-1943 and new IN Stations were also still opened.

> "Many stations are still awaiting improvements by the sappers." (Monthly notes to IOs, No 5, July 1943)

In February 1943 Major Jones had introduced a new scheme involving the use of what he referred to as "temporary stations". No detailed information pertaining to the exact whereabouts of these stations has found its way into Beatrice Temple's diary but she did jot down the date on which she set out to visit them (1 March 1943).

It may be assumed that a diary entry from a few days earlier, 25 February 1943, is also related to the above-mentioned new scheme: "New scheme stations assemble". On the following day Beatrice Temple travelled to Wendover, where she visited what might have been one of these "new scheme" stations, and on the following day she met Major Jones there, who, according to a brief note, explained the scheme to her. On the same day Beatrice Temple also visited her officers' billet "with all six, then to tent".

The ATS officer crews of IN Stations commonly consisted of three subalterns and it is not clear why a team of six would seem to have been required at the Wendover station. Furthermore, the reason for opening a new station, if only temporarily, which required a crew of six operators, so late in the war when the threat of an invasion had almost disappeared, has as yet to be fully understood. By 1943, any invasion was expected to have at least two months warning and the country was no longer on invasion alert. Seaborne and airborne raids were however still considered a possibility, and for this purpose a specific counter attack unit was still held for the relief of the Landguard.

In the first week of March 1943 all the billets were paid for, because the ATS crew had left. Inexplicably, their stay had lasted for only about one week. In August, however, operations were resumed so it seems, because Beatrice Temple busied herself with finding new billets. By September, Janette Norris, Wynne Read and Marjorie Barden were settled in their new "palatial" billet, where Doris White, who by then served as one of Beatrice Temple's clerks (the other was Mary Shaw), visited them. Perhaps the women were accommodated at Halton House, built for Alfred Charles de Rothschild and owned by the RAF since 1918, which indeed does have palatial dimensions.

Together they had tea in their billet and then they all proceeded to the site, which Beatrice Temple describes as "very well rigged-up, with 3-ton lorry and tent occupied by most mixed population". This would seem to suggest that the wireless sets and batteries were, perhaps only temporarily, being kept in the back of a lorry and the IN Station operated from there. By mid October the situation appears to have changed, because Doris White met two of the three aforementioned ATS officers at the "new station". According to the diary entries, Beatrice Temple last visited the site, which to date has not been identified, in January 1944 (see also page 107).

The station appears to have bridged a gap between two sites on the Inner Network: Coleshill House in the west and another as yet unknown location to the east of Hertford, further to the east. Due to the absence on Major Jones' map of geographical features commonly shown on maps such as towns, roads, rivers and railway lines etc, it is difficult to accurately place any of the marked locations, especially when no other information is available.

Major Jones' dot on the map would appear to mark a site to the north-west of the market town of Amersham, where the 45th Division HQ was based at a large manor house called "The Bury". Amersham is about 10 kilometres (6 miles) distant from Wendover. Cold Morham Farm, the base of Commander Ian Fleming's 30 Assault Unit, deployed to seize Axis secrets and weapons, was on the old A143 road just north of the current Old Town. The Special Training School XX (also known as Station 20), where Polish section SOE agents were trained in clandestine operations, was situated in Pollards Wood, also in the near vicinity.

It is of interest to note that towards the end of 1943, the OUT Stations were given an important new role, which might at least partially explain the opening of new IN Stations, some permanent and some temporary, so late in the war.

In June 1943 Major Jones discussed the introduction of a new policy, according to which two ATS officers were required to stay overnight at their place of duty. This new policy was implemented in autumn 1943; around the same time the OUT Stations were assigned their new task.

The following information originates from a letter written by Major Peter Forbes to John Warwicker (dated 31 January 2002, BROM Archive). Peter Forbes was the AU Ops IO in the Scottish Borders area before being promoted to major and posted to Coleshill as a staff officer in July 1943.

> "The important new role given to the OUT Stations was to report rumours circulating from East Anglia and all along the South Coast. The War Office wanted to know what was being picked up about concentrations for the (D-Day) invasion. These reports came to me for consolidation and were passed to General (sic) Frank Douglas for onward transmission. In the end it was probably the most important SD work."

A new IN/Relay Station was opened as late as August 1943 at Ousden in Suffolk with one of its crew, Marina Bloxam, having been commissioned in October 1943. For a detailed description of this station see page 142.

One month earlier, in July 1943, an IN Station had been opened at Elgin in Morayshire. Like Ousden and Wendover, the IN station at Elgin remained operational until closedown and Beatrice Temple paid her last visit to the ATS crew based there on 4 March 1944, two days after she had visited her officers at Ousden (see also page 178).

Dorothy Monck-Mason
(Source: BROM Archive)

The so-called Secret Sweeties

The author David Lampe in his book *The Last Ditch*, first published in 1968, would seem to have coined the phrase "Secret Sweeties", referring to the ATS wireless operators in the Special Duties Branch. He has recorded that male officers who served with the Auxiliary Units recalled that the women were exceptionally pretty and that in the Divisional HQ mess at Doncaster they were always referred to as the secret sweeties ("The Secret Sweeties", page 123 ff)). Barbara Culleton however, who in 1942 was based at Hickleton Hall (near Doncaster) for a couple of months has said that the term was unheard of in her time, and would certainly not have been appreciated.

The exact number of ATS subalterns recruited into SD is not known. David Lampe mentions 93 but documents that have since become available to the public suggest that there would seem to have been more than 150. The May 1942 Establishment records the number of AU ATS in SD at that time as having been 135. A year later authorisation was given for the recruitment of 25 more ATS officers. Personnel numbers fluctuated as they required to be adjusted so as to accommodate revised policies and hence not all the women remained with SD for the whole duration of the operation. At closedown in summer 1944 the number of AU ATS in SD had shrunk to 56. Thanks to the London Gazette and its Supplements, where not only all commissionings but also promotions and relinquishing of commands as well as retirement dates of military personnel are published on a regular basis, details concerning the great majority of the ATS officers concerned could eventually be unearthed. Some of the women left - either because they got married or were expecting a baby, or because of illness. Others were moved to different duties such as helping with administerial work at HQ or retained as Stores officers.

The names, details and service numbers of 90 of the ATS officers who served in SD, as well as the dates of their commissioning and when a commission was relinquished, can be found in the list below.

Adams-Beck (Mrs), Doris Elsie	227840	20 Feb 1942	30 Mar 1944
Alexander, Mary	211137	21 Sept 1941	25 July 1944
Astley-Cooper, Rosemary Anne	211144	21 Sept 1941	?
Atkinson, Queenie Purnell Freeman	230032	26 Feb 1943	11 June 1946
Badgerow (Aston), Priscilla Mary	234151	March 1942	?
Barden (Tarrant), Marjorie Lilian	196514	29 June 1941	25 July 1944
Bell, Heather Pauline	294922	18 Sept 1943	29 Sept 1944
Bloxam, Marina	301325	22 Oct 1943	17 Apr 1943
Promoted to Subaltern on 1 Jan 1947 WRAC: Capt M Bloxam is dismissed the service by sentence of a General Court Marshal on 17 April 1953			
Boitel-Gill (Grant), Joan Ursula	211164	21 Sept 1941	26 June 1944
Britten (Mrs), Phyllis Marion	230560	11 Mar 1942	8 Nov 1944
Bromley (Alston), Yolande Audrey Yvette	205953	20 July 1941	20 Apr 1943
Brown, Vivien Aline Deirdre McKerrel	246043	28 Aug 1942	22 Mar 1943

Browne (Trant), Phyllis Michelle "Mickey"	196536	29 June 1941	27 June 1948

Relinquished her commission on 27 June 1948 and was granted the honorary rank of Subaltern

Burbage, Marguerite	223872	15 Jan 1942	Oct 1948

Honorary Junior Commander in Oct 1948

Burton, Edwina Caroline Gearey	263932	12 Feb 1943	?
Buxton, Pamela Mary	248456	25 Sept 1942	1 Dec 1943
Campbell (Gascoyne), Airlie Abinda	234073	15 Apr 1942	15 May 1944
Campbell, Evelyn Doriel Mary "Dodo"	192703	30 May 1944	?
Chesney, Joyce Hazel	244726	21 Aug 1942	25 July 1944
Clifford (Mrs), Nina	230626	11 Mar 1942	15 Nov 1944
Cole, Florence Margaret "Waddy"	230660	11 Mar 1942	20 Dec 1944
Colson, Thora Margaret	227983	26 Feb 1942	?
Culleton, Barbara Marion	205716	7 Sept 1941	7 Aug 1957

Curtis (Olesinska), Sarah Henrietta	196567	29 June 1941	June 1947

Promotion to Honorary Junior Commander in June 1947

Dallimore, Edith Mary	244727	21 Aug 1942	25 July 1944
Davis, Angela Mary	211975	21 Sept 1941	7 Nov 1942

Dicken (Mrs), Betty Berkeley	205715	7 Sept 1941	8 Nov 1943

Committed suicide in "Met" hut/Heathfield Park (carbon monoxide poisoning) on 8 Nov 1943

Drake-Brockman (Mrs) Cicely May	244722	21 Aug 1942	?
Ellis-Hughes (Mrs), Ann	205714	7 Sept 1941	?
Filer, Marjorie Nora	218658	3 Aug 1941	25 July 1944
Fletcher, Elizabeth Ann Abbie	301326	22 Oct 1943	28 Apr 1946
Fox, Joan Marion	225125	15 Jan 1942	25 July 1944
Graham (Marsden), Gertrude Russell	301327	22 Oct 1943	29 May 1944
Graham (Gordon), Hilary	205710	7 Sept 1941	23 Feb 1945
Gregory, Winifrede	231888	31 July 1942	?
Gunter (Dielman), Ann Lettice Valborg	211976	21 Sept 1941	May 1952
Gwynne (Battersby), Prudence "Prue"	244661	21 Aug 1942	29 Aug 1946
Hackwood, Muriel Helen– 27 June 1942	238858	27 June 1942	30 Nov 1944
Hackwood, Edith Margaret	238904	27 June 1942	?
Harrington, Sheila Hames	294923	18 Sept 1943	15 Dec 1944
Hay-Whiting (Goodman), Pamela	225133	15 Jan 1942	5 Nov 1945
Hills (Mrs), Kathleen Marie "Kitty"	205954	20 July 1941	25 July 1944
Hilliers, Constance Mary Caroline	230584	11 Mar 1942	1949

Hildyard, Alma Vernon	225126	5 Jan 1942	1950

Dec 45: temporary Junior Commander. Dec 46: MBE & hon rank of Junior Commander. Dec 1950: Honorary Captain & promotion to Lieutenant

Holmes, Bettine Mary	211977	21 Sept 1941	?
Hopkins, Cicely – not found	-	Nov 1942	?
Hopkins, Eileen Margaret	294363	3 Sept 1943	29 Sept 1944
Hornsby, Pamela Margaret	301328	22 Oct 1943	?
Hough (Mrs), Lynette	294924	18 Sept 1943	24 Sept 1944
Irving (Ingle-Finch), Pamela Mary Forster	225127	15 Jan 1942	11 Nov 1944
Jones (Mrs), Christine Violet Lane	246044	28 Aug 1942	28 Apr 1943
Jensen, Olga Elizabeth	238929	27 June 1941	25 July 1944
Kaines, Wendy Monica Pax	205951	20 July 1941	15 Dec 1944
Knapp (Swan), Nina Patricia	306656	1 Jan 1944	1 Nov 1944
Lloyd, Marion Avis	223853	15 Jan 1942	25 July 1944
Monck-Mason (Rainey), Dorothy Eileen	230589	11 Mar 1942	?
Moss, Silvia Joan	244935	28 Aug 1942	25 July 1944
Norman-Butler, Eleanor Mary	205713	7 Sept 1941	25 July 1944
Norris, Elizabeth Janette	244644	21 Aug 1942	3 Mar 1948

Relinquished her commission on account of
disability on 3 March 1948 and was granted the
honorary rank of Junior Commander.

At closedown in July 1944 she had been attached
to HQ North Riding District.

Oliver, Daphne Margaret	297848	28 Apr 1943	?
Paddock (Pikts), Hilary Joan	216799	20 July 1941	3 May 1945
Paget, Joan – not found	-	May 1942	?
Pearce, June Isabelle	250080	9 Oct 1942	17 Mar 1945
Pratten (Mrs), Joan Priestley	248958	9 Oct 1942	29 Sept 1944
Purves-Smith (nee Wise), Myfanwy Janet	225114	15 Jan 1942	29 Sept 1944
Pye, Margery Anne	205952	20 July 1941	1 Jan 1943
Read, Winifred Audrey "Wynne"	216798	20 July 1941	25 July 1944
Relph, Margaret	244942	29 Aug 1942	?
Richards, Rosemary Beatrice	225112	15 Jan 1942	12 May 1942
Richardson, Sybil Hazel	211978	21 Sept 1941	19 Sept 1944
Rigby (Briscoe), Margaret Hamilton	291533	6 Aug 1943	25 July 1944
Robertson, Annie Kathleen	270347	26 Mar 1943	?
Ronald (Whigham), Patience Mary	230652	11 Mar 1942	24 Oct 1943
Rush, Elizabeth	218522	27 Nov 1941	28 Oct 1946

Relinquished her commission on account of
disability and was granted the honorary rank of
Junior Commander

Seaver (Mrs), Hope Leslie "Hopette"	205712	7 Sept 1941	24 Mar 1944
Shaw (Mrs), Mary Frances	238896	27 June 1942	?

On duty at SD HQ for OC AU ATS in Dec 1943

Stronach, Elizabeth Templer	230619	11 Mar 1942	?
Temple, Beatrice	192882	30 May 1941	Retired in the 1950s

Nov 1941 – Junior Commander ATS
May 1942 – Senior Commander ATS

Thomas, (Mrs) Vera Maxine	236916	6 June 1942	?
Thompson, Enid Mary	211413	21 Sept 1941	?
Thurlow (Ogilvie) Rosemary Margaret	270397	26 Mar 1943	1947
Trevaskis (Rappoport), Winifred Eve	211980	21 Sept 1941	1 Feb 1943
Turner, Mary Dorothy	244808	28 Aug 1943	?
Vaile (Mason), Marjorie Muriel Berkeley	205709	7 Sept 1941	19 Apr 1945
Ward (Mrs), Amy Dorothea "Thea"	218659	3 Aug 1941	23 Mar 1942
Waterhouse-Brown (Mrs) Sally Alice May	291443	6 Aug 1943	?
White (Mrs), Isobel Doris	205711	7 Sept 1941	29 Oct 1944
Whiting, Margaret Esme	196691	29 June 1941	15 Dec 1944
Williams (Mrs), Myfanwy	301329	22 Oct 1943	?
Wood, Millicent Mary Magdalene	221737	11 Mar 1942	?

As the great majority of the ATS officers who worked in SD would have come almost direct into AU Signals, with only a shortened training course following their recruitment, and without having spent time in the ATS before their commissioning, most of the women were unemployable in any normal ATS unit. Nevertheless, at least 20 (including Beatrice Temple) continued to serve in the ATS (and later in the WRAC) for a number of years after the end of the war, and some until their retirement.

Number of ATS officers recruited by Beatrice Temple between 1941 and 1944

Year	1941	1942	1943	1944
January		8		1
February		2	2	
March		9	2	
April		2		
May	2			
June	4	5		
July	6	2		
August	2	9	9	
September	17	2	1	
October		2	2	
November	1			
December	-	-	-	-
Total	32	41	16	1

The double doors separating the main chamber and the generator room (Norwich). Union cloth (anti gas), soaked in oil, was used to effectively seal these doors to prevent war gasses and lethal carbon monoxide fumes generated by the battery-charging engine from entering the main chamber, where the wireless operators worked. A similarly insulated door (at Alnwick IN Station) can be seen below. *(Photo: Colin Anderson)*

The secret door concealed behind a shelf unit, the frame of which is still in place, at Norwich IN Station. One of the two short sections of wood seen at the back of the top shelf could be moved, revealing a pull cord for operating the catch that opened the door to gain access into the main chamber.

The original hatch which covered the exit tunnel opening in the generator room of the Alnwick IN Station in Northumberland. *(Photo: Colin Anderson)*

The short, breezeblock-built emergency escape tunnel at Halstead (Essex) IN Station.

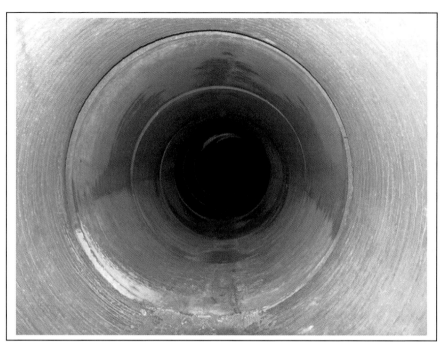

View up the 17 m (~55 feet) long emergency escape tunnel at Norwich (Norfolk).

The water tank, in its original position in the lobby at Norwich IN Station. Two sand-filled fire buckets can be seen to its left.

An unidentified piece of heavy canvas cloth with oil stains, found on the floor at the Halstead IN Station. It might have been part of an overall or perhaps of a kit bag.

Lighting conduit and two light fittings, with wiring still in place, at Norwich IN Station.

Codes

Much has been written (and speculated) regarding the secret codes used in the communications taking place between OUT and IN Stations. David Lampe, who was very fortunate to have met Colonel (later Brigadier) CR "Bill" Major, who had succeeded Colonel Gubbins as CO of HQ Auxiliary Units in December 1940, is quite clear about the issue. He writes that a friend of the Colonel invented a code sheet consisting of 500-odd military words and phrases. A single letter code matched these phrases and arrangements were made to change the code on a daily basis (*The Last Ditch*, page 134).

Stanley Judson - he had joined AU direct from the NCOs' Training Battalion in Harrogate and was posted to Sudbury (Bachelor's Hall, Hundon, Suffolk) and, together with his team of signallers helped to set up the wireless networks in Lincolnshire, Yorkshire and Norfolk – in a letter to his former colleague, Arthur Gabbitas, dated 11 Feb 1995 (BROM Archive), recalls:

> "I remember the code quite well. It was a sheet, divided into squares or oblongs, and in each square there was an Army term and a different description so somebody could say "Able Y" and the person receiving the message would look on the code sheet and it would say "50 tanks", or whatever. All these sort of things were put in the different squares so you related the top with the side and the letters and that gave the clue to what the message was." (J Warwicker interview, IWM ref: 29468, 1999)

In 1943/44 the Army introduced a hand-held, paper-based encoding system working on the same principles as described above. This system continued to be used up to well into the 1970s. Called "Slidex", it consisted of 204 boxes containing letters and words. The letters on the cursors were set each day in the daily Signals Instructions and the code is described as having been easy to use and well liked by its users.

The recollections of former ATS wireless operators are less clear and often conflicting, although all are agreed that Morse code was never used. Janet Wise (nee Purves-Smith) believed that they had to eat the code sheets after use (Stephen Sutton, IWM ref: 14817, 11 Aug 1994). Marina Bloxam thought that their contact telephone numbers changed according to the code they were using.

> "We had a code which we knew the "key" to. We had it in our heads or waistcoat pocket." (Stephen Sutton interview, 31 Oct 1994; IWM ref: 14816)

Jill Monk (nee Holman), the daughter of an OUT Station operator in Aylsham, Norfolk, recalls that her mother used to do the coding. She failed to remember the code, how often it was changed, and how it arrived at their OUT Station. She thought the AU Signals soldier who regularly called to change the batteries might have delivered it.

Yolande Alston (nee Bromley) remembers that there was a code and that it changed daily, but very little else:

> "Tanks and things were called 'cows' or 'bulls' so that if we'd been picked up it would be women having a silly chat about cows. I can't remember being given training in code work but we must have, we must have had the codes. We changed the code every day and then the sheet was thrown away or destroyed. I expect we had instructions but I can't remember any of that." (J Warwicker interview, IWM ref: 29457, 28 Feb 1997)

Wynne Read, who worked at the Heathfield Park IN Station in East Sussex, recalls that the codes used for their messages were based on various unlikely texts, including some of the comic verses contributed to the "*Punch*" magazine by Patrick Barrington (later the 11th Viscount Barrington), one of which began:

> "I had a duck-billed platypus when I was up at Trinity.
> For whom I developed a remarkable affinity.
> He used to live in lodgings with myself and Arthur Purvis,
> And we all went up together for the Diplomatic Service."

According to Subaltern Edwina Burton, who worked at the Hollingbourne IN Station in Kent, practice transmissions (to South-Eastern Command) involved the reading of various passages of text in 'plain' language - ie no code was used.

UA	OL	NJ	LE	ED	RB	QG	TP	X
	A / ATK	07 / ADVANCE	14 / AIRCRAFT	24 / AIRFIELD	AM CLOSING DOWN REOPENING AT	41 / AMERICAN	L / AMMUNITION	
	ASSUME CONTINUOUS WATCH ON FREQUENCY	08 / ATTACK	P / BARRAGE	25 / BE PREPARED TO	33 / BEARING/DIRECTION	42 / BLOCK	51 / BLOWN	
	SWITCH ON	H / BRIGADE	15 / CABLE	CANADIAN	34 / CANCEL	43 / CAPTURE	52 / CARRIER	
	D(hg) / CLOSE	Q / SWITCH OFF	Q / CODESIGN	26 / COLUMN	35 / COMPLETE(D)	44 / CONCENTRATE (CON)	M / CONFERENCE	
	DO / CUT OFF	I / D.R.	16 / DAY	V / DELAY	A / DEMOLITION	G / DIVERSION	53 / DIVISION	
	D1 / ENGAGE(MENT)	09 / ENGINEERS	SWITCH ON	27 / ESSENTIAL	36 / ESTABLISH	45 / ESTIMATED TIME OF ARRIVAL	N / EXCL	
	B / FORWARD	J / FORWARD TROOPS	17 / FREQUENCY	28 / FRONT	B / FULLERPHONE	46 / GAP	54 / GAS	
	C / HARASS	1(hg) / HARBOUR	R / HELD UP	SWITCH OFF	37 / HELP	H / HIGH GROUND	O / HOLD (ING)	
	2 / INFANTRY	K / INFORM(ATION)	18 / INTACT	29 / INTENTION	SWITCH OFF	47 / JUNCTION	55 / KILOMETRE(S)	

Part of a "Slidex" code sheet *(source and photographer unknown)*

Some interesting information about the codes used can be found in the Monthly Notes to IOs, issued by Major RMA Jones and distributed to all SD IOs, to the GSO III SD (operations and training), and to Royal Engineers *(RE):*

> "The code we use can be broken quite easily by experts, so even in code messages, great care should be observed, and references to the functions of this organisation should never be made, even if they are enciphered." (Monthly notes, No 1, March 1943)

> "The thing to remember is that our cipher is of the lowest grade (for the sake of simplicity), and that it provides security for a limited time only. Tactically, therefore, it is secure because by the time it will have been broken the information will be out of date or action will have been taken by the appropriate military command.

> A very different picture would be given to the enemy if, during present training, a daily interception of our practice traffic were taking place."

> "One IO has recently (presumably to save time and trouble) transmitted from the IN Station to all OUT Stations in his area the provisions of the new "captured drill" and how it works! Any further comment is unnecessary, except to express the strongest disapproval of such stupidity!" (Monthly notes, No 6, August 1943)

The wireless operators were told, and they believed, that their communications could not be intercepted. Ken Ward explains:

> "The reason that no signals were intercepted was two-fold: first the quench system and secondly the very limited and directional range of the sets."

This, however, appears to not have been quite the whole truth. The truth - that signals were in fact intercepted quite frequently, and were liable therefore to also be intercepted by the enemy - is revealed in the Monthly notes:

> "The first thing to remember is that at this HQ we can (and do) listen in to many Monthly Training Periods (the exercises) and that on "freak days" OUT Stations in remote parts of the country can often be picked up here. For instance, an OUT Station in Kent was recently heard at Strength 5.

> It seems not unreasonable, therefore to suppose that similar transmissions may be intercepted in enemy-occupied countries." (Monthly notes, No 6, August 1943)

The Base Stations

As already mentioned, Major Jones' memorandum lists 30 IN-Stations, 125 OUT Stations and 78 SUBOUT Stations. Every wireless network used a specific call-sign as a means of identification when communicating. Interestingly, almost all the call-signs that are known to date are names of locations far distant from where the network using it was operating.

As all OUT and SUBOUT Stations were run by civilians, often from their homes, the chances that one such location might coincidentally be stumbled upon in some remote location seven decades later are slim - unless the wireless set was hidden not in a box buried in the ground or in the attic or cellar of a dwelling house or in a chicken coop but in a sturdy dugout. In fact, a number of these dugouts have indeed been found, most in good condition. Stanley Judson, one of the AU Signals officers who helped setting up some of the wireless networks, recalls that originally the wireless sets were contained in boxes resembling small coffins, metal-lined inside and covered with a lid. They were sunk in the ground, mainly in woods or at other suitable locations; after removing the camouflage, the operator lifted the lid and worked on the surface. Fortunately, some of the civilian operators have come forward and talked about their activities in later years and hence some of the locations are now known.

Travel pass issued to Arthur Gabbitas, who as a member of one of the AU Signals maintenance teams spent a lot of time on the road collecting batteries for recharging, and checking aerials. *(Source: A Gabbitas)*

In 1941, 3-man crews of AU signallers were busy setting up new networks, first in East Anglia and then northwards up to the Scottish Borders, and westwards along the south coast to Devon. In 1942 there were five areas, each named after a letter of the alphabet (A to E) and controlled by an Area Officer or IO. The unit Alf Ellis was part of consisted of nine men (mainly OWLs and instrument mechanics) who were divided into three groups of three men each and commanded by a sergeant. The teams were responsible for the setting up and later for the maintenance of altogether 48 wireless stations on the "Chirnside" and "Golding" networks (Somerset and Devon), on the "Osterley" (Dorset) network, and on the "Omagh" (Hampshire including Isle of Wight) network. This task required the men to be almost constantly on the move. Sergeant Ellis' crew had a Humber staff car, a utility vehicle, an Austin two-seater car and a Matchless motorcycle at their disposal.

In order to maintain security at all times, a letter of the alphabet was substituted for each of the men's names. This included the commander, Major RMA Jones, who was "Y", whereas Captain OB Hall-Hall, the IO, was referred to as "Chaney". The sergeants were George Spencer ("D"), Scott ("M") and Alf Ellis ("K"); the names of the signallers and maintenance men involved were Crawley ("E"), Corporal RGA Gilbert ("H"), Brown ("J"), Foard ("N"), Orr ("Q"), Lance Corporal Robert Caldow ("S") and Bill Air ("X"), with "O" and "Z" as yet to be identified. (Alf Ellis' diary, 1942)

That security was taken very seriously indeed is also evidenced by the practice of referring to high-ranking military visitors by their surnames only and that they always wore civilian clothes on the occasion of a visit. The diary entry according to which Alf Ellis met "Mr Lloyd" at "Omagh", for instance, records the visit on 27 July 1942 of the GOC-in-C Southern Command, Lieutenant-General Sir Henry Lloyd (he was appointed in March 1942) to the Winchester IN Station. "Mr Lloyd" also features in Beatrice Temple's diary, together with Captain Coxwell-Rogers (the IO) and Captain Tracey, on the occasion of a visit, on 12 August 1942, to the Cheddon Fitzpaine IN Station "and farm" (Volis Farm, where the ATS officers were billeted) near Taunton in Somerset. In her diary Beatrice Temple too frequently refers to IOs (who were provided with appropriate cover stories and always wore civilian clothes) by their surnames rather than by their military rank and status.

Everybody involved, including the civilian spies and observers appear to have been continuously reminded (not to use the term indoctrinated) of the secret nature of their work. A number of eyewitnesses later stated that they were instructed once again, at closedown, never to tell anybody "because there might be an emergency, there might be the same situation again at some time in the future." (Jill Monk, Ursula M Pennell)

All the IN Station locations in use in June 1944 are marked on a map produced by Major Jones but some remain nevertheless elusive. As has already been mentioned, IN Stations commonly consisted of an everyday workplace which commonly was a small building - furnished to look like a meteorological hut, with barometric charts on the walls - and a well-concealed dugout nearby. There appears to have been no standard design according to which these huts were built. Some were described as wooden huts with a pitched roof, others seem to have been Nissen-type constructions and some were not huts at all, when an already existing buildings such as a folly tower, a summerhouse or a gazebo, was used instead. Each hut was equipped with two (sometimes three) wireless sets, operated in shifts by between three and five ATS officers or AU signallers.

IN Station huts were situated either within the grounds, or in the near vicinity of the Army HQ to which the IN Station was attached. Not only was such a location well protected but also the passing on of information from wireless operator to Intelligence officer would have been almost instantaneous. Captain Ken Ward recalls that at Halstead his wife, one of the ATS wireless operators, had to walk only about 50 metres. Field telephones would seem to have been used frequently and a GPO landline was commonly used for bridging longer distances.

Most IN Station huts appear to have been dismantled soon after the war. As none of them seems to have survived, and because details regarding their construction and interior are, for this reason, scarce and based entirely on recollections, and sometimes on hearsay, all information relating to their design ought to be taken with a pinch of salt, all the more so since, as already mentioned, a standard design does not appear to have existed.

The dugouts were intended to provide better protection for the stay-behind IN Station operators in the event of an invasion. The huts would have continued to serve for everyday use but they had to be situated close enough to a dugout so that the latter could be reached quickly, on foot, in an emergency. For reasons yet to be fully understood, a small number of IN Stations never seemed to have had a dugout.

It would seem that no dugouts were constructed before mid-1942 (Ken Ward interview 10 Aug 1999, IWM ref: 29472) and the appearance, for the first time, of Royal Engineers sappers in the May 1942 Establishment supports this. The same Establishment also lists four 8 cwt wireless trucks, presumably used for testing wireless links when searching for suitable new locations. Ken Ward's information is also supported by one of the first ATS officers to have been recruited for the job, which states that she has never seen or been in a dugout during the whole of her career, which lasted from January 1940 until 7 July 1942 (Yolande Alston nee Bromley; J Warwicker interview 28 Feb 1997, IWM ref: 29457).

IN Station dugouts are sometimes also referred to as 'Zero' Stations, so-called because, according to David Lampe (in *The Last Ditch*), whenever the operators transmitted from them they followed the station's call-sign with the code suffix 'zero'. Little evidence has been found that this was indeed the case, and a specific suffix would certainly not have been required to differentiate between operation from the everyday workstation hut and the dugout. Barbara Culleton, amongst others, does not recall the use of the term: "I don't recall the name 'Zero' but I think it was rather 'Control' stations for the OUT Station link-ups." (Letter by Barbara Culleton to John Warwicker, 8 May 2000; BROM Archive).

Interestingly, though, Alf Ellis in his 1942 diary would seem to refer to a newly constructed dugout site as 'Zero'.

Built by Royal Engineers sappers, who were unaware of their intended use, the dugouts commonly consisted of three chambers. Unlike the operational bases (OBs) constructed for the AU operational patrols, the entrance shafts of which had steel rungs set into one wall or across a corner to serve as a ladder, IN Station dugouts would seem to have been accessed by wooden steps or ladders which could be removed when not in use, as one of the drawings by Subaltern Sally Waterstone-Brown, who in 1943 was based at the Hollingbourne IN Station, confirms (see page 100). Denying an enemy intruder immediate access by removing the only means of getting down the shaft would certainly have given the occupants some valuable time to escape.

Apart from one (to date) known exception, the dugouts were built to a standard design and consisted of a buried elephant shelter, with dividing walls built from breezeblocks. Access was through a vertical shaft with the entrance openings being secured by a concealed trap door which was operated by a complex system of pulleys and counterweights. Trapdoors also secured the outer ends of emergency exit tunnels, some of which were of quite exceptional lengths. Ventilation was provided by a number of glazed ceramic and concrete pipes and followed the same principles laid out by Captain Nigel Oxenden for AU ops patrol bases' ventilation (*Auxiliary Units - History and Achievements*, pages 6 and 26).

A cleverly concealed door led from the antechamber or lobby at the foot of the entrance shaft into the wireless room which had another doorway at its far end, giving access to a small adjoining room which housed the generator required for the recharging of batteries. The emergency exit tunnel opening was in the end wall of the generator room, leading outside and to safety, some distance away from the site.

In this context it is of interest to know that initially only ATS within the Ack-Ack Command were issued Battle Dress, but with the onset of the construction of dugouts it appears to also have been available to AU ATS officers. The wearing of Battle Dress, ie trousers, especially during exercises which involved operating from and staying in the dugout for up to a week, became the norm. Illustrated instructions concerning these monthly exercises have been found amongst the drawings made by Sally Waterhouse-Brown (see page 99):

The Signals Instruction manual 55 contains several paragraphs detailing the actions to be taken in the event of discovery:

> "No action whatever will be taken by the crew until it is definitely ascertained that the enemy have discovered and are about to open one of the hatches. When there is no doubt upon this point, the code word "Scramble" will be transmitted three times.
>
> When the enemy have discovered the secret entrance to the op room all sets, valves etc will be carried into the chamber farthest from the hatch which the

enemy appear to have discovered, all papers destroyed by fire and the sets rendered unworkable.

When this action has been taken, the crew Detachment Commander will lead the party and will get out as quietly as possible, followed by the two other operators.

The OC Det (Officer Commanding Detachment) will make every effort to kill the enemy. If, however, the party is too large for him to tackle, he will endeavour to escape capture and to make his way to join up with the nearest BRITISH troops."

Interestingly, the text addresses male soldiers, indicating that Signals crews in the event of an invasion might have replaced the ATS crews, as has indeed been suggested (but not confirmed) by some of the signallers who were involved. According to the recollections of a number of ATS officers, however, the women received at least some basic training in the use of firearms. Barbara Culleton, for instance, was trained how to use a rifle and a pistol, but was never issued with either. Other ATS officers have confirmed that they were never armed and would hence have been unable to defend themselves.

In an interview broadcast by the BBC Radio 4 programme "Open Country" on 8 January 2004, Barbara Culleton however asserted that she was issued with a cyanide tablet, to be used in the event of capture.

"It was in a tin and if it had ever been opened they would have wanted to know why. All strictly secured but it was there, just in case. We were told the most horrific stories of what would happen if the Germans did invade. It didn't sound very pleasant, so maybe it was the best thing to do."

It is a well-known fact that SOE agents and resistance fighters parachuted into occupied Europe during WW2 were commonly supplied with a so-called suicide pill, a glass capsule containing a fatally poisonous substance such as cyanide. Putting the pill in the mouth and biting down on the ampoule released a concentrated solution of potassium cyanide, said to kill within a very short time. Heinrich Himmler, Hermann Göring and Eva Braun are known to have chosen this method and Field Marshal Erwin Rommel was forced to use it. It is not known whether any of Barbara Culleton's ATS colleagues were also given a cyanide tablet. Not one of the women did mention having been issued with a suicide pill when interviewed much later, and the ATS officers who are known to have committed suicide by gassing themselves with generator exhaust fumes would seem not to have had access to such a pill. Contemporary records contain no information regarding the issue of cyanide pills to Auxiliary Units either.

Ten of the thirteen IN Station dugout sites which have to date been identified and recorded are accessible and sufficiently intact so as to allow a detailed study of their design and layout.

Roy Russell, an AU Signals officer who is remembered by Jack Millie as having spent some time in Wales and who was later put in charge of two IN Stations in Kent, has provided a detailed account of the dugout design:

"A Royal Engineer officer came and took us to our two units. They had been built ready for our occupation. I did not see the stations being built, but when they were operating I went in a lot and I remember well what they were like. To get into the underground station you had to crank a shaft. You knew more or less where the entrance was and you had to find a particularly small flat stone. You moved that, and underneath you could see where the crank fitted. You could turn that, and up came a piece of grass which was like a manhole cover, covered with turf so no join could be seen. When it came up, it revealed a shaft and at a certain height you could swing it away and climb underneath it. You then used the crankshaft to reseal it. The shaft was 4-sided and about the size of a trap door and it was wood-lined. There was no ladder but wooden steps, fastened to one side. You climbed down about eight feet, on to a concrete floor.

The structure was a Nissen hut, but with corrugated iron arched across to form a roof. At the bottom (of the shaft) there was a room, about six by nine feet, with shelving all around, and on one shelf there was an empty shell magazine, which gave the impression that the place was an empty ammunition dump. On one of the shelves lay a piece of wire. If you knew what to look for, there was a small hole in the woodwork into which you could push the wire. Something activated the other side, and the whole of that side cantilevered. If you bent down you could walk in and close it behind you. You were now in a room where you would see two tables with wireless sets and three ATS officers operating them. Beyond the "Set" room there was a room with cooking facilities, and Elsans, and there was a room for battery charging. Everything was powered by batteries which had to be recharged by a little engine – a "Chorehorse" – petrol driven – in a tubular cage. The exhaust from that was led away by a duct and came out some way away, where you could only just hear it. The last room led to an emergency exit plus tunnel which was a heavy duty concrete culvert pipe measuring 30 inches in diameter."

"Some stations were equipped with paraffin heaters which had a tray along the top which contained water. Whether this was condensate I do not know, they were referred to as aircraft heaters so it may well have been."

"The stations would have been supplied with American K-rations when operational". (Stanley Judson)

The (to date) found and, where accessible, surveyed and recorded IN Station dugouts are listed below.

Ardingly (West Sussex) – partially collapsed	Call-sign: not known
Alnwick (Northumberland) - intact	Call-sign: Otley
Blorenge (Monmouthshire) - collapsed	Call-sign: Harcourt
Buckland St Mary (Somerset) - inaccessible	Call-sign: Chirnside
Cheddon Fitzpaine (Somerset) - inaccessible	Call-sign: Golding
Halstead (Essex) - intact	Call-sign: Buttercup
Heathfield (East Sussex) - intact	Call-sign: not known
Hollingbourne (Kent) – partially collapsed	Call-sign: not known
Norwich (Norfolk) - intact	Call-sign: Bowling
Ousden (W Suffolk) – concrete hut base only	Call-sign: Gorey
Salisbury (Wiltshire) - intact	Call-sign: Byfield
Shipley (West Sussex) - collapsed	Call-sign: Harston
Winchester (Hampshire) - intact	Call-sign: Omagh

In the following, some attention will be paid to the variation in detail. For instance, the escape tunnel opening is commonly situated at ground floor level (with the exception at Alnwick, Wilton and Winchester, where the opening lies a step or two above ground level). Apart from the IN Station dugouts on the Blorenge and at Halstead, both of which have square and very short tunnels with breezeblock walls, all other (known) tunnels were constructed from sections of concentric concrete sewage or culvert pipes.

Ventilation in almost all of the dugouts (there is one notable exception) was provided by two large concrete pipes, the lower being the inlet, the upper the outlet pipe. Fresh air entered the dugout through the bottom pipe, expanding and rising as it warmed until in reached the top pipe, from whence it would have been pushed outwards, all the time being replaced by fresh air. This process could be assisted by a fan or by the use of a Tilley lamp (Nigel Oxenden, *Auxiliary Units – History and Achievements 1940-1944*, page 26).

Both these pipes emerge through the wall and into the wireless room. The sections passing through the generator room have small rectangular openings allowing for the air to circulate. The openings in the outlet pipe could be sealed either with a lid of some sort or with a piece of cloth. No evidence was found that the opening in the air inlet pipe would also have been sealed. At Norwich and Alnwick a piece of oil-soaked fabric was found still in situ above the opening in the outlet pipe. This fabric was commonly used during the war for gas proofing doors and officially called Union cloth (anti-gas). It had to be soaked in oil for maximum effectiveness. At Halstead, a curved piece of sheet metal was used instead and the openings of both pipes at the Goathland OUT Station were sealed with a (flat, square) piece of metal sheeting.

The concrete ventilation pipes at Halstead and the inlet pipe at Winchester have a section of large glazed ceramic pipe joined onto them, providing an additional opening. Perhaps these Y-junctions helped to smooth the airflow and ensured roughly equal suction from both generator and wireless rooms. The fact that a fan assisted the air circulation at Halstead might have influenced this unusual design. A fan, operated by a 6V battery, has also been said to have been in use at Blandford, the "Osterley" network IN Station in Dorset (Dorothy Monck-Mason).

Most dugouts had at least one or two (but usually more) smaller, glazed ceramic ventilation pipes, one commonly emerging into the generator room through the wall above the tunnel opening. This pipe appears to have served the purpose of allowing expanded warm air to dissipate, especially when the generator was running and the air in the generator room was heating up. For charging batteries, the generator would have to be kept running for about nine hours, with its engine getting quite hot.

The wireless sets were powered by 6-volt 85 AH accumulators (Major Jones). It has been documented (by Alf Ellis and others) that three sets comprising two or three batteries each per IN Station were in regular use. It is also known that under training conditions (pre-invasion) batteries were collected and re-charged by a member of the AU Signals maintenance crew by rota. In the event of an invasion however, IN Station operators would have had to change and recharge the batteries themselves and for this they required a generator. Although it is now known that a number of dugouts were connected to mains electricity this could, of course, only be used until the supply failed and a generator was therefore vital for back up (see also page 98).

It has been documented (see page 102) that the generator room of the Hollingbourne dugout was equipped with a mains rectifier/battery charger, indicating that mains electricity was used for charging batteries for as long as it was available. The wooden battens it was mounted on are still in situ as is the dual output switch beside it.

A small pipe is frequently found near the right-hand corner in the end wall of the generator room, not far above floor level. This pipe is believed to have served the purpose of extracting the generator's exhaust fumes by inserting the end of its exhaust hose into it. Great care would have been taken to seal it with fireclay or asbestos matting so as to prevent any poisonous carbon monoxide from entering the generator room. The generator would in all probability have stood near this pipe, in a position where it would have been easy to crank, refuel and maintain. Remains of what appears to be the end of an exhaust hose or silencer are still in situ, firmly fixed, within a pipe opening in the generator room at Halstead. The set-up at the Wilton IN/Relay Station would seem to be unique in that it had not one but two generators, the exhausts of both of which terminated in a sealed concrete box functioning as an exhaust box, from whence the fumes were carried outside through an asbestos flue pipe.

A cast iron pipe of the type more commonly found in the dugouts used by the operational patrols or by the Home Guard ventilated the lobbies at Halstead and at Norwich. Presumably this was part of the plan of making the enemy believe the lobby to be a Home Guard store. The existence of similar pipes in IN Station dugouts has not been recorded from other locations where they might have been removed, overlooked or rotted away.

Space in the generator room was much restricted because batteries, petrol, oil and kerosene in cans would have been stored there, and additional space would have been taken up by fire buckets required for sprinkling sand over any spilled fuel on the floor, as a fire would have been lethal, not to mention the danger of an explosion. The risk of overfilling the generator when refuelling was great as there was no gauge.

The generator room was also used for charging and storing batteries. David Hunt (pers comm) observes that the process of recharging took approximately nine hours and was a messy and hazardous task. Cell vents had to be opened before charging so as to avoid electrolyte being forced out of the cells by gassing pressure. During the second phase of charging the accumulators started gassing as excess electrical energy was breaking down the water diluting the acid, into hydrogen and oxygen. This created a dangerous and explosive mixture. The fine mist of acid dispersing with the bubbles was even in those days considered a health hazard.

The following instructions, glued onto the inside of the lid of a wooden box containing a 6-volt 72 AH accumulator battery used in conjunction with WS19 sets, illustrate the tasks involved:

"Electrolyte must be best Accumulator Sulphuric Acid, diluted with distilled water to a specific gravity of 1.350 at 60° F. The level of the electrolyte should be one-eighth of an inch above the tops of the separators when the cell is in the discharged condition. The level will rise when the cell is charged. Quantity of electrolyte required is approximately four pints per battery. After filling with electrolyte it is desirable the battery should stand idle for 12 hours before being put in charge. It will be found that a quantity of electrolyte has been absorbed in the plates and separators and more electrolyte should be added again to bring the electrolyte level to one-eighth of an inch above the tops of the separators. A piece of glass or ebonite tube should be used for measuring height of electrolyte.

For the first charge, remove the vent plugs and charge at 8 amperes for approximately 50 hours unless temperature reaches 110° F, when charging rate should be reduced until temperature falls. Charge should be continued until the specific gravity and volts per cell remain constant for one hour. During first charge only, the level of the electrolyte should be maintained by adding electrolyte S.G. 1.350 and not distilled water. When fully charged, the volts should be approximately 2.7 per cell whilst charging current is flowing, and the specific gravity 1.280 to 1.290 at 60° F. If the specific gravity reaches a higher figure, adjust by taking acid out and replacing with distilled water.

Subsequent charging – Recharge at normal rate of 8 amperes for preference until the specific gravity and volts per cell remain constant for one hour. If recharging at higher rate than normal, which must not exceed 16 amperes, the rate must be reduced to normal when the plates commence to gas. The specific gravity at the end of charge should be between 1.280 and 1.290 at 60° F.

Gassing charge – Once every month when the battery is in commission an extra gassing charge should be given at 8 amperes for one hour. Once every three weeks when the battery is out of commission a short charge should be given at 8 amperes for three hours.

Never leave cells in a fully discharged condition. Keep electrolyte level above separators one-eighth inch by the addition of distilled water. Keep battery and surrounding parts, particularly the tops of the cells, clean and dry. Keep terminals and connections free from corrosion and coated with pure Vaseline – NOT GREASE.

The vent holes in the vent plugs must be kept absolutely clear after cell has been filled with electrolyte.

For the initial charge distilled water, if obtainable, should be employed for marking up the electrolyte. For topping up or for refilling cells previously charged, distilled water is also desirable."

Suggestions according to which generators might have been positioned on shelves are without merit because the height alone would have made cranking difficult if not impossible. David Hunt (pers comm) points out that of the various types of charging engines used only the Chorehorse had a starter button in addition to the pull-cord starter. But even if equipped with a starter button, the generator's weight (100 lbs), not to mention its vibrations when running, would have made it's positioning anywhere else but on the floor impracticable and dangerous.

David Hunt points out that refuelling would also have been problematic, considering that Jerry cans would in all likelihood have been used and that it was tricky even when using a funnel. At Halstead, the wooden generator block is still in situ. It was (and still is) held in position by four metal spikes, one at each corner, which were sunk into the floor underneath, preventing the generator being propelled across the floor by its vibrations. At the Wilton IN/Relay Station dugout the two Chorehorse generators were firmly mounted on concrete plinths. The rubber couplings both generators rested on in order to reduce vibrations when in use are also still in situ.

The double doors separating generator and wireless rooms were well sealed, usually with Union cloth, in order to protect the operators in the wireless room from the fumes of charging accumulators as well as from the exhaust fumes generated by the charging engine but despite all precautions accidents did occasionally happen. Arthur Gabbitas vividly remembers that during an exercise which required staying underground for a lengthy period, Alf Ellis had suddenly collapsed in the dugout, and how his unconscious body had to be manhandled up and out of the entrance shaft, accidentally breaking his nose in the process.

> "Early in the evening, Alf's eyes glazed over and he collapsed. Fortunately, two officers were present to supervise the exercise but it still proved difficult for the three of us to lift the dead-weight person up the vertical ladder. We managed to drag him across the field to the staff car and rushed to the General Hospital where we were revived with oxygen, though experiencing dreadful headaches. The next morning Alf and I were most annoyed because the attractive auburn-haired night sister had spent most of the night chatting to the officers and ignored us. Talk about pulling rank!" (Arthur Gabbitas's memoirs, BROM Archive)

Bearing in mind that the primary source of carbon monoxide comes from exhaust fumes and that CO is a colourless, odourless, tasteless and initially non-irritating toxic gas and hence very difficult to detect, the notion that generators were ever situated in wireless rooms is without merit. Despite the opinion of some researchers, there is no evidence in wireless rooms that the generators were ever accommodated therein.

The charging of batteries however would appear to have been controlled from within the wireless room. Unpainted areas that remained on the dugout walls after the removal of shelves give some idea as to their size and use. At Alnwick, Norwich, Hollingbourne, Shipley and Halstead, for instance, the outline of the generator control panel or (battery) charging switchboard, measuring roughly

50 x 60 centimetres (20 x 24 inches), can still quite clearly be discerned on the dividing wall in the wireless room, beside the door leading into the generator room. Evidence of the presence of cables having been fed through the wall (to connect with the generator in the generator room) in the near vicinity supports this.

The main chamber, wireless or operational (ops) room would appear to also have contained tables for the wireless sets, chairs for the operators to sit on and a number of bunks or camp beds to accommodate the crew when it was required for them to stay overnight. Remains of bunks or of simple camp beds have indeed occasionally been found, and metal barrack bunks which were returned to the depots together with everything else when the stations were closed down, may also have been used. Three operators' bays complete with partitioning walls have been found, in good condition, at the Wilton IN Station dugout where four bunk beds have also survived in fairly good condition.

A number of IN Station dugouts were situated surprisingly close to a dwelling. The significance of this interesting detail will become clearer on closer examination.

Alnwick	~ 170 metres
Buckland St Mary	~ 170 metres
Halstead	~150 metres (to transformer)
Heathfield	~ 170 metres to Hall
Norwich	– Garden
Shipley	~ 160 metres
Winchester	– Garden

At Norwich, Wilton (Salisbury) and Heathfield IN Stations, and to a lesser extent at Ardingly, the original wiring is still in situ, although the wires were cut and the switches and sockets removed from the panels and switchboards. Norwich is the first IN Station where the existence of two separate electric circuits, one powered by 6V batteries and the other by mains electricity has been documented (*Churchill's Secret Auxiliary Units*, E Simak and A Pye).

Mains power originated either directly from a nearby domestic source (dwelling) or was accessed by tapping into a nearby electricity transformer or substation. Two cables with two conductors each were used for this purpose. The cables were connected in parallel for the purpose of halving the resistance and to reduce the voltage drop under load. David Hunt observes that mains power would have allowed for decent lighting and fan-assisted ventilation, for heating to keep the dugout dry and remove condensation and for such possible luxuries like a small kettle (pers comm). A kettle has indeed been found in the Norwich IN Station. Further research has since brought to light evidence of the Halstead, Hollingbourne and Shipley IN Stations also having been connected to mains power (the cables are still in place) and presumably there were a number of other IN Stations as well where the evidence has simply been overlooked.

Yolande Bromley, for instance, recalls that the "Met" hut at Thornham Magna was connected to mains power and that mains electricity was used for charging the batteries. Stanley Judson, referring to an IN Station in Yorkshire, also mentions the use of mains power. One of the drawings made by Sally Waterhouse-Brown - perhaps the only surviving contemporary illustration – shows a wall-mounted battery charger comprising a transformer and a rectifier, with a meter and two battery leads, in situ, in the dugout in which she worked (Hollingbourne). The red and black wires seen emerging from it are shown to have spade fork terminals rather than crocodile clips. The wooden battens this rectifier was mounted on are still in place today and a box with two fused switches is also still on the wall beside it, proving the accuracy of the illustrations (see page 102). Similar wooden battens are also still in situ at the Halstead IN Station which too is documented to have been connected to mains electricity (*Churchill's Secret Auxiliary Units*, E Simak and A Pye).

In this context however, it is important to consider the reliability of mains power in wartime. Much of the electricity was not locally generated and the grid was very vulnerable to storm and battle damage etc. Also, mains power could easily have been cut and it could therefore never replace batteries and generators - the wireless sets were designed to run on 6V (batteries) only. There can be no doubt however that for as long as mains was available it would have enormously improved the working conditions in IN Station dugouts.

Dorothy Monck-Mason (left) and Ann Ellis-Hughes, having their lunch break (presumably) outside the Blandford IN Station in spring 1942. *(BROM Archive)*

Sally Waterhouse-Brown's drawings

Subaltern Sally Alice May Waterhouse-Brown was commissioned on 6 August 1943, after having passed the ATS training course at No.1 OCTU at Edinburgh as the best cadet – an accomplishment duly noted in Beatrice Temple's diary. She joined the SD together with Margaret Hamilton Rigby (married name Briscoe), like her a gifted artist. Many of their drawings and sketches depict scenes drawn from work that provide unique glimpses of the environment the ATS officers worked in.

(Estate of Margaret Hamilton Rigby/IWM Documents 3150)

Alluding to the biblical injuction to care for the stranger in our midst, the title of this drawing draws attention to a hairy caterpillar the ATS officers would seem to have encountered on the lid of the dugout's chemical toilet.

The Stranger within our 'midst

(Estate of Margaret Hamilton Rigby/IWM Documents 3150)

Sally Waterhouse-Brown's drawings provide a unique opportunity to view the Hollingbourne (Harrietsham) IN Station, where she was based in the autumn of 1943, through her eyes, as she saw it when she was there. In the above view, looking through the open 'secret' door, which pivoted, it can be seen that the Elsan (chemical toilet) stood in the lobby. The wooden steps in the background lead up the entrance shaft – an interesting detail often assumed but until now never confirmed. Wooden steps were far easier to manoeuvre than the steel rungs commonly found in the entrance shafts of operational patrols' OBs.

Freddie, depicted below sitting on the dugout's camp bed, was one of the AU Signals crew of three who in the second half of 1943 were billeted at Sevenoaks. Their task was to recharge batteries, inspect aerials and repair wireless sets. He also features in Alf Ellis' diary as one of the men who helped setting up the networks in the south in 1942. Beatrice Temple mentions him in her diary as the officer who accompanied Lieutenant Oakey to Heathfield IN Station on the night Betty Dicken's body was found, and again when she met him together with Subaltern Wendy Kaines at Hollingbourne.

FREDDIE at WORK.

(Estate of Margaret Hamilton Rigby/IWM Documents 3150)

This drawing is of particular interest in that it is almost certainly the only depiction of a TRD set. What would seem to be a voltmeter contained in a wooden box can be seen on top of the empty case at right. On the left, Freddie's tool kit and an assortment of tools spread out in front of it (part of a head and breast set and a wooden box presumably containing valves) can also be seen. The lit cigarette in the ashtray beside him evidences that Freddie liked to smoke when working, and he appears to be whistling. Freddie's shoulder flash was commonly worn by ATS personnel attached to Royal Signals units; the reason why he would have worn an ATS flash is not clear. (IWM, INS 6212)

Sally Waterhouse-Brown's ("S.W.B") colleagues at the Hollingbourne IN Station were Phyllis Marion Britten ("P.M.B.") and Airlie Campbell. (See also Beatrice Temple's diary entry for 24 August 1943)

(Estate of Margaret Hamilton Rigby/IWM Documents 3150)

The existence of a wall-mounted battery charger is a clear indication of the IN Station having been connected to mains electricity. The wooden battens are still in place.

(Estate of Margaret Hamilton Rigby/IWM Documents 3150)

In January 1943 she had fallen off her bicycle and broken her nose. Airlie Abinda Campbell was commissioned on 15 April 1942. Some time between the date of her commissioning and the date she left AU ATS, on 15 May 1944, she married and her name changed to Gascoyne. Her son, James Campbell Gascoyne, recalls that his mother never spoke about her wartime activities.

(Estate of Margaret Hamilton Rigby/IWM Documents 3150)

Florence Margaret Cole, known to everyone as "Waddy", joined AU ATS on 11 March 1942, and the first IN Station she worked at would seem to have been Norwich. She looks very young, and indeed the officer commanding the ATS Company at Doncaster thought her to be too young for a Mixed Mess. (Beatrice Temple's diary)

The Networks

By the time Captain Ken Ward joined the team at AU Signals HQ at Hundon in January 1941, five ATS officers - all hand-picked by Lady Carlisle - were already working as wireless operators on the trial network set up in Kent. In the following months, more networks were gradually established until the counties of Dorset, Hampshire (including the Isle of Wight), Sussex, Kent, Essex, Suffolk, Norfolk, Lincolnshire, Yorkshire, Durham and Northumberland were fully covered.

In March 1942 the existing networks were further expanded to include the Scottish Borders, South Wales and North Somerset. Major Jones' map shows that the networks eventually extended from the Scottish Highlands southwards across Berwickshire and all the way south along the east coast to Kent, and west from there to Monmouthshire and Carmarthenshire in South Wales

With the exception of East Devon, each of the above mentioned counties had at least one IN Station, served by its own network of OUT Stations. Some IN Stations had an outpost that served an Army HQ situated further inland. Hatfield Peverel IN Station, for instance, would appear to have been an outpost of the IN station at Halstead and the Bury St Edmunds station would seem to have been an outpost of Thornham Magna IN Station. None of these outposts or extensions were served by OUT Stations.

Some other IN Stations, all located a safe distance away from the coast, seemed to have functioned as relays between a number of other IN Stations, some handling several different frequencies, such as at Ousden (Suffolk). Similar IN/Relay Stations were located at Wilton in Wiltshire, at Wendover in Buckinghamshire, and at an as yet unidentified location near Hertford. None of these stations had OUT Stations.

Only three IN Stations were attached to Command HQs: the Wilton IN Station served Southern Command HQ based at Wilton House near Salisbury; the Reigate IN Station served South Eastern Command HQ, based at Reigate, and the Edinburgh IN Station served Scottish Command HQ, based at Edinburgh. All other Command HQs were situated further inland and hence not covered by the wireless networks.

Most of the IN Stations were operational until closedown in July 1944, and Beatrice Temple's diary confirms that most of these sites were manned by AU ATS subalterns throughout the whole time during which they were operational. A closer investigation reveals that the probably decisive common denominator of the ATS-manned IN Stations appears to have been that all these stations were located at or in the near vicinity of an Army HQ, which no doubt provided the reasonably secure environment required by ATS regulations for their personnel.

All of the IN Stations manned by AU Signals crews were located a considerable distance away from the nearest Army HQ, with some being situated in very isolated areas such as on the Blorenge mountain or at Crwbin in South Wales.

AU Signals also manned the IN Stations at Hume Castle (Berwickshire), at Buckland St Mary (Somerset) and at Danby Lodge (North Yorkshire), as well as two as yet unidentified IN/Relay Stations, one near Beukley Farm to the west of Newcastle upon Tyne, and one in Hertfordshire. Intriguingly, Beatrice Temple's diary entries show gaps of approximately six months between her visits to two ATS-manned IN Stations, namely Harrietsham/Hollingbourne and Heathfield Park, both located in the then Canadian Corps District. The Canadians had taken over from 4th Corps in November 1941 and it is possible (but to date unverified) that AU Signals crews might have taken over the running of these stations for the duration of the Canadian troops' stay in the area. At Thornham Magna in Suffolk the IN Station would indeed appear to have been taken over by AU Signals when circumstances changed, ie when the Divisional HQ was moved out of the area and the ATS were subsequently posted to another location for security reasons.

From left: Unknown ATS officer, Phyllis Marion Britten, (unknown Signals officer), Sally Waterhouse-Brown and Airlie Campbell (the photographer at right) - autumn 1943 at Hollingbourne. *(Estate of Margaret Hamilton Rigby/IWM Documents 3150)*

The following table lists the longest-serving ATS-crewed IN Stations, based on Beatrice Temple's diary entries, using the dates of her first and her last visits.

Salisbury (Alderbury + Wilton)	817 days	28 months
Halstead	771 days	28 months
Doncaster (Hickleton Hall)	803 days	27 months
Reigate	774 days	26 months
South Dalton	661 days	22 months
Thornham Magna	648 days	21 months
Taunton (Cheddon Fitzpaine)	619 days	20 months

Buckinghamshire

One of the dots on Major Jones' map would seem to mark a location in the vicinity of <u>Wendover</u>, a market town at the foot of the Chiltern Hills in the Aylesbury Vale. That an IN/Relay Station had indeed been located in this area is evidenced by entries in Beatrice Temple's diary, made on the occasion of visits to her ATS officers who were based there. No other details are known and the station, which had wireless links with a station near Hertford (further to the north-east) and another at or in the vicinity of Coleshill House (further to the south-west), has as yet to be found (see also page 73).

Nothing is to date known about the IN Station at or near <u>Coleshill House</u> although it is reasonable to assume that it served the HQ of the Auxiliary Units.

Devon (see Somerset)

Dorset

The <u>Blandford</u> IN Station was situated in Buzbury Wood, near the 3rd Division HQ at Langton House in Blandford. According to Adrian Monck-Mason the War Department had requisitioned the whole wood. The call-sign of the Dorset network was "Osterley" (a district in Greater London). Beatrice Temple's last visit to the station was in August 1942 and it would seem that AU Signals took over and continued operations until closedown.

One of the ATS officers working at Blandford was Dorothy Monck-Mason (nee Rainey) who recalls:

> "We lived in a lovely country house belonging to Colonel and Mrs. Percy Brown. I think the woods (where the IN Station was located) were within short sighting distance and it was the same set-up there and we carried on the same exercises. We covered the Dorset and Hampshire area to the coast. Our IO was Owen Hall-Hall, who lived at Tarrant Hinton, I think. I don't think we were meant to meet the IO - oh yes, we did of course, they did call didn't they? I went to have dinner with them, he and his wife Jocelyn, yes.
>
> I can remember the aerials because they drilled a little hole up the tree didn't they, or whatever, you know and they sunk the aerial into it, didn't they, and then they covered it with moss and bark. We were training with the OUT Stations - we just switched on and we kept watch the whole time and we were all the time searching to pick up call-signs and then we'd answer them. The Royal Corps of Signals came to service our sets and it was they who brought the 6-volt batteries and they came to change them from time to time."

Two of the network's OUT Stations – "Osterley 1" and "Osterley 2" were never able to directly communicate with their own IN Station and consequently their messages had to be relayed using the IN-Station on the Somerset ("Chirnside") network, which they had no problem of contacting. When "Osterley 1" called the "Chirnside" IN-Station near Taunton in Somerset, an operator took down the message and then another operator sent it over to the other network using a wireless set on that network. A different wireless set would have been required because the frequencies were fixed and the Dorset network worked on a frequency of 60 mcs, whereas the Somerset network used 65 mcs (David Hunt, per comm).

The wireless set at <u>Hawkchurch</u> was kept in a box concealed in a hut on Briscoe's Farm. The station had the call-sign "Osterley 1".

The OUT Station at <u>Bridport</u> was situated on the north side of Watton Hill. It was a dugout and had the call-sign "Osterley 2".

The wireless set of the <u>Frampton</u> OUT Station was concealed in a box buried at an as yet unknown location on Hampton Hill. The station had the call-sign "Osterley 3". A Major Heath from Martinstown was the operator.

AU Signals officers Stan Judson, Alf Ellis and others have provided detailed descriptions of how initially the wireless sets and batteries were concealed within sturdy wooden boxes with detachable lids, buried in the ground at an isolated location near the operators' homes, and given explanations as to why, after a number of discoveries and arrests, not to mention the flooding of some of these boxes, all these sites were either abandoned or converted into purpose-built dugouts equipped with bunks and heaters, and stocked with Army rations (see also page 27).

The <u>Dorchester</u> OUT Station was located at an as yet unidentified location to the south of the hospital. According to some sources the wireless set was kept in an attic whereas others think it was concealed in a dugout. It had the call-sign "Osterley 4". Reg Perry recorded this station for the DoB project.

The <u>Milborne St Andrew</u> OUT Station (sometimes referred to as Dewlish OUT Station) was a dugout situated to the south of the A354 road near Puddletown. The station had the call-sign "Osterley 5". Reg Perry recorded its location for the DoB database without offering any further information.

The OUT Station at <u>Wool</u> was a dugout using the call-sign "Osterley 6".

The <u>Broadstone</u> OUT Station is believed to have been a dugout on Yaffle Hill (near the water tower); it used the call-sign "Osterley 7.

The OUT Station at <u>Lytchett Matravers</u> had the call-sign "Osterley 8" and was in an outhouse.

The OUT Station at <u>Stoborough Heath</u> had the call-sign "Osterley 9" and was in an attic.

The <u>Portesham</u> OUT Station ("Osterley 10") was in Beneke Wood, near Hardy's monument; the <u>Colehill</u> OUT Station was "Osterley 11".

The <u>Avon</u> SUBOUT Station had the call-sign "Osterley 8A"; the <u>Poole</u> SUBOUT Station used the call-sign "Osterley 7B" and was in an attic, whereas the <u>Wareham</u> SUBOUT Station ("Osterley 9A") was in a cellar. The station at <u>Kingston</u> was in an attic and used the call-sign "Osterley 12A".

The <u>Uplyme</u> SUBOUT Station had the call-sign "Osterley 1A". It was in the attic of a house located near the junction of Sidmouth and Upper West Hill Roads on the western fringe of Lyme Regis. (Alf Ellis, Arthur Gabbitas, Dr Will Ward, Reg Perry)

Essex

The Essex wireless network used the call-sign "Buttercup". The IN Station was located in the vicinity of the 42nd (East Lancashire) Divisional HQ at Dynes Hall, near the village of Little Maplestead. Although Halstead is about five kilometres (2.6 miles) distant, the station was always referred to as <u>Halstead</u> IN Station by Beatrice Temple and Ken Ward.

The existence of an underground structure in the vicinity of Little Maplestead would seem to have been known, perhaps from the time it had been built, by at least some locals including the gamekeeper. In his book *500 Years of Village History along the Suffolk-Essex Border,* Ashley Cooper briefly mentions a dugout which "is reliably reported to have been sited in a wood some two miles (three kilometres) from the village of Gestingthorpe". The source of this information was Mr Benjamin Perkins, the co-author of said book, who from 1959 until 1979 had been the manager at Dynes Hall. In a letter to Colin Durrant, the then chairman of the British Resistance Organisation Museum at Parham, he recalls that it was indeed the old gamekeeper who took him to the site, which was believed to have been an underground Army HQ that had been kept secret – "so secret that not even the Royal Dorset Regiment, based at Halstead during the war, knew of it". Mr Perkins' memory is of "a well-hidden dugout of evident military use, in the middle of a remote wood." (Letter to Colin Durrant, dated 4 December 1997; BROM Archive)

No trace was found of the everyday workstation, the "Met" hut (see page 141). Captain Ken Ward however recalls that it was only about 50 metres distant from where the Intelligence officer - to whom all the information gathered at the IN Station was hand-delivered - was based. (Captain Ward and his wife Thea, one of the wireless operators at Halstead, left the organisation at the beginning of 1942.)

Like almost all other known IN Stations dugouts, the Halstead IN Station was constructed to a standard design by units of the Royal Engineers who would have been unaware of its intended use. Situated on the edge of a wood immediately above a steep natural bank, the location was obviously carefully chosen. New trees have long replaced the original ones and it is hence no longer possible to find the aerial tree/s. The bank onto which the emergency exit emerges is presently heavily overgrown with brambles forming an impenetrable barrier. The vertical entrance shaft leads into a small anteroom or lobby designed to look like a Home Guard store. Originally it would have been furnished with shelves containing boxes of ammunition, effectively concealing a doorway leading into the main chamber. No shelves or doors have survived at Halstead. The floor of the wireless room is covered with concrete paving slabs which were originally covered by a layer of brown linoleum (some still in situ). The openings of two large ventilation pipes can be seen in the wall separating wireless and generator room. One of the aerial feeder cables enters the room through the roof, shielded within a metal conduit. A second feeder cable, a short length only, was found embedded in a broken piece of concrete that formed part of the construction of the entrance shaft.

Two two-cored 240 Volt mains power cables enter the wireless room through the opposite wall, each one contained within its own conduit. As no lighting conduits and very little original wiring have survived at Halstead it is not possible to establish whether the station also had two separate lighting circuits as has been documented at Norwich IN Station but the power cables confirm that the station was connected to mains electricity.

In all probability the doorway leading into the generator room was originally secured by twin doors - with a raised concrete threshold between the two (in situ). Two concrete ventilation pipes traverse one end of the generator room, sporting the characteristic rectangular openings. At Shipley (West Sussex) the opening was covered by what appears to have been a wooden board. At Norwich and Alnwick (Northumberland) a piece of Union cloth was used to close the opening (found still in situ at both locations). At Halstead a piece of slightly bent sheet metal (in situ) served as a cover. It is still firmly held in place by the original steel circlips. The pipes are painted white and both have a section of large glazed ceramic pipe, opening into the generator room, connected into them. Perhaps these Y-junctions served to create some additional airflow or they helped to smooth the airflow and ensured roughly equal suction from both generator and wireless rooms (or both), as without a doubt did the extractor fan, part of which is still in situ - an unusual feature that had not been previously documented. Similar vent pipe configurations were found at the Winchester IN Station (call-sign "Omagh"'- on the Hampshire and Isle of Wight wireless network).

A glazed ceramic pipe of slightly smaller diameter, believed to have served the purpose of extracting the generator's exhaust fumes, is in the generator room's end wall and it appears that the end of the generator exhaust hose was inserted into this pipe and permanently fixed in place with fireclay or asbestos matting. This prevented poisonous carbon monoxide fumes from entering the generator room. Above it the word 'CHARGED' - no doubt referring to batteries – can still be seen, pencilled on the wall in capital letters.

On the floor, next to the escape tunnel opening, the wooden generator block is still in situ, in its original position. Constructed from sections of square timber, this is the only intact original specimen known to have survived. Four metal bolts on its underside, one near each corner, not only prevented it from being propelled all over the smooth paved floor by the generator's vibrations when it was running, but also held it firmly in place when pulling the starter cord. The bolts, albeit quite corroded, are still contained within the holes that were drilled into the paving slab that the block is resting on. At the Halstead IN Station (also at Norwich, Heathfield, Alnwick and Shipley) the outline of a Lyons generator charging switchboard can still quite clearly be discerned and evidence of wires having been fed through the wall (to connect the generator in the generator room and the batteries under charge) in the near vicinity supports this. The charging panel was designed specifically for the use with a Lyons 550 W generator.

The emergency escape tunnel, an unusually short passage of only about three metres in length - being cut short by the steep slope of the earthen bank it was built into – has breezeblock walls, with some brickwork filling the gaps, with a roof constructed of paving slabs. The exit opening appears to either have collapsed or was deliberately blocked.

Dorothy Monck-Mason spent a short time at Halstead, apparently on the occasion of an exercise. Due to other problems encountered on her arrival she does, however, not mention the IN Station.

> "From Salisbury I was whisked off to Halstead and on my way I stopped off in London with all my luggage, including a trunk and my sleeping roll, my bedroll on top of my taxi, outside the Berkeley, to see if anyone had arrived and were going up to Scotland and to say that, unfortunately, I wasn't going to go be there and while I was in there, I told them I couldn't go and I came out and the taxi had driven off with all my luggage, absolutely everything. I'd lost my battledress, I think. I was in full dress uniform. I went up to Halstead and I was met by a driver - this was New Year's Eve - who said 'Ma'am, every hotel is full because its New Year's Eve but we have got a requisitioned house I'm taking you to' - which was unfurnished, unheated and I was just left there, and I found a huge pile of newspapers, stuck in a corner and I had to spread out on the floor and sleep there." (Interview by John Warwicker, 1999)

The IN Station had wireless links with OUT Stations north-east of Hadleigh, near Alresford, in the Stutton area and near Bradwell on Sea, and a SUBOUT Station at Dovehouse Farm near Mistley, the latter operated by Chris Jaggs, the farmer.

Another known OUT Station operator was RG Potts from the village of Great Braxted. Interestingly, Mr Potts was also a member of the Wickham Bishops AU operational patrol. (See page 156 for a similar case at Bury Hill, West Sussex). Mr Potts told David Lampe that he was advised at the time that his wireless transmissions were impossible to pick up by the Gestapo's locators. This turned out to be not quite the truth in that regular Army units did in fact occasionally pick up these signals – at times leading to the arrest of an operator. But because operators were provided with a War Office telephone number, to be called in an emergency, they were never detained for very long. (*The Last Ditch*, page 125)

The Halstead IN Station was linked with the IN/Relay Station at Ousden. It also had a wireless link with its outpost at <u>Hatfield Peverel</u> which served the HQ of the Essex Division, stationed at Berwick Place – a large manorial house located about one and a half kilometres to the west of St Andrew's church. The Hatfield Peverel IN Station had no OUT Stations and its location has to date not been found. Presumably it consisted of a "Met" hut in the grounds of Berwick Place. The station was closed before stand-down and is not marked on Major Jones' map.

Hampshire

The <u>Winchester</u> IN Station used the call-sign "Omagh" (the county town of County Tyrone, Ireland). The dugout was (and still is) located in the garden of Pitt Manor, with its entrance concealed beneath a cold frame. It served the 4th Division HQ which was based nearby at West Downs School in Romsey Road.

The dugout has been recorded and surveyed. It is in good condition (but currently inaccessible), with its design following the standard layout known for almost all other IN Stations, with a lobby at the bottom of a vertical entrance shaft; a secret door concealed behind shelf units leading into the main chamber, and a generator room and emergency exit passage at the opposite end. The IN Station was served by nine OUT Stations and six SUBOUT Stations all the locations and call-signs of which are mentioned in Alf Ellis' 1942 diary. In March 1943, Arthur Gabbitas was posted to Winchester, where he formed part of a three-man crew of signallers. While one man maintained radio watch, the other two visited the OUT Stations once a week in their scout car, replacing the batteries with freshly charged ones and inspecting the aerials. Beatrice Temple last visited the IN Station in January 1943 and it would seem that an AU Signals crew took over because the station is shown as still having been operational until closedown in July 1944.

> The <u>West Moors</u> OUT Station, call-sign "Omagh 1", was situated at the St Leonard's Hotel on the A31 road between Ferndown and Ringwood, about 15 kilometres (10 miles) north of Bournemouth. The operators were the landlord, Mr Harvey, and Mrs Betty Howe, the barmaid. The wireless set was kept in a dugout at the back of the hotel.

> The OUT Station at <u>Wootton</u> was in a shed and had the call-sign "Omagh 2". The operator was a Mr Taylor.

The Wickham and Denmead OUT Stations were dugouts. Wickham had the call-sign "Omagh 5"; the operators were Mr Pell and Mr Longland. Denmead ("Omagh 6") was operated by Mr Clarke, Mr Ship and Mr Bell.

The wireless set at Swanwick OUT Station was kept in an attic; it had the call-sign "Omagh 7". The operator was Mr Kelsea from Locksheath.

No details are known about the Norton and Wise End OUT Stations. Norton had the call-sign "Omagh 8" (operated by Colonel Pentwood) and Wise End was "Omagh 10".

The Bitterne OUT Station had the call-sign "Omagh 9". The wireless set was hidden in an attic.

The Setley SUBOUT Station was in a private house and used the call-sign "Omagh 2B".

The SUBOUT Station at Rowlands Castle had the call-sign "Omagh 6A"; Botley SUBOUT Station, "Omagh 7B", was in an attic; Burchen (call-sign "Omagh 7A") too was in an attic.

Some of the network's OUT Stations were located on the Isle of Wight, where Billingham Manor, near Newport, served as the base of the 214th Infantry Brigade.

The OUT Station at Shorewell was a dugout and had the call-sign "Omagh 3".

There appear to have been two stations in Newport, "Omagh 4" and "Omagh 4A", indicating that the latter was a SUBOUT Station. The operator of "Omagh 4" was a Mr Alexander.

The Ringwood SUBOUT Station ("Omagh 8A") was in an attic. A SUBOUT Station is said to have been at Ningwood. (Alf Ellis, Arthur Gabbitas, Dr Will Ward)

Hertfordshire

The 54th (East Anglian) Division as well as the Hertford Area & Hertfordshire Sub-Area HQs were stationed at the barracks in (Old) London Road, Hertford. The wireless path shown on Major Jones' map points to a location in or near Hertford, but the exact location of the IN Station has to date not been found. Interestingly, 11th (XI) Corps HQ was at Albury Hall, near Bishops Stortford, about 13 kilometres (8 miles) to the north-east. Albury Hall, when it was made available by the Glyn family to the Army and RAF for the duration of World War 2, played a vital role for Eastern Command in secret service work with the

Special Operations Executive (SOE), with agents behind enemy lines in France and the low countries, and work with the French Resistance, masterminding air drop operations out of the airfield at RAF Sawbridgeworth. Winston Churchill is known to have visited Albury Hall on a number of occasions. Sadly, like so many of the grand houses requisitioned during the war, the Hall was demolished in 1950. The IN/Relay Station had wireless links with the Ousden IN/Relay Station in Suffolk, further to the north-east, and with an IN/Relay Station in the vicinity of Wendover in Buckinghamshire, further to the west. It was not served by any OUT Stations. Beatrice Temple appears to never have visited this station.

Kent

The Kent Area HQ (and later the Home Counties Area HQ) was based at Shenden Manor in Weald Road (just west of Knole Park). The exact location of the IN Station in <u>Sevenoaks</u> has to date not been found and the fact that Major Jones' map does not show an IN Station at Sevenaoks indicates that it was either closed or moved to another location before closedown. Indeed, Beatrice Temple noted in her diary that on the occasion of a visit to her ATS officers on 1 January 1942, she was unable to find them because they had moved to Tunbridge Wells. A map created by Arthur Gabbitas (with the help of some of his former colleagues), based on recollections dating from before 1944, does however show the Hollingbourne IN Station linked with a site at or near Sevenoaks. The map also shows a wireless path from the Sussex IN Stations at Shipley and Ardingly terminating at the same location.

Major Peter Forbes too remembers the Sevenoaks IN Station:

> "My job was to write exercises to test all the networks and then go round to see them carried out. In my six months there (at Coleshill House) I visited by car every area and IO in the UK. I must therefore have visited all the IN Stations etc but I cannot now remember where most were. I remember visiting Captain Fraser at Sevenoaks and Canterbury. There was one, I think, in Wilton, Salisbury, and one on top of Reigate Hill. I remember the one at Hume Castle on the Borders. Funnily enough, much earlier I had looked at Hume as a possibility of an (AU ops) OB and might inadvertently have come across the station!" (Letter to Arthur Gabbitas, dated 1 February 1998; BROM Archive)

In his "Adventures in WW2", Lieutenant Roy Russell mentions an IN Station near the village of <u>Brasted</u>, about six kilometres (three miles) west of Sevenoaks. It would seem quite implausible for two IN Stations, both operating at the same time, to be built at such a short distance of each other. It may be that the Sevenoaks station was moved to or replaced by a station in Brasted, but to date no information has been unearthed to confirm this location, for which Roy Russel would appear to be the only source. Beatrice Temple makes no mention of the station in her diary and would seem to never have visited it.

One of the well-documented Kent IN Station sites is the dugout near the village of <u>Hollingbourne</u> (referred to as Harrietsham in Beatrice Temple's diary), located a few miles to the south-west of Maidstone. The dugout was built in a strip woodland bounded by fields. The entrance shaft is currently covered with corrugated metal sheeting, and the emergency exit tunnel opening is hidden under shrubbery about 30 metres further to the south. According to the local farmer, a small building originally stood right above the entrance (Brian Drury, pers comm). It is not known if this was the "Met" hut, with a trapdoor in the floor leading into the dugout (similar set-ups are known to have existed at the Blorenge and Wilton IN Stations and at the OUT Station in Goathland) or perhaps a dilapidated shed used for camouflage. In 1944, the IN Station had 11 OUT Stations and was linked with the Southern Command HQ IN Station in Reigate.

The structure, which apart from a few minor details is identical in design to all other known IN Station dugouts, is in good condition. One of the aerial trees still stands nearby, the long scar running up its trunk denoting the position of the aerial feeder cable, concealed underneath the bark. Interestingly, the secret door giving access into the wireless room operated on a pivot (as shown in several of Sally Waterhouse-Brown's drawings – see page 99), and a mains rectifier would appear to have been used for charging the batteries (see page 102) although the station would, of course, also have had a backup generator.

A concealed trapdoor originally covered the entrance shaft, with wooden steps leading down into a lobby made to look like a Home Guard store. As at all other known dugouts, the floor is covered with paving slabs, and a pair of large concrete pipes provided ventilation. A switchbox (beside the battens to which the mains rectifier was attached) is still in situ in the generator room, and several aerial feeder cables, contained within a small steel pipe, emerge into the wireless room. Interestingly, there is a sump in the floor of the generator room, just in front of the opening of the not quite five metres (16 feet) long emergency escape tunnel (see page 151). A similar sump was found at the Wilton IN/Relay Station.

Auxiliers had instructions to use Elsans for the evacuation of faeces only, and that drainpipes or sumps in their OBs were to be used for urination. Perhaps the same applied for male occupants of IN Station dugouts. AU signallers operated some of the IN Stations and some believed that they were to take over from the ATS in the event of an invasion. Most dugouts, however, did not have a sump. At Hollingbourne, the Elsan toilet stood in the lobby (see page 100).

One of the ATS officers was billeted on a house at West Leas to the north of the Ringlestone Road. Several of the women who worked at the Hollingbourne IN Station have many years later shared their memories. Sally Waterhouse-Brown, has produced a number of highly interesting drawings whilst based there (see pages 99-104). Edwina Burton, features in one of the episodes of Peter Williams' "Secret Army" film, which was commissioned by Meridian Television and transmitted in eight 30-minute episodes during 2003 (IWM, TV 149). Miss Burton says that she spent 18 months at Hollingbourne, sharing her duties with another ATS officer. She believed that the wireless sets they were provided with were the standard Army WS17 R/T sets. She recalls that the dugout had two camp beds and that the wireless operators were provided with a supply of food and water. Miss Burton thought that her transfer to AU ATS was perhaps due to the fact that her sister Mary was the civilian secretary of Major Petherick. (Mary Burton later became the secretary of Major Charles E Randell, who succeeded Major Petherick at Hannington Hall.) She was transferred back to ATS general duties at some time in 1944. Records show that Edwina Caroline Gearey Burton was commissioned on 12 February 1943.

Marjorie Barden (married name Tarrant) was another ATS subaltern who is believed to have worked at Hollingbourne:

> "In June 1941 I attended an officer training course in Edinburgh and on graduation returned to this special unit, having signed an official secrecy document. We worked as a group of two operators in various locations, mostly in Kent and Sussex but also served in various areas throughout the country until the summer of 1944. In addition to the Nissen hut we worked in, we had a well-hidden underground station in the same general area, where we would operate if the country were invaded. It was well stocked with supplies and extensively used during Army exercises. The stations were in isolated areas and the nearest Army HQ supplied our transportation" (Adrian Westwood, Kent Auxiliary Units).

The Canterbury IN Station is said to have been located 'near the barracks'. In this context it is of interest to note that in 1940 an underground Brigade HQ was constructed for South-Eastern Command within the grounds of a large detached house that stood in close vicinity to the Old Park Army barracks. "The Cherries", as it was called at that time, was located in a secluded spot on the outskirts of the city, and had been in private use, as was the neighbouring property, which too was requisitioned. (South East Defence Photos, January 2011). As the underground battle HQ - dug into a steep bank beside the house by the 171st Tunnelling Company RE and finished in 1940 – were never used, it is not unreasonable to assume that an IN Station might have been located in the grounds of either "The Cherries" or the adjoining property, called the "White House". Beatrice Temple visited the location 14 times between 1 January 1942 and 16 June 1943, which would appear to have been her last visit.

Another IN Station is believed to have been situated near Hill Top in the village of Challock, where the as yet to be confirmed site is described as having been a bungalow near the top of the hill. According to the information published on Adrian Westwood's "Kent Auxiliary Units" website, Captain Norman Field (the then AU ops patrols IO for the area) is said to have recalled having met two young women in FANY (First Aid Nursing Yeomanry) uniforms at the property on the occasion of a visit to the area with the then Commander in Chief Home Forces, General Sir Alan Brooke. According to an entry in the *War Diaries* of Lord Alanbrooke he did indeed visit the area (on 29 August 1941) but as the ATS had their own uniforms they would hardly have worn FANY uniforms on that particular occasion. The presumption that a dugout might have been nearby, perhaps in King's Wood, can be discounted, since it has been established that no dugouts were built before 1942. Beatrice Temple appears to

have visited the site only once, and the fact that it is not shown on Major Jones'
1944 map suggests that the IN Station was closed before stand-down.

No details are currently known regarding the exact location of the IN Station at
Tunbridge Wells which served 12th (XII) Corps District HQ, and in 1944 would
seem to have reported to Reigate. There has been much speculation regarding
the extensive labyrinth of underground passages and chambers known to still
exist only about 500 metres distant from the Corps HQ. The underground
structure is believed by many to once have been the underground battle HQ
used by Lieutenant General (later Field Marshal) Bernard Montgomery, who
has however asserted that he never used it and had, in fact, never known that it
even existed. The tunnel entrances are currently sealed and any military
records would seem to have been destroyed.

> "I know nothing whatsoever about the underground D-Day command HQ. It
> was not built for me, and I never gave any orders for it to be built. At no time
> during the 1939 – 1945 war did I ever have an underground HQ. I do not
> believe in such HQs; they are wrong and bad for morale." (Letter to CA
> Symonds, editor of the Kent and Sussex Courier)

> "In 1941, the War Office became alarmed about a possible invasion in Kent,
> so I was transferred to command 12th Corps. I arrived in Tunbridge Wells on
> 12 April 1941 and King George VI came and had lunch with me one day. On
> 17 November I was promoted to command the south eastern army, all the
> troops in Kent, Surrey and Sussex and left that day for my new headquarters
> in Reigate." (Letter dated 7 October 1969 to a Mrs Finch, who lived at 16
> Broadwater Down at the time.)

Ian Todd who researched the history of the Broadwater Down tunnels and
produced a report in May 1976 (an edited version is published on the
Subterranea Brittanica website) had contacted Lieutenant General Sir Nigel
Ritchie, who commanded 12th Corps from December 1943 to May 1945, and Sir
Nigel too would seem to have been unaware of the structure's existence:

> "The operations room to which you refer was not, to the best of my
> knowledge, in use during the period I commanded 12th Corps. I never heard
> of its existence. It was probably constructed during the period of threatened
> invasion from 1940 to 1941, when the late Sir Andrew Thomas commanded
> the Corps."

The tunnels, which are believed to have been dug in 1941 and to be almost 30
metres (100 feet) deep, are located in Hargate Forest in East Sussex, to the
south of Tunbridge Wells and just across the border, in an area known as 'The
Wilderness'. Intriguingly, Royal Corps of Signals soldiers are reported to have
occupied them for some time and the location of a wireless station in the
vicinity is marked on Major Jones' map. Beatrice Temple visited her ATS
officers at Tunbridge Wells regularly between January 1942 and June 1943.
Some of the subalterns known to have worked at the Tunbridge Wells IN
Station are Marjorie Barden, Mary Alexander, Ann Gunter, Priscilla Badgerow
and Phyllis Britton.

One of the OUT Stations on the Kent network is known to have been at Nash Court Farm on the Isle of Thanet. Mr Lamont, the operator, whose wireless set was hidden in a dugout in a corner of his farmyard, convinced the members of the local AU patrol that all he ever did was to pass on messages retrieved from holes in the ground to other people 'down the line'. Only after the war did the patrol members find out that a wireless set had been used (*The Last Ditch*, page 126). No details are to date known about the OUT Stations at Ripple near Deal, Buckland near Dover and Etchinghill near Folkestone.

The Charing OUT Station was operated by Adrian Monck-Mason, a chicken farmer, who kept his wireless set concealed underneath a chicken hut on his farm on Charing Hill. When one day he was on his way to the dugout he noticed a Royal Corps of Signals soldier wandering around nearby, a tall fish pole aerial extending from a knapsack radio slung on his back. He asked him what he was doing and the soldier explained that signals from a strange station had been picked up in the area. The Army did not recognise the code and as it had been unable to break it, had decided that German spies were at work in the area. (*The Last Ditch*, pages 125/126)

Dorothy Monck-Mason (an ATS wireless operator who worked at the Alnwick, Halstead, Blandford and Salisbury IN Stations) has offered a little more information regarding Adrian Monck-Mason (who, contrary to her belief, had never joined the Royal Signals):

> "I was married to Monck-Mason in 1941, who I recall, had been working with two brothers named Hacker (they were Finns) in the field of wireless technology, and which, I think, lead him to working somewhere within the Watson-Watt team. (Sir Robert Alexander Watson-Watt, KCB, FRS, FRAeS, contributed significantly to the development of radar. In September 1936 he became the Superintendent of the Bawdsey Research Station at Bawdsey Manor near Felixstowe in Suffolk.) At some stage after this I think he joined the Royal Corps of Signals and the operation within Auxiliary Units, setting up OUT Stations in Southern Command." (Letter to Arthur Gabbitas dated 20 January 1998; BROM Archive)

In the mid 1990s, an as yet to be confirmed underground structure, which might have been used as an OUT Station, was located in what is currently known as the Ham Street Woods National Nature Reserve, an ancient woodland near Ashford. The findings at the site were, however, inconclusive when volunteers of the Defence of Britain (DoB) project visited in 1997. (The purpose of this project was to record the 20th century militarised landscape of the UK and to inform the responsible heritage agencies at both local and national level, with a view to the future preservation of surviving structures. The DoB databases were created from field and documentary work carried out by volunteers between April 1995 and December 2001.)

Nevertheless, a detailed description was produced. The entrance shaft is said to consist of sewer pipes covered by a concealed hatch, which opened up to reveal steps leading down into a dugout ventilated by three glazed ceramic pipes. Duckboards covered the floor of a small room which still contained a table and a bench. The table rested on a concrete slab presumably used to cover the entrance. Several names and the date '1941' were found engraved in the wall but none of these names correspond with any of the known names of AU Signals and AU ATS officers – not really surprising considering the fact that OUT Station operators were civilians. A second, smaller and cruder vertical circular shaft was discovered some time later a short distance away. It was full of engineering bricks and overgrown with tree roots as well as flooded and therefore inaccessible. The site was subsequently also excavated and recorded by the Kent Underground Research Group. (Dr Will Ward, Arthur Gabbitas, Kentish Express)

No information is to date known about the OUT Station at Cranbrook or the stations near Rye and Lydd. Arthur Gabbitas also mentions a station at Guston and another near Ramsden Farm, to the south-west of Ashford.

Lincolnshire

The Lincolnshire IN Station, the call-sign of which is not known, was located in the grounds of Canwick Hall where the 1st Division HQ was also based. Arthur Foljambe, the 2nd Earl of Liverpool, owned the Hall. Both the 1st and the Lincolnshire Division were stationed at Canwick Hall (the latter was disbanded in autumn 1941). The men of the AU Signals crew were billeted at Canwick House (then a vicarage and presently a retirement home), with the grounds having been utilised for sheltered accommodation.

Arthur Gabbitas, however, recalls that when he was based in Lincolnshire from summer 1943 until closedown, he was billeted with the family of a lay preacher of the local Wesleyan chapel, near the Lincoln town centre. In the near vicinity, Canwick also had a Royal Signals office, which had been built in a disused quarry near the centre of the village. The building has long since been converted into a private residence (Lindum House).

The main Signals camp, originally used by the staff, later became a POW camp (known as Canwick Camp), utilising a number of already existing Nissen huts. The prison camp's number was 1012. The high registration number and also the fact that it is recorded as a German Working Camp suggest that it was opened fairly late in the war.

Stanley Judson, who for some time was based in Lincolnshire, recalls that there was what he refers to as a surface station (presumably a "Met" hut) in the grounds (the garden) of "a rather large house". One day the owner, a Lady

Liverpool, caught him in her garden when he was testing the site, and understandably, she wanted to know what he was doing.

The dugout was in the wood across the road. Stanley Judson has described it as having had a horizontal door supported on poles and counterweighted (the trapdoor), and a small room containing a set of shelves (the lobby). A secret catch opened the concealed door into the wireless room. An escape tunnel led out the opposite end. ATS officers operated the station, which was linked with the Hickleton Hall IN Station in the West Riding district of Yorkshire, but Beatrice Temple's last visit in October 1942 suggests that AU Signals then took over. Major Jones' map shows that in 1944 five OUT Stations served the IN Station.

> The wireless set at the OUT Station near <u>Donington-on-Bain</u>, to the south-west of Louth, was kept in a box buried in the ground within a wood. One day the local coal merchant and his assistant were overheard making a transmission. Consequently, an Army unit stationed nearby surrounded the wood and both operators were arrested.

> "The station at Donington-on-Bain was in a wood and the operators - one was the manager of a knackery and the other one was the village coal merchant by the name of Grey - were operating there in the wood one evening when a RAF (Royal Air Force) officer and a WAAF (Women's Auxiliary Air Force) doing a bit of courting heard this odd phonetic transmission. The officer, or one of them, crept down to the local Army unit which was stationed nearby, and they came up and surrounded the wood.

> The operators then noticed that they had been discovered but they managed to conceal the set before they were arrested under gunpoint. They did as they were told and phoned the Chief Constable. They were kept over night under arrest and released the next morning. After that it was decided to no longer use that site." (John Warwicker interview with Stanley Judson, IWM ref: 29468)

> The <u>Woodhall Spa</u> OUT Station is also well-remembered by Stanley Judson:

> "The operator was the local doctor, whose house was surrounded by an extensive garden looked after by a gardener. There was an empty garage and adjacent to it a tool shed which was used as a dog kennel. The wireless set was hidden under the floor of this shed and the dog had his bed on top of the hatch. Every time we had to change the batteries and test the set to make sure it was operational, the dog, a Red Setter, would escape through the door and we had to get it back inside without the gardener or anybody else noticing. The aerial was on a tree growing at the back of the empty garage but later on the Army decided to put an Ack-Ack unit and all their guns in this garage. When one day their cook chopped some branches off the tree, severing the aerial feeder cable, we decided to remove the aerial and put it up another tree but on trying to retrieve it, we noticed that the guttering on the garage, which was very old, had began to leak. If there were a rainstorm, the

water would pour down onto the shed and right into the wireless set contained in a box. The set was eventually moved into the house." (John Warwicker interview, IWM ref: 29468)

Another OUT Station was located at the mausoleum on the south side of <u>Brocklesby Park</u>, close to the Brigg Road and High Street and only a short distance to the north of the village of Great Limber.

Charles Anderson Pelham, the First Baron Yarborough, built the mausoleum in the late 18th century as a memorial to his wife Sophia. The Architect was James Wyatt who based his design on the Temples of Vesta in Rome and Tivoli. The building is situated in Mausoleum Woods, which are open to the public during the summer months. No trace of its covert use during the war has survived. Several operational patrols were also active in the vicinity but there is no written record of any of the local auxiliers having been aware of the existence of a secret wireless station in their area.

Aux researcher Dennis Walker, who has published a study of the operational patrols' OBs and the SD wireless stations in Teesside and maintained close contacts with Arthur Gabbitas, mentions wireless stations near Barton-on-Humber, Immingham, Mablethorpe, Skegness and Wainfleet (Source: Aux Units News website). SUBOUT Stations are believed to have been in or near Horncastle and Louth. In addition to the above mentioned, Arthur Gabbitas has also recorded a station to the north-east of <u>Willerby</u> and another which would seem to have been located at or near an Army HQ in <u>Bishop Wilten</u>.

Arthur Gabbitas, who remembered the area well, has confirmed the existence of a station at <u>Barton-on-Humber</u>. As this station is not shown on Major Jones' map it would seem to have been a SUBOUT Station.

> "There were several airfields under Bomber Command in the Lincoln area and most evenings the sky was full of Lancasters circling into formation at Barton-on-Humber. The wide verges of the narrow country lanes leading to our station were stacked with massive assortments of bombs. Obviously this was considered to be the simplest method of maintaining the supply of such a great aerial offensive. Needless to say, we drove very cautiously and with a firm grip on the steering wheel!"

> "Returning from Barton, we would call at Brigg for dinner at the British Restaurant, one of the diners set up by the government where people could have a meal off-ration." (Arthur Gabbitas's memoirs, BROM Archive)

GPO telephone junction box (above) and aerial feeder cables (below) at Norwich

Heap of rubble at the bottom of the entrance shaft at the Norwich IN station, created when the top rows of breezeblocks were knocked off for better concealment when the entrance was capped at closedown. The disc-shaped object seen at bottom left is one of the lead counterweights.

View into the entrance shaft at Halstead IN Station.

Wooden generator block and remains of an extraction fan at Halstead IN Station.

Sealed openings in ventilation ducts. Oil-soaked Union cloth (anti gas) was used at Alnwick IN Station – above *(Photo: Colin Anderson)* whereas at Halstead the opening was closed with a curved piece of sheet metal, held in place by circlips.

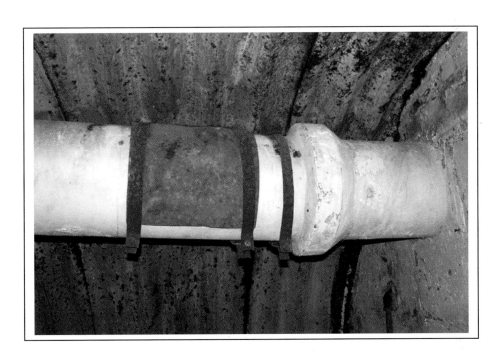

Concrete outlet pipes at Halstead (above) and at Norwich IN Stations (below). In addition to the usual square opening the outlet pipe at Halstead has the addition of a glazed ceramic drainage pipe near one end. At Norwich, the opening was sealed with Union cloth (anti-gas) which has fallen off. The darker colouring of the pipe is staining created by the oil-soaked cloth.

Norfolk

As the <u>Norwich</u> IN Station was discovered and surveyed by the authors, a detailed description can be provided - starting at the exit, which was the point of entry. The station used the call-sign "Bowling" (a village in Dunbartonshire). It is situated on high ground, possibly the highest ground in the area. The Forward HQ of the Norfolk Division (later 76th Division) was based nearby at Sprowston Hall, in the extensive grounds of which the first IN Station (a "Met" hut) presumably stood. The Hall later became the HQ of the 18th Division (of II Corps). When the dugout site was chosen at sometime in 1942, however, there was no need for finding a suitable spot for, or to build a hut, because an ideally suited folly tower already existed. Beatrice Temple visited the new site (the dugout), situated a short distance away from Sprowston Hall, on 10 July 1942, and again on 11 August. Then her visits stop. The reason for this would appear to have been that AU Signals had taken over the running of this IN Station.

A plausible explanation as to why the chosen site was located in the grounds of a civilian-owned property, which was not used by the military, has as yet to surface. It is probably due to its private and secluded location that seven decades later the dugout was found in a very good and undisturbed condition. The exit opening was secured with concrete slabs covered by a thick layer of soil, and the entrance opening was found still solidly capped with the original reinforced concrete. A concrete culvert pipe, the escape tunnel, emerges into a manhole-like shaft with breezeblock walls. The top row of breezeblocks has been knocked off in order to lower the shaft for better concealment when the dugout was sealed in 1944. The hatch consisted of wooden or plywood boards, nailed onto two lengths of timber. The door would have been attached to two metal pipes - passing through wooden battens for support and then through the boards - and fixed in place by a nut at each end. Each of the pipes was contained within a sleeve made from shorter lengths of slightly larger diameter steel pipes that were clamped to a wooden frame with two C-brackets. When activated, a counterweight started to descend downwards until it had reached the bottom of a rectangular hole in the floor. Simultaneously, the two long pipes, held within their sleeves, were pushed upwards, resulting in the trapdoor being gradually raised horizontally above ground level. Above ground, the trapdoor would have been hidden under a layer of earth. (See Appendix A)

There is evidence of the existence of two two-cored 240V cables, running parallel to each other along the whole length of the exit tunnel, suggesting that the dugout was connected to mains power. A length of about 10 metres (33 feet) of this cable was found on site. There is also evidence of altogether three switch units, with the wooden panel situated immediately next to where the exit tunnel enters the dugout. This appears to have been the main point where both external (mains) and internal (batteries) power was connected into the internal wiring. The main isolating switches for turning off all the power would have been on this panel but no trace remains. The wires were fed through conduits with inspection covers at each bend. The conduit running along the ceiling of the wireless room contains two pairs of ceramic ceiling roses from which, it would seem, flexes were leading down to bulb holders with bulbs.

The exit tunnel leads into a buried Nissan-type hut consisting of three rooms separated by breezeblock walls. The rooms were accessed through wooden doors that are still in place, functional and in good condition. Facing the tunnel opening, evidence can be seen that the opening could be closed where it emerges into the generator room. The cover appears to have been made from wooden boards and some of the screws to fix it to the wall are still in place, embedded in the surrounding breezeblocks. This small room would appear to have been used for housing a battery-charging engine (generator) for storing and charging the batteries used for powering the wireless sets as well as the lighting. The whitewashed wall above one of the two small glazed ceramic ventilation ducts in the breezeblock end wall appears to be soot-stained, indicating that the pipe was probably used for externally ventilating the generator's exhaust fumes. A fire bucket - a sand-filled ration container with an improvised wooden handle - stands by the wall beside the twin doors leading into the wireless room.

The generator room is traversed on one side by two large concrete ventilation ducts, one near the bottom (the inlet pipe) and one near the roof (the outlet pipe). Both of these pipes have a small rectangular opening, which provided ventilation in the generator room. The inlet pipe opening would have been blocked – in this case by a homemade collapsible screen constructed from sections of Union cloth nailed to wooden battens – when the generator was running to prevent fumes entering the ventilation system of the wireless room.

The wireless room is separated from the generator room by sturdy wooden twin doors with a raised threshold in-between. "DANGER – 250 VOLTS – KEEP OUT" can be seen written in capital letters onto the inner door with a red crayon, confirming the presence of a source of mains electricity in the generator room. Both doors have a layer of Union cloth affixed all the way around their outer rims, effectively sealing them. The doors had to be well sealed to protect the operators in the wireless room from the toxic gasses created by the charging of the batteries as well as from the exhaust fumes generated by the charging engine or explosive vapours from petrol cans. Janet Purves-Smith, an ATS officer who worked at the Alnwick IN Station for about 18 months, recalls that when the generator was running these doses (see picture on page 79 were always kept tightly shut.

> "A charging engine produces an awful lot of carbon monoxide fumes and we had these enormous felted doors which closed through to where the Elsan and the charging engine stood. When you put on the charging engine the doors were completely closed and the vents came into full use and got rid of the exhaust fumes." (Stephen Sutton interview 18 Nov 1994, IWM ref: 14817)

Three aerial feeder cables disappear through the wall at about 40 centimetres (16 inches) above floor level near the entrance doorway. The table for the wireless sets would probably have stood near this corner in the vicinity of the aerial feeder cables as it is assumed that the wireless sets were positioned nearby. The following information comes from Arthur Gabbitas:

> "The wireless set used was code-named TRD. It was housed in a metal case measuring about 0.40 x 0.24 x 0.23 cm and powered by a large conventional

6-volt 85 AH accumulator battery the voltage of which was boosted to 240V by a vibrator contained within the set. The frequency used ranged from 48 to 65 mcs, nowadays commonly used by BBC1 TV. The aerial terminals were connected inside via a piece of flat twin feeder and to a 72-ohm flat twin feeder outside the front panel, leading to the dipole antenna hidden in a tree." (Memoirs, BROM Archive)

The interior side of the entrance door was also covered entirely with Union cloth. The other side of this door however, appears to be something different entirely (see below). Coming down the entrance shaft, the uninitiated would have found themselves in a small room that to all intents and purposes was used for storage, with a small water tank standing against the wall on one side. On the wall facing the entrance shaft an intruder would have seen a shelf unit stacked with boxes and tins. This shelf was designed to have the appearance of a bookcase, with a frame extending to both sides of the doorframe (overlapping it) and also to above the door. The wooden brackets supporting these removable shelves are still in place and the door itself has small recesses so that the shelves fitted partially into it, perfectly concealing both the door and the doorframe when the shelves were in place and the door closed. The shelf boards are missing but the bookcase-style frame is in situ – and it is the only complete one known to be still in existence.

The section extending to above the door lintel has two lengths of wood affixed to the panels covering the wall. These battens, one on each side, appear to be fixed in place by two screws, one at each end. Only the top screw, however, holds the piece of wood on the right hand side. The bottom 'screw' is in fact a nail, and a dummy at that. This piece can be moved sideways and in doing so it reveals a small carved out recess and a hole drilled through it. The hole is just large enough to allow for a piece of string to pass through. The other end of this string is still tied to the door catch (on the wireless room side), which could be released by pulling said string, and the wireless room could then be entered by swinging forwards the door - but not without first removing at least some of the shelves. The shelves could then be replaced to conceal the door, and the door closed.

The lobby by the entrance shaft still houses the original 50-gallon water tank, covered with a piece of sheet metal. Beside it there are two fire buckets filled with sand and improvised wooden handles. The walls of the entrance shaft, the breezeblock end wall of the lobby and the corrugated sheeting in this room were not painted. The floor is covered with concrete paving slabs. The drop down entrance-shaft faces the secret doorway into the wireless room. A wooden or steel ladder appears to have been used for access. A large heap of concrete rubble is lying at the shaft's floor. This rubble has come from removing the top layers of breezeblocks. Running down the wall to the left of the entrance shaft there is a cast iron pipe which ends at about 50 centimetres (20 inches) above floor level. It appears to have been the only source of ventilation in the lobby.

Viewed from below it can be seen that the entrance opening is covered with wooden boards. Almost at the top of the shaft there are several small rectangular recesses in the breezeblock wall. They would seem to have held the wooden frame surrounding the opening and probably supported the entrance hatch. After removing the hatch and the top layer of breezeblocks, the wooden frame appears to have been pulled off the walls and smashed. Pieces of it, intermingled with lumps of shattered breezeblocks in all sizes, rest in a quite a formidable heap at the bottom of the shaft. Buried amongst it were a couple of pulleys, and the cast lead counterweights used for operating the hatch. When the station was closed down in 1944, the top of the shaft was capped with reinforced concrete. Once set, this concrete cap was covered by a thick layer of soil. It is still as solid as it was on the day it was capped seven decades ago.

The Norwich IN Station was served by five OUT Stations and linked with the IN/Relay Station at Ousden. Beatrice Temple's last visit to the station was on 10 July 1942, when she saw the 'new site'. As the location is marked on the 1944 map, evidence that the station was operational until then, it would seem that AU Signals took over from the ATS in the summer of 1942.

Jill Monk, nee Holman, in 2012 *(Photo: Katie Hart)*. The Holmans' former family home, "The Beeches" (photographed in 2012) was later converted into two separate dwellings and access to the coal cellar housing the wireless set has long since been blocked.

The probably best-documented OUT Station in Norfolk was located in a house called "The Beeches", on the outskirts of the picturesque market town of Aylsham, near Blickling Hall in the Broadland district. "The Beeches" was the home of Dr Alec George Holman and his wife Kathleen, who was one of the town's ambulance drivers during the war.

Dr Holman is still well known in the historic market town of Aylsham, where he is fondly remembered as a no-nonsense doctor who had little patience for malingerers but was fully committed to his calling - so much so that on one occasion he interrupted a family holiday, driving several hundred miles back to Aylsham, where one of his patients about to give birth had requested his assistance. The road where the family used to live has since been renamed Holman Road in his honour.

The doctor's daughter, Jill, was 16 years old when she was enrolled:

> "Colonel *(sic)* Collings, the local commanding officer *(sic)*, asked my father if he thought I'd fold up at the sight of a German. My father told him I didn't fold up at anything - horses, bulls, and schoolmistresses - so the Colonel recruited me. He thought a brat on a horse was unlikely to be suspected of anything. So I was to ride out and spot any choice targets, in terms of troops or supply dumps."

Major John Collings was a professional soldier and an accomplished equestrian, horse trainer and breeder, and a valued member of the Army Polo Team. What Jill did not appear to have known is that Major Collings was employed by Special Operations Executive and had already spent some time abroad. When Jill Holman met Major Collings he was, unbeknown to her, serving as the Special Duties Branch IO for Norfolk. He was replaced in spring 1944, when Captain Douglas Ingrams from Taunton, Somerset, took over. The Major was a frequent guest at the Holman family home, often enjoying a hack on one of Jill's horses. After initially being kept hidden in their garden shed, the wireless set was later installed in the coal cellar, which during the war had been converted to an air raid shelter. It was situated below what at the time was used as a billiard room, and accessed through a hatch in the floor, concealed beneath a rug. The wireless was placed in the former coal chute (which had been sealed on the outside) and hidden behind an asbestos board with an electric fire fixed to it. By operating a concealed catch, the board plus the adhering stove could be lifted off. Messages could be dropped from the yard above down a pipe leading into the chute. The aerial was disguised as a lightning conductor on the roof.

Just as at Aylsham, where the wireless operator was a doctor, the SUBOUT Station at Aldborough too was operated by a medical practitioner - Dr James Angwin Eddy. The two doctors had in fact known each other for quite some time and until 1933 owned a joint medical practice. Aldborough is a small village in the Broadland District, located about seven kilometres (~ four miles) to the north of Aylsham, as the crow flies. Dr Eddy worked as a general practitioner in the village from 1923 until 1973. In 1959 he was elected president of the Norwich Medico-Chirurgical Society and for many years, even after his retirement, he served on the Norfolk Local Medical Committee. In his obituary (October 1995) it is mentioned that Dr Eddy had many interests, particularly music. What the obituary did not mention is that in the 1940s, Dr Eddy had a wireless set hidden in his surgery which would seem to have served as a relay between the Norwich IN Station and the Weybourne OUT Station further to the north-west, operated by a schoolmaster. Interestingly, Dr Eddy features in auxilier John Everett's (corporal of Alby Patrol, Norfolk Group 3) memoirs:

> "Although meant to be secret, the location of our OB was certainly known to one or two other people, including Dr Eddy, a local doctor whose job it was to carry written messages to the patrol by placing them into a buried tin canat the foot of a telegraph pole near Hagon Beck bridge, about 50 metres distant from our OB." (Private papers, 2012)

Dr Eddy's former home and surgery in the village of Aldborough in 2012

AU operational patrols and AU Signals worked independently and did not usually know of each other's existence even when operating in the same area. This is one of the rare occasions where it can be confirmed that they did in fact interact with each other. Although John Everett knew Dr Eddy as a local doctor, and would in all likelihood have even been registered with him as his local GP, and although he was aware of the doctor carrying messages from and to the dead letter box near the Alby patrol's OB, he never knew that the doctor's main involvement was in running a secret wireless station for the Special Duties Branch. That at least some of the Operational IOs (IOs in charge of AU operational patrols) were aware of the existence of SD activities is evidenced by the recollections of Captain Peter Forbes, the AU ops IO for the Borders area, who was posted to Coleshill, promoted to major and then put in charge of all the SD IOs in June 1943. Similar transfers have been documented from other areas:

> "It was decided to re-allocate the Glamorgan Operational Area, presently run by Major KW Johnson, between Captain G Woodward and Captain HLF Buckland. Major Johnson will cease to be an Operational IO but will continue as IO SD in Glamorgan. Additionally, he will take over from Captain Bucknall the duties of IO SD Herefordshire and Worcestershire. These changes will take effect as from midday on 12 November 1943." (Colonel Norman Bruce Ramsey, Commander Auxiliary Units, 26 October 1943)

Major Oxenden records a meeting in May 1941 between an AU Operational Group commander and a key man (see page 9) from the Special Duties Branch:

> "The latter saw no near prospect of getting an OB and was invited by the other to share his. The commander was approached through the IO, with the

result that a special conference on the link-up question was held in July. It was decided that this should only take place on a fairly high level – group commander to key man – and in special circumstances; in no case would OBs be shared. Following this, a few exercises were run jointly by the IOs of the two sides during the ensuing year, but they seemed to lead nowhere, and with our changing operational policy, the link-up was allowed to die a natural death." (*Auxiliary Units History and Achievement, page 11*)

Because of her father's acquaintance with Dr Eddy, Jill Monk too had met the doctor, but like John Everett, whom she also knew, she had - until 2012, when the authors told her - never known of the clandestine wartime activities of either. Jill was also unaware that yet another gentleman with whom she is acquainted had acted as Dr Eddy's runner - the same task that Jill had been carrying out for her father at their Aylsham OUT Station. George Hammond still lives only a short distance from the former doctor's surgery. He recalls that he used to frequently accompany Dr Eddy when he was out in his car visiting patients, and his eyes light up on describing Dr Eddy's car, a foreign car which was like no other in the area: on opening the door an inside light would come on. But more often than not he used his pushbike for transport, always carrying with him a tennis racket so that in case he was stopped and questioned, he could explain why he was carrying tennis balls.

The tennis balls had a small slit cut into them so that a message could be inserted and concealed within, and his job was to take these messages to pre-arranged drop-off points, of which, so he says, he had used two. At least one other location he was unaware of was a tin can, buried at the foot of a telegraph pole near Hagon Beck, near the Alby patrol's OB. Patrol member John Everett, who had always wondered about what he might be doing there, recalls seeing Dr Eddy repeatedly at this location, as recounted on page 131.

Mr Hammond, who is now 86 years old, kindly took us to within a few yards of each of 'his' message drops, the locations of which he found without the slightest hesitation. Both dead letter drops, of which no trace remains, were small square holes in the ground with a wooden or fibrous (non-metal) cover concealed under grass or leafmould, perfectly blending in with the surrounding ground. The tennis ball containing a message was dropped into the opening of a glazed ceramic pipe contained in this hole, like an ordinary drainpipe would be. Both locations are on a downward slope, and Mr Hammond recalls that he could hear the ball bouncing on its way downhill. As it has been established beyond any doubt that there was neither an OB nor an OUT Station dugout the pipe could have connected with, the conclusion must be that the ball ran into another 'drain gulley' a little further down the slope, as indeed there was (and still is) a farm track about 10 metres away at one of the sites. From there an informed passerby could easily have picked up a message without attracting undue attention. Mr Hammond recalls having delivered only about four or five messages to each one of the two drops. He was never asked to collect a message, indicating that other runners unbeknown to him must also have been involved.

It is of interest to note that one of the message drops was ten kilometres (seven miles) distant from Dr Eddy's surgery, in an area in which several operational patrols are known to have operated, whereas the other site was located about nine kilometres (six miles) distant from the surgery but only about three kilometres (two miles) away from the Southrepps OUT Station, with no AU patrols in the vicinity.

The visit made by Dr Eddy to the then Norfolk AU HQ at Beech House on the outskirts of Wroxham, witnessed by Mr Hammond who accompanied the doctor on one occasion (of course without knowing what Dr Eddy did there or whom he met) is another example of the cooperation between AU ops and SD. (GW Hammond, interview on 4 October 2013)

Edgar Coe, the headmaster of Kelling School, operated the OUT Station at Weybourne, presumably from his house, which adjoined Kelling School. The picturesque North Norfolk village had been considered a possible invasion site because of the deep water offshore, and landmines and extensive scaffolding barriers blocked its beaches. Nearby was a highly secret anti-aircraft artillery range (Weybourne Camp), which, together with a complementary camp in the neighbouring village of Stiffkey represented the main live firing training ranges for Ack-Ack Command. Weybourne would seem to have been an important location for the siting of a wireless station but apparently a direct wireless path to link it with the Norwich IN Station could not be established. The problem seems have been overcome by setting up Dr Eddy's SUBOUT Station in Aldborough, which relayed messages from the schoolhouse at Kelling and the Norwich IN Station.

That the area was attractive for spies of all sorts is supported by a rumour according to which the residents of Weybourne Mill were spying for the Germans. One night when on patrol local policemen noticed a light flashing from the top of the windmill's 13 metres (42 feet) high tower out towards the sea and suspicions arose in the village about Mr Dodds and his strange wife who lived at the mill. Mrs Dodds, who is said to have had a strong foreign accent, descscribed by some as having been German or perhaps Austrian, apparently took a lot of interest in the military camp. She used to ride around the village on a bicycle, as many did at that time, and always had a very large bag in the basket in front of the bicycle. One day Mrs Dodds left her bicycle unattended and it fell over. When a local picked it up, he looked inside the bag that had fallen out of the basket and in it found a wireless transmitter. The police were duly informed, and the authorities arrived and took the couple away. Mr Dodds, who is indeed listed as the miller at Weybourne in 1942, returned a few weeks later but Mrs Dodds was not seen again. (Jim Baker, 2005)

Another OUT Station was located near the village of Rougham (north of Swaffham in West Norfolk). In this context it is of interest that Captain Jocelyn Leslie Hardy DSO, MC, the CO of AU Norfolk Group 8, also lived in the vicinity. He farmed at Washpit Farm, about two kilometers (1.5 miles) south-west of Rougham. Robert "Ray" Mallett, one of the members of the Narford Patrol, recalls (unfortunately without disclosing the exact location) that there was a "communications centre unit", with wiring (aerial feeder cable) hidden under the bark of a tree, and that the wireless set was concealed inside an oil drum.

(*Standing up to Hitler*, page 246). The description would seem to indicate that the station was in a wood. Primrose Wood, Roger Plantation and Ash Plantation are all situated within the area encompassing the highest elevation, 85 metres (280 feet) above sea level, to the north of Rougham Hall.

Southrepps, one of the larger villages along the coast, is situated between the towns of North Walsham and Cromer in the North Norfolk District. The village is located three kilometres (1.8 miles) inland and consists of Upper and Lower Southrepps. The wireless set of the Southrepps OUT Station is reported to have been hidden in the belfry of the parish church of St James, but it is more likely to have been the aerial that was concealed there (Jill Monk, pers comm). The set was operated by the vicar, Dr Reverend Humphrey Gordon Barclay, CVO (Commander, Royal Victorian Order), MC (1882 – 1955), who lived in the nearby vicarage.

The Reverend Barclay was born in 1882 in Bletchingley, Surrey, and read Theology at Trinity Hall, Cambridge Theological College. In December 1914 he went to war where - attached to 1st Cavalry Division serving in France - he was a temporary chaplain to the Forces from 1914 to 1919. Earning several campaign medals, including a Military Cross in 1917 "for care and comfort of the wounded under fire" when in action with a front line unit, he did not apply for his medals until 1928. Reverend Barclay died in 1955 in North Walsham and is buried near the Barclay family home, Hanworth Hall, where a memorial in the south aisle of Hanworth St Bartholomew's church commemorates him.

Northumberland

The IN Station, situated in a wood near the village of Heiferlaw, had the call-sign "Otley" (a market town in West Yorkshire). Built within the remains of ancient earth works, the dugout is located to the north of Alnwick, not far from the old A1 road and close to the medieval tower at Heiferlaw. Mature trees still surround the site. The station served the Alnwick Sub-District HQ.

The dugout, built to the same design as all other known IN stations, is in good condition although a considerable amount of leaf mould now covers the floors of the three chambers.

On the occasion of a survey conducted in 2010 by Ian Hall and Colin Anderson, a number of original features were found to be still in situ, and some of the wooden fittings could be identified despite being in a much-deteriorated condition. Interestingly, most of the woodwork appears to have been painted blue. There also remain three doors and what would appear to have been one of the hatches, as well as one of the wooden plugs used to block the ventilation ducts. The doors were covered with Union cloth; the doorways all had spaces where wooden lintels would have been but these were found either missing or in a very deteriorated condition. The shelves and the secret door leading into the wireless room are missing. Several metal ventilation pipes were apparently used for ventilating the lobby. The floors were covered with paving slabs. The entrance shaft and the dividing walls were constructed from breezeblocks, most of which had been plastered over and painted off-white. Two large concrete pipes traversing the generator room ventilated the wireless room. Both end walls show evidence of shelving. The 14 metres (46 feet) long emergency escape tunnel, constructed from concrete drainage pipes, leads out of the generator room, terminating in a vertical shaft. A scarred tree, with some of the aerial feeder cable still in place, was discovered in the near vicinity. (Ian Hall & Colin Anderson, 2010; Stephen Lewins, BR Archive)

ATS subaltern Dorothy Monck-Mason (nee Rainey), who worked at the Heiferlaw IN Station, remembers:

> "One of my postings was to Alnwick - to Doxford Hall near Alnwick. That was the home of Lord Runciman, who had decided to leave Doxford Hall and go to his home on the Isle of Eigg - his other home. So this is where we were billeted, in part. I think it was more or less the servants' quarters, as you would expect. We had a batwoman to look after us, so there were three of us there. Our IO was a man called Victor Goss, Captain Victor Goss, who was a pain in the neck, oh, I shouldn't say that should I? (Captain John Victor Goss was the IO for Northumberland.) The butler had gone with Lord Runciman to the Isle of Eigg but the gamekeeper remained at Doxford Hall, and he used to bring us in the most wonderful goodies from the garden. We had a hut and a dugout." (Interview by John Warwicker, 1997)

Another ATS officer familiar with this IN station was Janet Purves-Smith:

> "I was posted to Alnwick, in private "lodgings" for a while. Then we were sent off to Doxford Hall, which was the house of Lord Runciman. Our Station in Alnwick was, I think, extremely good. We were right up on a hill about five miles outside of Alnwick on the site of some old Roman castle. A part of the old Roman wall was the entrance to our dugout. What happened was, that one pressed something in the wall and it just sort of "came out" and down we went, 30 feet or so, to what we hoped looked just like an underground petrol store. It was a small area which was lined with these shelves all stacked with this petrol. Then you pressed something and one of these things just swung-out and then you had two chambers behind. Our ordinary station above ground was a Nissen-type hut and we would have to take our radios down below with us when we went into the dugout, which was about one hundred yards away. Lampe hasn't got it right you know! What he said was "Oh, they had a 'charging-engine'" Well, a 'charging-engine' has an awful lot of carbon-monoxide fumes coming from it. So, it's not just "Oh they had a charging-engine," - I mean, we had one of these chambers which was big enough for two beds, a table and cupboard... and then you had these enormous felted-doors which closed through to where the sort of Elsan was and the charging-engine, all sorts of little tiny vents going on up to the surface you couldn't see. But when you put the charging-engine on, the doors were completely closed and these vents came into their full use and got rid of the exhaust fumes. Beyond the charging engine was this tunnel, escape tunnel. Rather claustrophobic going through it. Quite a big tunnel which went a long way – I can't remember how far but as this was on top of a hill here is your Roman camp and our escape tunnel got out right down the hill, well, I think it was jolly efficient. When we went on an exercise we had to cart the wireless sets down with us, we had to take them with us because you couldn't leave them.

Lampe has also got it wrong where he says that we had long hours on duty and were "on air" all the time. Well, we weren't. We had ten minutes exactly. Ten minutes from the hour to ten-past and from the half-hour to twenty-to. So the men would always know that's when they could get us. Because, I mean, for secrecy's sake you don't want to be on the air for longer than you have to. So, that was our "watch" and that was when they could contact us."

"I was in Alnwick for – I think about 18 months. Alnwick was my last post. I had already been in Halstead, Knepp Castle and in Bury St Edmunds, and then up to Alnwick for a long time. We got leave, we were ordinary military officers. Just a frightfully interesting job. On an ordinary working day we would get to our station at 9 in the morning, we would be on 09:00 till 09:10, then half past to twenty to for the rest of the day. Till 18:00. Up in Alnwick quite a lot of the time we bicycled to work. Our cover story was we were Signals. Then we would go down the dugout two or three days a week where we would continue our watches. This was seven days a week." (Interview by Stephen Sutton on 18 November 1994).

In 1944, four OUT Stations served the Alnwick IN Station, with the most northerly having been located at Whiterig Farm to the south of Ayton. The IN Station was linked with the IN Station at Hume Castle in Berwickshire; with the Scotch Corner IN Station in North Yorkshire and with an as yet unidentified IN Station located to the north-west of Hexham, about 29 kilometres (18 miles) west of Newcastle-upon-Tyne. Beatrice Temple occasionally met Victor Gough and Cyril Grover for lunch in Newcastle when she was in the area.

The fact that Captain Victor Albert Gough's name was on Beatrice Temple's list of contacts would seem to be yet another indication that at least some of the Operational IOs knew about SD locations and activities in their areas (see also page 132). In the spring of 1943 she met Captain Gough, who had taken over from Captain Anthony Quayle (the actor) as the Operational IO in March 1942, and Captain Cyril E Grover (the SD Area IO) several times. In the autumn of 1943 Gough left AU and several months later joined the Jedburgh Force of SOE, forming part of team "Jacob". His cover name was "Arran". In the autumn of 1944, Captain Gough was captured while on a covert operation in France, and executed by the Gestapo.

During late 1943 and early 1944, Beatrice Temple regularly met Captain John Rupert Hunt Thouron, an officer in the Black Watch, who is believed to have been Captain Gough's successor, although according to his obituary published in the *University of Alabama Almanac* on 20 February 2007 (Vol 53, No 23), he was seconded to the General Staff, Scottish Command, to undertake responsibility for instructing the Glasgow Home Guard battalions in the tactics of street and house-to-house fighting, and later to the SOE, where he was based at Station X - a wireless interception station co-located with the Code & Cipher School at Bletchley Park.

No details are known about the IN Station located west of Newcastle. It is reported to have been situated in Beukley Covert, a small wood to the west of the Stagshaw transmitter station (Radio BBC, Northeast and Cumbria) by Beukley Farm. As this location is not mentioned in Beatrice Temple's diary it would seem that an AU Signals crew operated it. This station presumably served the Tyne Valley Sub Area HQ (9th Corps) based at Hexham, about eight kilometres (five miles) to the south-west. Four OUT Stations, only one of which has so far been identified, served the IN Station.

This OUT Station was situated in the ancient battlemented peel tower at Longhorsley, since converted into a private residence. The small room where the wireless set was kept was accessed through a garage that had a secret doorway; the aerial was on a nearby tree. The operators were Mr Charles Webb, a solicitor, and as a member of the Royal Observer Corps in charge of the Longhorsley post. The Reverend Father Wright, who at the time also was an Air Raid Warden, assisted him. (WA Ricalton, Longhorsley Local History Society website)

Somerset

The two Somerset IN Stations at Cheddon Fitzpaine and Buckland St Mary - on the "Golding" (a hamlet in Shropshire) and "Chirnside" (a village in the Scottish Borders) networks respectively - were served by a vast network of OUT and SUBOUT Stations, five located in East Devon and two in Dorset. The IO for the area was Captain Coxwell-Rogers MC, who was based at 13 Mount Street in nearby Taunton. He had served in the Gloucestershire Regiment and was given the honorary rank of captain when he relinquished his commission in January 1944 due to ill health. Captain Douglas Ingrams, a farmer in Membury who operated the remote OUT Station on Bewley Down, replaced him. Beatrice Temple met Captain Ingrams on 30 January 1944 at the Cheddon Fitzpaine "Met" hut and has described him as "very ineffectual".

The "Golding" IN Station was situated at Volis Hill in the parish of Kingston St Mary, to the north of Taunton and the ATS wireless operators were billeted to the nearby Volis Farm. Nothing is known about the construction or layout of this dugout except that it was necessary to blast the bedrock on the site to bury the dugout. It is inaccessible and might still be intact. The station used the call-sign "Golding 0". (David Hunt/Somerset County Council 2012)

The following details were taken from a record sheet the original of which is held by the DoB. The DoB's site surveyor and recorder was Mr RW Mead, who, having been born at Volis Farm, which he later farmed until 1986, had an intimate knowledge of the area and of the sites described by him in November 1995. Furthermore, Mr Mead was the Cheddon Fitzpaine Home Guard sergeant at the time of stand-down. According to his record, the everyday work hut stood 15 metres (50 feet) west of Volis Hill Road. The remaining concrete platform measures 10 x 4 metres (33 x 13 feet) and is about 30 cm (1 foot) high on the south side of a high stone bank. The hut is described as having been constructed from wood.

The dugout is located in West Combe near Hestercombe, approximately 520 metres to the south of Volis Farm. It is situated inside a wood, approximately 30 metres south of a stone wall and about two metres away from a boundary bank. The chamber is described as being filled with earth and leaves reaching up to about 30 cm (1 foot) below roof level. The entrance opening is about 60 centimetres (2 feet) square and covered by a slab. A glazed ceramic ventilation pipe emerges into the vertical shaft. Fallen trees were at the time (in 1995) considered to pose the main threat to the structure. The station served 8th (VIII) Corps at Pyrland Hall (the Rear HQ was based at Hestercombe House). HQ South Western District took over from 8th Corps in early 1943 and Hestercombe House became the HQ of XIX (19) District US Supply Services.

Of particular interest is Mr Mead's recollection that the two sites were linked by an underground cable running alongside the north side of a nearby stone wall. A former switchboard operator at Hestercombe House recalled that during the war the two sites were linked by phone to Pyrland Hall and Norton Manor Camp, which in 1943 became the HQ of V US Corps. Until well into the 1990s part of an aerial feeder cable was said to have still been in place, running up the trunk of a tree growing near the dugout.

Major Jones' map shows that the station was served by four OUT Stations:

The West Hill OUT Station had the call-sign "Golding 1". The station was operated by Dr Francis Sidebotham - occasionally helped by his daughters Gerty and Ann - from his property at Bendarroch House where the dugout was concealed underneath a chicken hut. Ann Traill (nee Sidebotham) recalls that the wireless set was kept in a small underground room, about 1.80 metres (6 feet) square, accessed by a ladder. Dr James Sidebotham, the son of Dr Frances Sidebotham, remembers having watched what he presumed to be regular soldiers fixing an aerial to the tallest tree in the vicinity – a Wellingtonia that is still in place. (Nina Hannaford, BR Archive)

The OUT Station at Pinhoe had the call-sign "Golding 2"; the wireless set was kept in a dugout. (Alf Ellis, diary)

The OUT Station at Hemyock was a dugout and used the call-sign "Golding 3". The dugout has been found intact and in good condition. Part of the trap door opening mechanism and two lead counterweights were also recorded. (Dr Will Ward & Nina Hannaford, BR Archive)

The wireless set of the Wiveliscombe OUT Station was hidden in an attic; it used the call-sign "Golding 4". (Alf Ellis, diary)

A SUBOUT Station - "Golding 1A" – is said to have been located at the Hare and Hounds public house in Ottery St Mary, near Putts Corner by the junction of the A375 road. The then landlord of the pub was Henry John Smith. (Nina Hannaford, BR Archive). Arthur Gabbitas, who was based in the area for some time during 1943, however says that the wireless set was kept concealed in the summerhouse on the roof of Lord Coleridge's mansion near the church. (Stephen Sutton interview, IWM ref: 14819/2)

The Bishop's Clyst (Broadclyst) SUBOUT station used the call-sign "Golding 2A".

Another IN Station was located on the site of Castle Neroche, near the village of Buckland St Mary. It was linked with the "Golding" and "Osterley" IN Stations. There was, however, a communication problem at the latter, concerning two OUT Stations on the "Osterley" network ("Osterley 1" and "Osterley 2"), which were unable to communicate directly with the IN Station on their own network and messages had hence to be relayed via the "Chirnside" IN Station (David Hunt, pers comm). AU Signals officers, billeted at Castle Neroche Farm, operated the IN Station. The dugout is believed to be intact albeit currently inaccessible. (David Hunt/Somerset County Council 2012)

In his memoirs, Arthur Gabbitas has provided some insight about his time at this station:

> "The station was set in a hollow, on the site of an old Roman encampment, 900 feet (275 metres) up, at the end of the Blackdown Hills. The farmer was typical Somerset-born, his dialect barely understandable; his wife was from Birmingham. They introduced me to the delights of home-produced ham and cider." (BROM Archive)

The Bewley Down OUT Station is known to have used the call-sign "Chirnside 1". Captain Douglas Ingrams who later succeeded Captain Coxwell-Rogers as the SD IO for Devon and Somerset, and in 1944 served as the SD IO in Norfolk, operated it. Two ATS officers, Priscilla Mary Badgerow and Mary Alexander, both at the time based at the Cheddon Fitzpaine IN Station, would seem to have made frequent visits to the Ingrams family and are said to also have helped with the hay harvest. Captain Ingrams' son David, who in early 1941 had witnessed the construction of the dugout, recalls having met said officers in 1943 when home from boarding school during holidays.

The wireless set was hidden at the bottom of a pair of cottage gardens (since merged into one) where there used to be two back-to-back earth-closet privies. In one of these the whole seat (including surround and bucket) was fixed to a steel frame which could be raised vertically from below. As unusual as this might at first seem, it is known from history that secret rooms were frequently hidden beneath privies, one example being the so-called priest holes used by Roman Catholic clergy fleeing from Protestant pursuivants in the 16th century. One of the special features of the dugout, as described to J Warwicker by David Ingrams, would appear to have been a battery-operated lamp. Its outside switch was to be used (by the few in the know) for giving a pre-arranged Morse code signal before entering the dugout.

Built from curved sections of corrugated iron sheeting resting on a low concrete wall, with an end wall of old railway sleepers, the OUT Station dugout was divided into two small rooms, the first containing a hinged bed and a hinged table. A second chamber, access to which was gained by activating a secret catch, which pivoted two of the sleepers in the dividing railway sleeper wall, adjoined this room. The wireless set was kept in the back room. (Derek Warren, *Now You See It – Then You Didn't*). The dugout was found to be in good condition and is currently in the process of being restored.

The Axminster SUBOUT Station had the call-sign "Chirnside 1A" and was hidden in an attic; the OUT Station at Widworthy (in East Devon) was a dugout and had the call-sign "Chirnside 2".

The OUT Station in the village of Puriton had the call-sign "Chirnside 3". The wireless set was kept in a box hidden in a shed. The Puckington OUT Station had the call-sign "Chirnside 4" and, like at Puriton, the wireless set was kept in a box in a shed. The Edgarley OUT Station had the call-sign Chirnside 5"; the wireless set was kept concealed in the farmhouse at Edgarley Manor Farm. No details are known about the Spaxton SUBOUT Station ("Chirnside 3A").

The Brent Knoll SUBOUT Station ("Chirnside 3B") is reported to have been hidden under the stairway of a now derelict farm cottage adjacent to a property known as "The Laurels" in the village of Brent Knoll. Neville Charles Leonhardt, occasionally helped by his sister, operated the wireless set. One of the consultant surgeons at Burnhams War Memorial Hospital, Dr Harold Whewell Hogarth Holmes, is believed to also have been involved. (T Wray & Donald Brown, BROM Archive)

Suffolk

The county of Suffolk had three IN Stations, with the station at Ousden - using the call-sign "Gorey" (a village in Wexford, Ireland) - apparently functioning as a relay. Characteristically, none of the IN/Relay Stations had OUT Stations. Ousden is a small village in West Suffolk, situated about 12 kilometres (7 ½ miles) south-west of Bury St Edmunds and 10 kilometres (six miles) east of Newmarket, near the Suffolk – Cambridgeshire border. It is only about 11 kilometres (7 miles) distant from Bachelor's Hall in the village of Hundon, where the AU Signals HQ was based until 1942. The nearest Army HQ – 2nd (II) Corps HQ - was at Lower Hare Park near Newmarket, about 15 kilometres (10 miles) distant. Sergeant Les Parnell, who was based in the area for some time, confirms that information was indeed passed on to 2nd Corps HQ, and that this was done via a GPO telephone line. (Letter to Dr Will Ward, 28 March 1999)

According to an eyewitness account, the ATS wireless operators' workplace was a wooden hut located in the north-eastern corner of Littly Wood, near the small village cemetery. The hut was situated on high ground at approximately 130 metres (426 feet) above sea level, which is almost as high as anybody can get in Suffolk. Captain Ken Ward has confirmed that at least some of these huts were supplied with a daily weather forecast as a cover story in case somebody asked, and hence these huts are sometimes referred to as "Met" huts. A small shed housing the generator stood near the south-east corner. Brian Drury confirms that the wireless links between the Ousden and Norwich, Halstead and Thornham Magna IN Stations all were line of sight wireless paths (pers comm).

Beatrice Temple, who visited all IN Station sites regularly, and diligently took note of the names of the people she met there and of the issues discussed with them, mentions Ousden for the first time on 23 August 1943, the day on which billets were found at Dalham Hall for the ATS wireless operators. Beatrice Temple's first visit to the IN Station, which was operational until closedown, was made on 19 October 1943.

The following information originates from an interview with Mr Ted Knights, conducted by Dr William Ward (BR Archive) in 1999. Mr Knights lived in the house adjoining the small cemetery situated near the IN Station. The ATS subalterns - billeted at Dalham Hall, three kilometres (two miles) away as the crow flies - stored their bicycles in the disused washhouse in his garden.

> "Commonly two of them would arrive in the morning and stay all day, to be replaced by two others at night. During times of heavy troop movements (Army exercises) altogether five of them would arrive. Occasionally a man called round to deliver water."

Mr Knights recalls that the hut was built from wood and stood on a concrete base (see also the drawing below).

> "Soldiers had arrived in trucks and felled the absolute minimum of trees, leaving the remainder for cover. They then laid a concrete base and brought the materials required for building the hut in a couple of trucks."

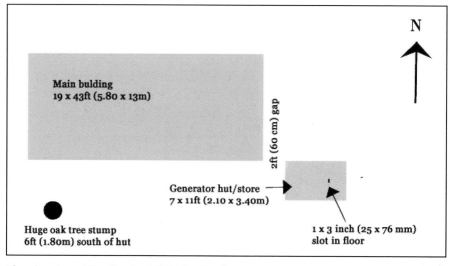

Plan drawing of the Ousden IN/Relay Station

After completion, a few strands of barbed wire on stakes were set up to surround the compound. After the war, Mr Knights went into the hut before the Army dismantled it. He described it as a large room with a few windows, containing a toilet and a stove. He believes that the hut had a pitched roof. The wood was felled in 1955 and replanted in 1966 and Mr Knights was certain that there was no dugout: he used to regularly walk in the wood and was sure that he would have found it.

One of the ATS officers who worked at the Ousden station, Marina Bloxam, thought that there was a dugout. Her description, however, does not conform to any of the known designs of IN Station dugouts. Having been opened that late in the war (in October 1943), when the threat of an invasion was no longer considered to be realistic, it can reasonably be assumed that a dugout would not have been deemed necessary. Regarding the aerial, Les Parnell remembers that it was up a tree, with the feeder cable hidden in a groove cut into the tree's trunk and then covered over, whereas Mr Knights remembered having seen it on the hut's roof. Memories are often clouded, especially when recalled many decades after the event.

Interestingly, a close examination of the original map made by Major Jones, the original of which is held at the National Archives, reveals that a wireless path linking the Halstead IN Station with an as yet unidentified IN/Relay Station on the Inner Network, near the town of Hertford, has been erased. Some sources suggest that the erased link might have been drawn in error. An alternative interpretation would be that the Norfolk and Suffolk networks were not connected with each other prior to the opening the Ousden IN/Relay Station, nor were they linked with the Essex network and the Inner Network. The Halstead IN Station would, however, appear to already have been linked with the Inner Network through a wireless path that had since become redundant. It would seem that the station at Ousden for the first time connected the Norfolk, Suffolk and Essex networks not only with each other but also with the Inner Network.

Before the Ousden station was opened, there were, of course, no wireless paths leading to it; the draftsman would simply have added these to the map once the station was up and running, in the colours representing the respective frequencies used. The obsolete old link between Halstead and Hertford had to be erased so as to bring the map fully up to date, and a handwritten annotation at the bottom confirms that indeed the map had been corrected to 28 June 1944, the date on which Major RMA Jones wrote his "TOP SECRET and PERSONAL" report to Brigadier RE Barker CBE, CSO at GHQ Home Forces (TNA, WO199/1194 – SD/1/1460). Unless older maps predating the final version can be unearthed this theory cannot, of course, be verified, but the fact remains that a wireless path was erased, a path that would seem to have been replaced by another with the opening of the new station at Ousden.

The Ousden IN/Relay Station handled three different frequencies: the Norfolk network operated on 60 mcs, both the Suffolk and Essex networks operated on 65 mcs and the wireless link between Ousden and the next station 'down the line' near Hertford operated on 52 mcs. As TRDs are reported to have been set to a specific frequency which could only be changed in a workshop, one wireless set per frequency and almost certainly each with its own aerial, would have been required, unless the versions referred to as TRF and TRM were tuneable and available. Interestingly, the acronym 'TRF" commonly stands for "Tuned Radio Frequency", but the tuned radio frequency receiver had nothing in common with the TRF set mentioned in the context of TRD. The 28 TRFs and 36 TRMs reported to have been in use in June 1944 would not appear to have been used in OUT Stations. They might have been tuneable and could have been reserved for the use at IN/Relay Stations but this theory has as yet to be confirmed.

Four of the altogether 56 AU ATS officers who were still working in SD at closedown came from the West Suffolk Sub-district. A Part II Order (Officers ATS), Serial No 42 - published on 21 July 1944 by authority of WOUM 112/ATS AG 16 (o) [War Office Unclassified Memorandum, Adjutant General's Branch, 16 (officers)] - records their names as Marina Bloxam, Eleanor Mary Norman-Butler, Joyce Hazel Chesney and Joan Priestley. This would appear to have been the crew based at Ousden. The officers were struck off the strength of Auxiliary Units and posted to No.1 War Office Holding Unit, and also struck off the Lodging List and Food (allowance) with effect from 25 July 1944.

Marina Bloxam remained with the ATS (and later the WRAC) and was promoted to subaltern on 1 January 1947 until, with the rank of a captain in the WRAC, she was dismissed by sentence of a General Court Marshal on 17 April 1953. By then attached to the Amphibious Warfare HQ, she was accused of stealing a railway warrant and obtaining a 1st class ticket from King's Cross to Fort William with a warrant she knew had been forged. (Glasgow Herald, 24 March 1954)

The Thornham Magna IN Station was located within the perimeter of the 15th (Scottish) Division HQ, which it served. The Division HQ was housed at Thornham Hall and Park. The network used the call-sign "Chariot".

According to Yolande Bromley, one of the first ATS wireless operators to work there, the hut was equipped with a toilet and had cooking and rest facilities. It was connected to mains electricity, which would appear to also have been used for charging the batteries. The AU Signals crew assigned to 15th Division were stationed in Eye, about 6½ kilometres (4 miles) distant, and the ATS officers were billeted in the so-called Red House - the home of the Honourable John Henniker (Lord Henniker's youngest brother) and his first wife, Molly. The Red House, currently home to Julia, Lady Henniker, is situated at the southern edge of Thornham Park. The station's two long-term wireless operators were Yolande Bromley (married name Alston) and Margaret Whiting.

Yolande Bromley, who was commissioned as a 2nd subaltern on 20 July 1941, remembers barometric charts and other weather data on the walls of their hut and also that they did not have a dugout:

> "I have never been down one of these dugouts because there wasn't one at Thornham." (Interview by John Warwicker, 1997; BROM Archive)

The ATS officers stayed at Thornham Magna until October 1942, after which time the IN Station hut was moved out of the park and into a nearby private wood situated further to the east. The reason for the relocation appears to have been that the 15th Division was moved to another location and that a prisoner of war camp was to be established within the park, in autumn 1942. The Italian, and later German prisoners lived in huts in the old garden and in the surrounding woods (Lord John Henniker, *Painful Extractions*). The ATS subalterns were consequently moved to a new location (Hardwick Manor near Bury St Edmunds), where Waddy Cole, who had previously worked at the Norwich IN Station, joined them.

In a letter dated 24 March 1942, General Sir Bernard Paget, the C-in-C of GHQ Home Forces, had advised AU HQ of his decision that AU Signals crews should take over from ATS the running of all the Divisional IN Stations, and Thornham Magna was such an IN Station. The probably most convincing evidence that AU Signals continued operations from the new location at Thornham Magna is the record of a fatal accident, which is documented to have occurred there six months after the ATS had left the site.

One of the AU Signals maintenance men, Corporal Laurence Tee, had climbed up an oak tree to check the aerial when the rope broke and he fell, landing on his back. He was taken to Ipswich hospital where he died. Stanley Judson, who clearly remembered it in letters to colleagues and in taped interviews conducted by John Warwicker, confirms the accident. The date of Corporal Tee's death, 16 April 1943, is carved into his gravestone in the churchyard of St Michael's at Boldmere near Birmingham.

In his "Adventures in WW2", Lieutenant Roy Russell has provided a detailed description of the dangerous work involved when checking or repairing aerials:

> "High winds or even branch growth could alter the delineation and lose wireless contact. It would then be necessary for one of our signalmen to go up the tree. He would be hauled up, standing in a noose of rope thrown over a high branch. The other end was attached to a Humber car, and by slow backing, he would be drawn up the tree. Sometimes he had to climb the last few feet, carrying a bag of tools on his back. This was a job we shared in view of the risks involved." (See also Stan Judson's account on page 24.)

It was seven months since the ATS had left before Beatrice Temple made a few more visits to Thornham Magna during the summer of 1943; on at least one occasion she stopped for a cup of tea with Molly Henniker.

Both available maps – one by Major Jones, the other created in about 1995 from recollections by Arthur Gabbitas with the help of some of his former AU Signals colleagues – are agreed on there having been five OUT Stations. Two of these stations are mentioned briefly (in Alf Ellis' 1942 diary) as having been located at Uggeshall (call-sign "Chariot 3") and at Peasenhall (call-sign "Chariot 2").

Another OUT Station is known to have been at Great Glemham. It was a mobile chicken shed and the wireless set was operated by Charles Kindred, unbeknown to his cousins Percy and Herman Kindred, both of whom were members of an AU ops patrol whose operational base was nearby. (*With Britain in Mortal Danger*, page 206)

The Thornham Magna IN Station was linked with the Ousden IN/Relay Station, which also had links with the Halstead IN Station ("Buttercup") in Essex and with the Norwich IN Station ("Bowling") - two of the first three IN Stations that were set up in East Anglia. (Captain Ken Ward)

In September 1941, the counties of Suffolk and Essex (and others) were divided into sub areas, resulting in the establishment of a Sub-Area HQ West Suffolk, based at Bury St Edmunds. In a letter (to John Warwicker, dated 22 Feb 1997; BROM Archive) Yolande Bromley mentions a new IN Station that was opened in the Hardwick area of Bury St Edmunds, where the Ministry of Defence (MoD) had requisitioned a former flax factory site, at the time occupied by the Bury Hand Laundry. Contemporary documents show that the Command Supply Depot of the RASC was stationed there during the war.

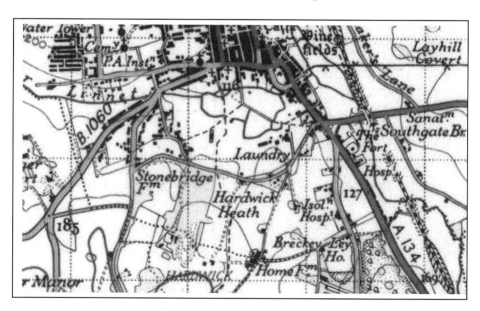

Adjoining the site in the south was a camp, housing first Italian and later German prisoners of war (Hardwick Camp, POW camp No. 260). The officer in charge of the prison guards was stationed at Hardwick Manor, the grounds of which adjoined the camp in the south-west. The Laundry site buildings were recently demolished to make way for a new housing development, and part of the former POW campsite is currently occupied by the West Suffolk Hospital.

Hardwick Manor is the name of a former gardener's cottage on the Hardwick Estate, which after the sale of much of the estate in the 1920s was purchased and enlarged into a mock-Tudor mansion by Mr HW Hewitt (a High Court judge) of Kensington. Hardwick Manor was set in 50 acres of the former park and it can reasonably be assumed that this is where the IN Station, presumably no more than a hut, was located. The Suffolk Sub-Area HQ (11th Corps) to which the station would seem to have reported were based at 12 Risbygate (Gibraltar Barracks), only about two kilometres (1.2 miles) away.

Captain (later Major) Wilf Bradley (referred to by Beatrice Temple as "Mr Bradley" because SD IOs commonly wore civilian clothes) who was in charge of Suffolk, Norfolk, Essex and Lincolnshire and based in Bury St Edmunds in 1942/43, recalls:

> "After interviews in London and Coleshill with Lord Glanusk and others, I was taken on a country walk by Major Jones who told me all about the unit and I was soon sent to my HQ at Bury St Edmunds, where I also met the "Queen Bee" (Beatrice Temple) of the ATS.
>
> In summer 1943 I was sent to the North where I took over from about Newcastle to John O'Groats with my HQ in Edinburgh." (Letter to Arthur Gabbitas, dated 21 November 1995; BROM Archive)

Bury St Edmunds was considered a safe zone for evacuees, which probably explains why there was no dugout. The Bury St Edmunds IN Station - of which Yolande Bromley says that she opened it – would appear to have served as a link from the Thornham Magna IN Station to the newly created Sub-Area HQ at Bury St Edmunds. It had no OUT Stations of its own. When the HQ moved, the site would appear to have been closed down; it is not marked on Major Jones' 1944 map which shows all the stations that were still operational at that time.

Yolande Bromley
(Source: BROM Archive)

Trapdoor counterweights: a length of railway track (above) at the Halstead IN Station and a bundle of sash weights found at the Norwich IN Station.

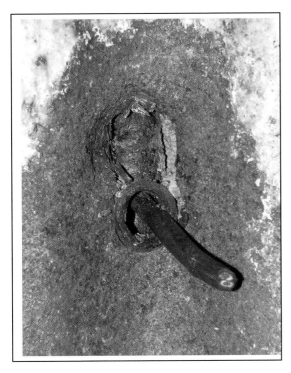

Mains power cables at Halstead (above), and exposed on the perimeter of the Shipley IN Station dugout which can be seen in the background *(Photo: Brian Drury)*

Evidence of the existence of mains power on the remains of a switch panel at the Halstead IN Station (above) and on the inside of a door at Norwich IN Station. The writing on the door says: "DANGER – 250 VOLTS – KEEP OUT"

Wooden plug used to blank off the ventilation when the generator was running in the adjoining room, at the Norwich IN Station.

Sump at the escape tunnel mouth at Hollingbourne IN Station *(Photo: Brian Drury)*

Switch box at Hollingbourne *(Photo: Brian Drury)*, right, and wiring - still in situ in 1975 - at Ardingly (East Grinstead) IN Stations. *(Photo: Harry Townsend)*

Exposed ventilation chamber at Shipley IN Station *(Photo: Brian Drury)*

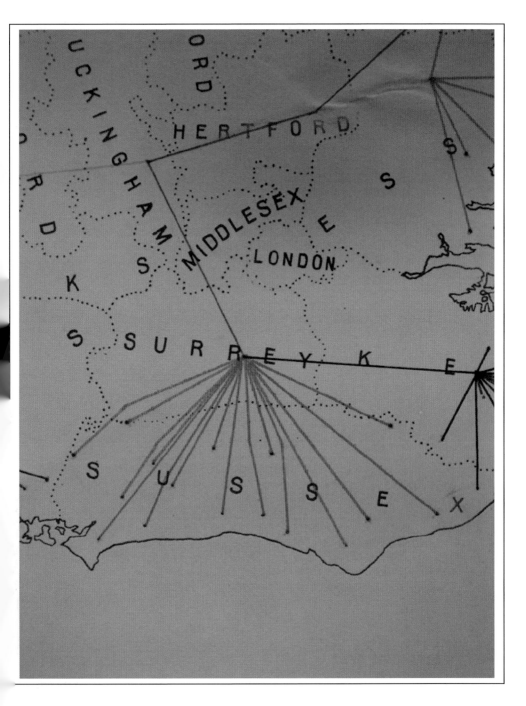

The Surrey and Sussex networks in June 1944 as depicted by Major Jones
(TNA, WO 199/1194). See Arthur Gabbitas's map on page 164 for comparison.

Surrey

Reigate and the North Downs have always played an important part in the defence of Great Britain and during WW2 Reigate Hill was again chosen as the location for a defence post in the event of an invasion. It also became the location of the HQ of South Eastern Command.

Beatrice Temple did visit the <u>Reigate</u> IN Station on many occasions and also recorded the names of the ATS officers stationed there. On 15 June 1943 she noted in her diary that she had visited the new hut and described it as "very grand". The location of the site has to date not been found but one of the ATS operators has shared her experience of working there in an article published in the Hampshire Chronicle (on 21 March 2003), many years later. "I never told a soul at the time and have never spoken publicly about it," said the then 81-year-old Prudence Battersby (nee Gwynne). Mrs Battersby recalled that she was first based at Doncaster, then in Suffolk and finally in Reigate. She said that they worked in eight-hour shifts around the clock and part of their duties was to communicate with other "cells" of the organisation.

> "Conditions were spartan, with just two beds, two chairs and two wireless sets, and the three women in each unit just had each other for company. Perhaps not surprisingly, they often fell out. It was terribly lonely and it really got me down after a bit. I did almost two years. It was boring work and tremendously claustrophobic. A lot of the women committed suicide."

In fact, there is only one documented case of a suicide (in November 1943 at Heathfield Park IN Station). Miss Gwynne was commissioned in August 1942 and remained with the ATS until August 1946, when on relinquishing her commission she was granted the honorary rank of Junior Commander. Captain (later Major) Peter Forbes, who from August 1941 until July 1943 was the IO in charge of East Lothian, Berwickshire, Roxburgh, Selkirkshire and Dumfries & Galloway operational patrols, and later based at Coleshill HQ where he was put in charge of all the SD IOs, remembers visiting an IN Station "on top of Reigate Hill". Major Jones' map shows no less than 16 wireless paths from stations in East and West Sussex as well as the entire Kent network (via the Harrietsham IN Station), all reporting directly to the Reigate IN Station. Another path links with the Wendover IN/Relay Station in Buckinghamshire which was a station on the Inner Network.

Sussex

Sussex had been at the frontline of Britain's defences ever since Prime Minister Neville Chamberlain on 3 September 1939 at 11:15 BST announced that the deadline for the withdrawal of German troops from Poland had expired and that Britain was at war with Germany. The beaches were closed for most people; barbed wire barriers had been erected between the sea and the promenades, and heavy artillery lined the seafronts. The Home Guard were formed and put on alert. Several months later, 24 operational patrols of the Auxiliary Units based a few kilometres inland had formed a defensive belt comprising about 140 local men trained in unarmed combat and sabotage techniques, ready to spring into action in the event of an invasion.

The Sussex wireless network had three IN Stations, two of which would seem to still have been operational in mid-1944. Of the various OUT and SUBOUT Stations fourteen have to date been identified. Due to the changing military situation, resulting in the formation of South Eastern Command in February 1941, the creation of sub area HQs, the arrival in the area of Canadian and American Forces and the increased Army presence during the run up to D-Day, the local SD networks required constant adjustment. As the only official and hence reliable contemporary document available is the map created by Major Jones in June 1944 (see page 153) there is to date no clear understanding of any of the developments which pre-date it.

Two of the three IN Stations were located in West Sussex (at Ardingly, and near the village of Shipley) and a third was at Heathfield Park in East Sussex. Arthur Gabbitas's map (see page 164), which was created in the 1990s with the help from some of his AU Signals colleagues, shows the Shipley IN Station served by seven and Heathfield Park IN Station by eight OUT Stations. The IN Station at Ardingly would appear to have functioned as a relay and was not served by a network of OUT Stations. Going by Major Jones' map however, none of the Sussex IN Stations appear to have been served by OUT Stations. By the summer of 1944 all the wireless stations in Sussex, whether IN or OUT Stations, would seem to have reported to and been linked directly with the Reigate IN Station.

The IN Station near <u>Shipley</u> (Beatrice Temple refers to the location as West Grinstead) is situated near the site of Knepp Castle (a 12th century motte and bailey fortress of which only a short section of wall with a doorway in it remains). The ruined castle is located near Horsham, where the 47th (London) Division was stationed. By spring 1942, the 1st Canadian Division HQ had moved into Knepp Castle. The network used the call-sign "Harston" (a village in Leicestershire or Cambridgeshire). The dugout, now partially collapsed, was constructed following the same standard design known for almost all other IN Station dugouts and a detailed site survey was published in Sussex Aux Units researcher Stewart Angell's book *The Secret Sussex Resistance*. What would seem to have been overlooked are two 240V power cables - evidence that the IN Station, like a number of others, was connected to mains electricity.

Major Jones' map shows the IN Station with a wireless path to Reigate, whereas the map created from memory by Arthur Gabbitas presents a very different picture. Drawn from recollections pre-dating 1944, it shows that at some earlier time the Shipley IN Station was linked with what would appear to have been another IN Station near Sevenoaks, which also had wireless links with the IN Stations at Heathfield Park and at Ardingly (East Ginstead). In Arthur Gabbitas's time, the Shipley IN Station appears to have been served by seven OUT-Stations.

One of the ATS officers who worked at the Shipley IN Station was Janet Wise (nee Purves-Smith):

"We had to go up to somewhere in Essex (possibly Great Yeldham) and there was a Major Hills there, at that time, and we had to go for a "voice-test" (at Bachelor's Hall, Hundon). I think they were just looking us over though, actually, but anyway we squawked into this thing and then they said we were suitable applicants. Then I went to Halstead as an 'other rank' *(interestingly, if true, this was against ATS regulations)* for about six weeks, and then up to the OCTU at Edinburgh. And then one was appointed. I was appointed down to Knepp Castle which was the Divisional Headquarters of one of the Canadian Divisions at the time. From Knepp Castle we had our OUT Stations. What I think was quite clever was, there was no question - we knew their voices. We didn't know where they were; all we knew was that it was "Harston One;" "Harston Two;" and "Harston Three;" which were the "OUT Stations". It would be: "Hello Harston, Harston Two calling". (Interview by Stephen Sutton, 18 November 1994).

Little is known about the OUT Station at <u>Birdham</u> which was in the garden of a private dwelling house called "Elmstead", to the north-east of the village of Birdham near Chichester. The operator's name was Ernest Allman. Mr Williams, a tractor driver from <u>Sidlesham</u>, kept his wireless set in a marshy area at Church Norton near Selsey, about five kilometres (three miles) to the south-east of Birdham, as the crow flies.

No details are known about the OUT Station at <u>Crossbush</u> but the aerial tree has been found to be still in place and the bricked up tunnel that once connected the OUT Station to the hotel across the road from it can apparently still be seen in the hotel cellar. (Brian Drury, pers comm)

Another OUT Station is believed to have been located at an as yet unidentified location on <u>Bury Hill</u>. The operator was Reginald Pitts of North Stoke Farm, who was also a member of the Warningcamp AU operational patrol. The only other known case of an individual having been involved with both at the same time is Mr RG Potts, an auxilier and OUT Station operator from Great Brasted in Essex (see page 111)

Mr Baron, a farmer from <u>Clapham</u>, kept his wireless set tucked away at the back of his bullpen.

Walter Langmead, a farmer from <u>Runcton</u>, concealed his wireless set in the loft of a barn near the main road to Pagham. When he left the area, a retired Admiral called Palmer took over. His wireless set was hidden within a large tank installed by a special unit of Canadian soldiers under the floorboards of a disused chapel.

Frank Campbell, a retired electrical engineer from Manchester who at the time owned the "Warming Pan" restaurant, operated the OUT Station in <u>Arundel</u>. His wireless set was hidden in a dugout underneath a clump of trees on the opposite side of the road. The site was accessed from the restaurant's cellar where, underneath a slate shelf, a small section of the cellar wall was mounted on rails. When a nail was pushed into a certain crack in this wall, a locking catch lifted, allowing the wall to be pushed aside. The operator then had to crawl along a tunnel that ran under the main A27 road. When the road above the tunnel started to subside, the site was abandoned. At the new site the set was kept within a large tank similar to Admiral Palmer's at Runcton. (*The Secret Sussex Resistance*, page 77)

Another IN Station in West Sussex was (and still is) located in the grounds of Wakehurst Place, <u>Ardingly</u>. The dugout was discovered in the 1990s by estate workers and it has since been surveyed and subsequently made inaccessible by the National Trust who currently owns the property. Beatrice Temple refers to the location as East Grinstead. Arthur Gabbitas's map shows a link from Ardingly to the same location at (or near) Sevenoaks that the Shipley IN Station too was linked with for some time, and it shows a second link between Ardingly and Shipley - evidence that Ardingly had perhaps functioned as a relay from Shipley to the HQ it was attached to. 4th (IV) Corps Advanced HQ was based at Worth Priory in Paddockhurst and 4th Corps Rear HQ was stationed at Fenn Place, Turners Hill. In September 1941, however, the area became part of the new Canadian Corps District, and on 17 November 1941 the Canadian Corps took over both HQ buildings. By spring 1942, the Advanced HQ of the 1st Canadian Corps had moved into Wakehurst Place; the Rear HQ remained at Worth Priory.

After having declared war on Germany on 9 September 1939, Canada's commitment was at first limited. Nevertheless, the 1st Canadian Infantry Division was dispatched quickly, arriving in Aldershot in December 1939. The arrival of the 2nd Canadian Infantry Division in the summer of 1940 brought the number of Canadian troops in Britain up to 56,000, and on Christmas Day 1940 the Canadian Corps (commanded by Lieutenant General McNaughton) came into being. With the arrival of three more divisions and two tank brigades during the following eighteen months, a second Corps was formed.

Both Corps were eventually put under the command of the newly created First Canadian Army which fought alongside the British 2nd Army throughout the NW Europe Campaign, forming part of the 21 Army Group commanded by Field Marshal Montgomery. Initially Aldershot was the main centre for all Canadian units arriving in the UK and due to the sudden influx of both British and Canadian troops a large number of hutted camps were built, houses were commandeered and parks were taken over for stores and vehicle depots.

The IN Stations and wireless networks, now in the Canadian Corps District, would seem to have continued operating uninterrupted. The West Grinstead (Shipley) IN Station, however, appears to have been taken over by AU Signals because it is shown on Major Jones' map, ie was operational until close down. On her last recorded visit to West Grinstead, on 9 September 1942, Beatrice Temple met the Canadian Camp Commandant to talk about transport for returning the ATS officers based there.

After the Canadians had left, the area became the Sussex District, with the North-Sussex Sub-Area HQ based at Horsham. On 26 May 1942 Beatrice

Temple wrote in her diary (referring to East Grinstead): "Canadian Corps gone, British to take over". On the same day she also visited Heathfield Park where she encountered "troops everywhere".

The East Sussex IN Station was located in the grounds of <u>Heathfield Park</u>, which, like most other estates and many large houses in the area at the beginning of the war, was requisitioned by the War Office and turned over to the military authorities. The park was converted into a military camp and the house was used as the Divisional HQ by a succession of units both British and Canadian. The 55th (West Lancashire) Infantry Division were among the first regular troops to be stationed there, with their artillery and signals commands billeted nearby in Heathfield House. The Canadians who arrived in the summer of 1941 and were to be the main occupants of the park in the following years replaced them. By spring 1942, the HQ of the 3rd Canadian Division had moved in. In June 1944 Heathfield became the HQ of the Guards Armoured Division, and housed a battalion of the Worcestershire Regiment, as well as some elements of the 55th Division, which by that time had returned for home defence duties.

HEATHFIELD PARK, SUSSEX.

When researching for a book he had planned to write about the history of Heathfield Park, author Roy Pryce happened to meet Winifred "Wynne" Read, one of the ATS subalterns who had been posted to work there on the completion of her training in the early autumn of 1941. Wynne Read had been recruited with the first volunteers in the summer of that year when she was working near Sidcup as a private in the Pay Corps. Once commissioned, she was trained in wireless telegraphy at Challock Lees, north of Ashford.

After a brief spell at the No.1 ATS OCTU at Craigmillar in Edinburgh, and an overnight stay at Bachelor's Hall at Hundon (where she recalls that she had to sleep on bare boards, despite her new officer status), Wynne Read was posted to Heathfield, together with two other young ATS officers: Marjorie Lilian Barden and Marjorie Nora Filer. All three were billeted with families in the vicinity; Wynne Read stayed with the Angoods family in Tower Street.

She described the everyday workstation as having been an unobtrusive hut, equipped with wireless receiving and transmitting equipment, situated just inside the perimeter walls of the Park, to the left of the entrance from Tower Street. The dugout was located a short distance further into the park. Pulling back a loose piece of bark on a tree, and pressing the switch concealed under it gave access to the dugout. The earth about 15 metres (50 feet) away then opened up to reveal a trap door which in turn led via a ladder into a small room. The walls of this room were packed with explosives and ammunition, but under a shelf another catch gave access to a further room equipped with an R/T wireless set, food, clothing and bunks. Beyond this there was another small room with a chemical toilet and an emergency escape tunnel. (Winifred Read in: *Heathfield Park, A Private Estate and a Wealden Town* by Roy Pryce)

It was in the hut just inside the perimeter walls of the Park, where Subaltern Betty Berkeley Dicken took her life on 8 November 1943, by inhaling carbon monoxide fumes generated by the small charging engine kept in the generator room. Betty Dicken had been moved from the Salisbury IN Station to Heathfield Park in the autumn of 1943. She was billeted at "Ivydene" in Hailsham Road; her colleague, Kitty Hills, stayed at "Heatherville".

Due to the secrecy surrounding the activities of the Special Duties Branch, the local police officer, Constable Stanley Newman of the Heathfield police station at Broad Oak was denied access to the place of death, the exact location of which was also not disclosed.

With the permission of HM's Coroner, the SD IO, Lieutenant Frank Oakey, assisted by Lance Corporal Robert Caldow (known to his colleagues as "Freddie"), and two other AU Signals soldiers moved Mrs Dicken's body to a local mortuary. Robert Caldow also features in Alf Ellis' 1942 diary; in Beatrice Temple's diary; in several drawings made by Sally Waterhouse-Brown and in the stand-down photo on page 28.

Commissioned on 7 September 1941, together with Barbara Culleton, Eleanor Norman-Butler, Doris White and five other women who served in SD, Betty Dicken, who was married to a lieutenant serving overseas with the Royal Engineers, was one of the longest-serving AU ATS officers, and the work would seem to have worn her out. She had therefore requested to be moved to other duties, a request which had resulted in a summons to Coleshill by Senior Commander Beatrice Temple, rather than in the desired transfer. A railway warrant, authorised by the HQ of the Auxiliary Units and issued by Subaltern Doris White, who by then no longer served as a wireless operator but as one of Beatrice Temple's administrative assistants (the other was Subaltern Mary Shaw, also a former wireless operator) was included in the letter.

But instead of taking a train to Highworth, where a car would have been waiting to take her to Hannington Hall, Betty Dicken obtained the key for the "Met" hut from Kitty Hills, started the generator, and sat down on a blanket on the floor until the poisonous exhaust fumes overwhelmed and eventually killed her. In order to achieve this, she would first have had to disconnect the generator's exhaust hose. On the discovery of her body the generator's petrol tank was checked, and found to be empty.

A suicide note was found when her body was discovered by Beatrice Temple two days later. The note had been left on the folding table "in the next room", as SD IO Lieutenant Frank Oakey put it. The note was written underneath the text of Beatrice Temple's summons, which she had received earlier that day. At the inquest, held on 12 November at the Half Moon Hotel, the coroner reached the conclusion that the cause of death was carbon monoxide poisoning, and that Mrs Dicken had committed suicide whilst the balance of her mind was disturbed. The coroner's fee amounted to 10/6 (10 shillings 6 pence); the letter accompanying the cheque to pay for it was typed and signed by Subaltern Mary Frances Shaw, for the OC (Officer Commanding) ATS Auxiliary Units. A year earlier, in December 1942, Mary Shaw had been working at the Bury St Edmunds IN Station in Suffolk. (The inquest papers, closed until November 2018, are kept at the East Sussex Record Office: ESRO SHE 2/7/808).

"Found Betty gassed," wrote Beatrice Temple in her diary. Because of Subaltern Dicken's request to be moved just before a scheduled exercise it had been decided, between Beatrice Temple and Major Jones, to write an adverse report, hence the summons to HQ. It would seem that this was not the first time that the Betty had tried to go against the regulations, as mention is made of an "ultimatum" given to her in June when working at the Salisbury IN Station.

Several more diary entries detail what happened in the following days: "Cleared hut with Kitty (Hills), packed all Betty's belongings, then to inquest from which press was excluded (Nov 12). Went to funeral with Doris (White) – very quiet cremation at Brookwood. Spoke to no one (Nov 16). Mind between numb and shut off from tragedy (Nov 20)". No mention is being made of the poignant suicide letter found by Lieutenant Oakey, presumably because he handed it straight over to the coroner. Beatrice Temple's diary entries also reveal that on 4 November 1943, four days before the tragic suicide of one of her officers, she had received a phone call from Major Jones to say that Heathfield IN Station was to be closed by the end of the month. No trace appears to have survived of the hut. The dugout is still in place and apparently in very good condition, with much of the fittings and wiring still in situ. It is, however, inaccessible.

In Arthur Gabbitas's time the station would seem to have been linked with an IN Station at (or near) Sevenoaks, which also had links with the Ardingly and Shipley IN Stations. Furthermore, Arthur Gabbitas's map shows the station at Heathfield Park as having been served by a network of eight OUT Stations (see page 164). This map was produced during the 1990s from the memories of some of the AU Signals officers who were involved. Understandably, none of the men were able to remember exact dates after such a long time, but thanks to Beatrice Temple's diary there is at least a reliable contemporary record for the closedown of the Heathfield station.

Stewart Angell (in *Secret Sussex Resistance*) has recorded a number of OUT Stations which would seem to have been part of the Heathfield network:

The Telham OUT Station was described in some detail in an essay authored by Sussex Aux Units researcher Stewart Angell which has been published on the Subterranea Britannica website. Henry Thomsett, a gamekeeper at Crowhurst Park, operated the wireless set and Mr Calder, who farmed at Breadsell Farm, which adjoins Crowhurst Park in the east and is situated just to the south of the Hastings Road, now the A2100, assisted him. Both men had less than one kilometre to travel in order to get to their wireless station.

The set was kept in a dugout (now collapsed) situated on the slope of Blackhorse Hill near a footpath along the edge of Ring Wood, to the west of the present Beauport Park golf course. The site was excavated and found to have a ceiling and walls made from corrugated sheeting and timber. After removing the collapsed roof it was discovered that the main chamber had a concrete pit with a sump in its floor, where the operator is believed to have worked; this was the only area in the dugout where it was possible to stand upright. The dugout had two escape tunnels, the longest measuring 12 metres (40 feet). The aerial feeder cable is still embedded in a nearby maple tree's trunk.

The site is about two kilometres distant from Telham Hill, from where it is believed that William the Conqueror's army first caught sight of Harold's soldiers forming up for the famous battle between William (who at the time was the duke of Normandy) and the Saxon King Harold, which took place on 14 October 1066 and has entered the annals of British History as the Battle of Hastings.

Sydney Dinnis operated the OUT Station at Parkwood Farm in Upper Dicker. The wireless set was kept inside a cupboard in a locked room in his house and when Mr Dinnis later moved to Priory Farm (near Wilmington) the wireless set was again kept in his house. The aerial ran up the inside of the chimney.

The Cadborough OUT Station was a solidly constructed dugout with a concrete floor and two Anderson shelter-type chambers resting on low sidewalls. Each room was about 1.80 metres (six feet) long and 1.50 metres (five feet) wide. A narrow wall with a low doorway divided the two rooms. The dugout was accessed through a vertical shaft, and it had a 10 metres (30 feet)) long emergency escape tunnel leading out the opposite end. A great number of glazed ceramic pipes provided ventilation.

Edwin Trangmere, farmer at Priesthawes House near Stone Cross, kept his set in a dugout in his garden. The dugout is described as having been constructed from wood and measured about 3 x 4.50 metres (10 x 15 feet). It contained a table for the wireless set and a chair for the operator.

Another OUT Station operator, Dr Stuart Hogg from Westham, is said to have carried his set around with him in a small briefcase. This idea was presumably borrowed from the SOE, who during WW2 supplied their agents and resistance groups in German-occupied Europe with a portable transmitter receiver station called Type 3 MKII (commonly referred to as Type B2).

The operator of the Telscombe OUT Station was Harold West who farmed at Bevendean Farm near Brighton. His wireless set was initially kept in a dugout located on the outskirts of the village, where a poacher discovered it. The wireless set was subsequently moved to a new dugout in the garden of the vicarage but there it was discovered yet again. Consequently, the whole area was deemed to be unsafe and it was eventually decided to move the wireless set to a safer location further away, although the location appears to still be shown on Major Jones' 1944 map.

A secret radar station would also appear to have been in the vicinity: Mr Geoffrey Ellis, a schoolboy at the time, recalls seeing a military trailer with a dish aerial, parked just off-road at the top of Telscombe Tye where there was a chalk track leading north. Mr Ellis has since found out that this was a top-secret experimental radar installation. There would also seem to be a number of documents currently held in the National Archives, recording the great consternation that its presence caused to the local military authorities that were not allowed to know anything about it. (WW2 People's War, Article ID: A7489597 dated 3 December 2005)

The wireless set was moved from Telscombe to Falmer, to a dugout situated in Half Moon Wood (presumably Moon's Plantation) near St Mary's Farm to the north of the village and about nine kilometres (five miles), as the crow flies, to the north-west of its previous location. The local farmer, Lawrence Pye, was the operator and the aforementioned Harold West assisted him. (*Secret Sussex Resistance*, pages 74-79)

Locals are familiar with a story according to which there used to be a WW2 listening post or an underground store situated at the top of a steep slope not far distant from the bridle path leading through Half Moon Wood. The DoB database has a record of an "Auxiliary Unit Special Duties Outstation" (site reference: S0011764).

A local man has described the site as "basically an underground location with a cantilever device to open and close the door entrance. It was quite snug and warm and well hidden and was used after the war for brewing up. Jim (an acquaintance) was there the day that the fire eventually burned through the wooden floor and onto ammunition that was still there and lying below. The firework display lasted for two days, and it was a miracle that nobody was killed or injured. David West, the farmer, filled in the shelter after the event as it became quite dangerous, and there were health and safety issues for people wandering about Stanmer Woods. The debris is still visible. There is another listening post somewhere in Stanmer but I am not sure where." (Kip Oliver, Stanmer Preservation Society Forum, May 2011)

If the location which researchers have since discovered should indeed be the OUT Station site, only a pile of moss-covered stones is left of it today. Might David West have been a relative of Harold West, the wireless operator from Telscombe?

A number of Auxiliary Units operational patrols were active in East Sussex, and the remains of some of their dugouts are still in place today. In this context it may be of interest to note that in July 1942 a competition was held at St Mary's Farm between the Cooksbridge, Bishopstone and Firle operational patrols. The Cooksbridge patrol won (Diary of patrol leader Bill Webber in: *The Secret Sussex Resistance,* page 33). There was also a large military presence in the area. In 1942 Stanmer House, located only about one kilometre to the south-west of the dugout site in Half Moon Wood, was requisitioned from the Pelham family to provide billeting and fire ranges for a Canadian tank regiment. Stanmer Park was also used as a D-Day marshalling camp (Camp J2) with a capacity of 2,800 personnel. In the run up to D-Day, soldiers were also camped at Firle Place, Ditchling, Plumpton, Seaford, Lewes and Eastbourne.

To summarise the networks in Sussex: fundamental changes were made, presumably in the run-up to D-Day, which, uniquely, resulted in all Sussex stations, IN and OUT, reporting directly to the Reigate IN Station in Surrey. A number of OUT Stations (presumably all those which could not be linked with Reigate) would appear to have been closed. New stations were opened further inland. No information is to date known about these new stations and who manned them, and their exact locations have not yet been identified. One such station would seem to have been situated about two kilometres (1.2 miles) to the south-east of Haslemere on the Surrey-Sussex border, near Black Down - the highest point in the South Downs National Park. Less than a kilometre distant is Aldworth House, built for the poet laureate Alfred Lord Tennyson. During the war the Admiralty had requisitioned the house. Other sites were located in the Rake/Brow Hill area to the north-east of Petersfield; at Slindon House, HQ of the 1st Canadian Infantry Brigade, and near Petworth where the Canadian Army, prior to D-Day, had moved into Petworth House and used the adjoining Park as a tank holding area. Tottington Manor, near Small Dole, appears to also have been part of the wireless network. The manor housed the regional AU HQ and Stewart Angell reports that it had two lookout posts, one of which with a telephone line connecting it to the dugout at the manor.

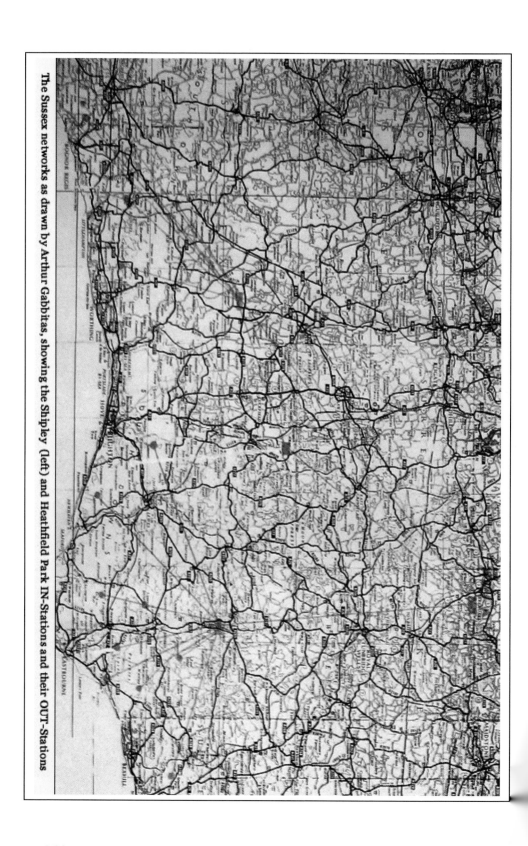

The Sussex networks as drawn by Arthur Gabbitas, showing the Shipley (left) and Heathfield Park IN-Stations and their OUT-Stations

Wiltshire

The Alderbury IN Station served 5th (V) Corps HQ, based at Longford Castle, about two kilometres west of the village of Alderbury. There was also a reinforcement camp for 5th Corps Signals. In his handwritten contemporary notes, Adrian Monck-Mason refers to the station as "Byfield I.S." and describes it as "a Corps-type station without B.S." The network used the call-sign "Byfield" (a village in Northamptonshire). According to an accompanying footnote dated 14 July 1942, work yet to be done included the setting up of duplicate aerials. On 28 June 1942, Alf Ellis took three wireless sets to "Byfield" (Alf Ellis diary). Adrian Monck-Mason described the hut at Alderbury as being situated in a copse "at the back of the rectory" (BROM Archive). Apart from having been the operator of an OUT Station near Charing in Kent it is not clear in which other capacity Adrian Monck-Mason was involved, but involved he certainly would seem to have been. Beatrice Temple repeatedly met him in the company of other SD officers at Blandford, at Dorchester and at Bachelor's Hall in Hundon. Perhaps this is the reason why his wife Dorothy believed that he had joined the Royal Signals.

The Alderbury IN Station in 2013

The location (in a copse adjacent to the Old Rectory) is not marked on Major Jones' map, indicating that the site was abandoned before closedown. A new station near Wilton would, however, appear to have replaced it, presumably after the HQ the station was attached to was moved elsewhere: on 8 November 1942, 5th Corps was included as part of the Allied land forces (First Army) in "Operation Torch", the amphibious landings in French-held Morocco and Algeria.

The Alderbury site is only about 12 kilometres (7 miles) distant from the Wilton IN Station. Beatrice Temple referred to both locations as "Salisbury", which suggests that they operated at different times. Dorothy Monck-Mason (nee Rainey) who worked at "Salisbury" in late 1942 recalls:

> "One of the stations I worked at was Blandford where we were billeted at Tarrant Keynestone. After this (in autumn 1942, according to Beatrice Temple's diary) came Southern Command, with Wilton Castle (sic) as our attachment and Captain Owen Hall-Hall as our IO." (Letter to Arthur Gabbitas dated 20 January 1998; BROM Archive)

The new IN/Relay Station served Southern Command HQ based at Wilton House. In this context an account from an officer who worked at said HQ at the same time might be of interest. Lance Corporal Alice Catherine Hunt (nee Griffith), an ATS teleprinter/keyboard line operator, was posted to the 3rd Command Signal Company (stationed at Wilton House) in October 1942:

> "At HQ, teleprinters received signals constantly and these messages were then redistributed to their intended destinations, either by teleprinter, telephone or dispatch rider, some of whom were ATS. We worked in three shifts in the underground cellars of Wilton House. Most of the signals were Orders. These were in code and had to pass through the cipher office before they could be issued. Signals marked "PP" (Priority) had to be dispatched immediately." (WW2 People's War, Article ID: A4233863/21 June 2005)

In the run up to D-Day Wilton House was the HQ of General Dwight David "Ike" Eisenhower. Documentary evidence shows that the Wilton station had direct wireless links to the IN Stations at Blandford (covering the Dorset coast) and at Winchester (covering Hampshire including the Isle of Wight). The station also had a link to an as yet unidentified location at or in the vicinity of Coleshill House and hence indirect access to the Somerset IN Stations.

Beatrice Temple first mentions the new location on Tuesday, 8 June 1943 ("visited hut and took Ann out to show her the new site") and she would seem, from now on, to refer to this new location as "Salisbury". The dugout was re-discovered in 2013 by an urban explorer. The site is located within a wooded area on the Wilton Estate, which is owned by the Earl of Pembroke. Steel grilles to keep the resident bat population safe from predators secure both the entrance and the exit openings, with much of the original capping still in situ. The structure was built into the chalk rock and is in fairly good condition, although part of the roof above the entrance lobby has started to collapse and plans are currently underway to preserve it. Not only are many of its original features and all the wiring still in place, the structure is also unique in that it is considerably larger and more sophisticated in its design than any other known IN Station dugout. In the transcription of Beatrice Temple's diary the dugout is referred to as a "Super Zero Station" – 'Zero' perhaps being an addition made by Barbara Culleton who occasionally added her own terms and comments.

The wall separating the entrance lobby from the adjoining rooms was constructed from railway sleepers, with a door also built from sleepers and cleverly integrated into the wall so that an intruder would have been unable to recognise it as such. Two heavy locks secured it. A small area on the other side of this wall still contains what appears to be a crudely made stand for a water tank. In all likelihood this lobby also housed a chemical toilet, of which no trace remains. At right angles to it a doorway leads into a larger room still containing four bunk-beds. Unusually, several glazed ceramic ventilation pipes can be seen emerging from underneath the beds. No other known IN Station dugout is known to have had an equally sophisticated ventilation system which would seem to even have incorporated below-floor-level ventilation. The Royal Engineers sappers who installed it obviously made improvements on earlier stations.

A short passage leading past what seems to have been a small cooking area leads to the wireless room. The cooking area is denoted by a sturdy worktop and above it, at roof height, there is a boarding which forms a pelmet surrounding a glazed ceramic ventilation pipe quite similar to a cooker hood. There is also a light fitting above the worktop and a light switch fitting on the wall beside it. One side of the wireless room is taken up by three workstations, separated into bays by partitioning screens for noise reduction. The existence of three bays suggest that three wireless sets were used simultaneously, each operating to a different station. The Wilton IN Station did indeed have three wireless links –two working on a 60 mcs frequency and the third on 53 mcs, a frequency used exclusively on the so-called Inner Network. All the wiring, including the aerial feeder cables and a heavy-duty mains electricity cable, is still in situ – an important and rare find. The emergency exit passage turns off at right angles by a short wall separating the wireless room from cooking area and bunkroom, leading to a tunnel constructed from segments of concrete culvert pipe. There is evidence that the tunnel was provided with its own lighting and information provided by Bert Davis, whose AU Signals crew was based in the area from 1943 until closedown, adds a few interesting details:

> "I spent many days fitting and wiring that station – one fact I will never forget is running electric wiring through the concrete pipes *(ie the 17 metres long escape tunnel)*. I cannot remember the distance involved but I do remember fitting the cable clips with rawlplugs. In those days we had no drills or masonry bits, just a hammer and an old rawlplug punch. Blisters and backache bent up in a 48' (1.22m) diameter pipe." (Letter to Dr W Ward)

A manhole-like structure, covered with a lid, and with what would seem to be two glazed ceramic pipes set into it for ventilation, was sunk into the floor of the short passage leading to the escape tunnel. The 'manhole' is situated at the foot of a raised step leading up to the tunnel opening. A sump or soakaway at the foot of the opening prevented rainwater trickling down the tunnel from entering the dugout proper. The tunnel, which abruptly changes direction about half-way up, is 17 metres (56 feet) long and ends at a shaft which contains yet another unique feature in that what appears to be a small water tank was sunk into its floor near one corner. Its exact purpose remains a mystery. Concealed trapdoors operated by a system of pulleys and counterweights covered both the entrance and the exit shaft when the dugout was in use. On 8 February 1944 Beatrice Temple spent a long time there, testing the hatch opening mechanism with "Mr Gardiner" Beatrice Temple's diary) – it is not clear who Mr Gardiner was.

The end room housed not one but two generators, one on each side of a large rectangular stone 'box' with a heavy stone lid that would seem to have originally been sealed. The box appears to have functioned as an exhaust box, as indeed sections of steel pipes can be seen emerging from it, and the remains of flexible generator exhaust hose which fitted onto them were also found nearby. An asbestos pipe mounted on top of this box was presumably used, similar to a flue pipe, for carrying the deadly poisonous generator exhaust fumes safely outside and out of harm's way. The cover of the oval cutout in the elbow of this pipe could be removed for easy cleaning with a flue brush. Concrete plinths with the generator mountings in situ flank the exhaust box. The generators were mounted on rubber couplings so as to better absorb their vibrations when in use. The presence of a heavy-duty armoured cable as well as of mains power cables however suggest that the dugout was connected to mains electricity (and ran primarily on mains power) and that the generators were for backup only.

The three operators' bays with partitioning walls (above) and what appears to be the remains of a switchboard, and various cable entry points, with all of the wiring still in place. *(Photos: "BD")*

Bert Davis recalls that the AU Signals crew's workshop was in an empty shop in Fisherton Street, Salisbury (*The Mercian Maquis*, page 122). When he revisited the IN Station site in the 1960s he found it very overgrown with shrubs and brambles and he failed to find any sign of the hut that he remembered to have stood nearby:

> "The hut was just fitted out with a telephone. I had to tap into the phone line and run concealed wiring to the buried Nissen hut (the dugout). I think that the tunnel led to the Nissen hut – hence the electric cabling."

Considering that the "Salisbury" site (initially at Alderbury) was first mentioned in Beatrice Temple's diary in December 1941, and that it operated (albeit at a different location) until March 1944, it would seem to have been the longest-serving IN Station in SD history.

Yorkshire

Some of the Command and District HQs appear to have been served by an IN Station which seems to have functioned as the extension of another IN Station, such as the station at <u>Hickleton Hall</u>, about ten kilometres (six miles) distant from Doncaster, in the West Riding district of Yorkshire. Beatrice Temple refers to the location as Doncaster. The wireless sets were apparently kept in a gazebo in the grounds of the Hall (Barbara Culleton), which at the time was the base of 1st (I) Corps HQ.

As the main invasion threat was always considered to be from the Wash south to Portland, Hickleton Hall was in a relatively safe part of the coast, some 130 kilometres (80 miles) inland, where an invasion would have been impossible to conceive and airborne raids unlikely to land that far inland – presumably this explains the absence of a dugout. Barbara Culleton spent several months at Hickleton Hall in late 1941, and the SD IO, Captain Michael James Farrer, was also based at the Hall. Hickleton Hall also accommodated a camp for Italian and German prisoners of war, and later for displaced people from the Ukraine and Poland. The camp was first built in 1941 and finally closed in 1948. Archaeological remains of the camp hut bases can still be found at the site.

The <u>South Dalton</u> IN Station was located near the Yorkshire Division HQ based at Dalton Hall near Beverley, in the East Riding district of Yorkshire. It had four OUT Stations and was linked with the Hickleton Hall IN Station in the West Riding district. The station was manned by ATS officers and would appear to have served the Yorkshire Division based at South Dalton Hall.

The station's dugout was discovered, structurally intact, by local Aux Units researcher Alan Williamson, 53 years after it had been sealed. Access was through a vertical shaft leading into a Nissen-type structure consisting of three rooms divided by breezeblock walls. Ventilation was provided by a number of glazed ceramic pipes and by two large concrete pipes traversing the generator room. The small room at the foot of the entrance shaft still contained wooden shelf units, stacked with tins and bottles when Alan Williamson visited it. The shelf unit swivelled outwards to reveal a hidden door leading into the main chamber. The door appeared to have had an inner core of loose sand, perhaps for soundproofing - an interesting detail which has to date been recorded from only one other IN Station dugout, namely Wilton, where soil was used.

The main chamber contained a desk with a writing slope and a table covered with a thin metal sheet. A brass bulb holder, short sections of aerial feeder cable, two metal pipes and part of the wooden hatch covering the entrance shaft were also recorded by Williamson but most of the wiring and shelving appears to have been ripped off the walls.

The end room contained what was deemed to be a crude wooden bench with mounting blocks for a generator, and a fire bucket. A sliding wooden hatch concealed the emergency escape tunnel opening. The tunnel was 9.40 metres (31 feet) long and built from concrete culvert pipes.

The above-ground Nissen hut serving as the everyday workstation was located about 300 yards away from the dugout. It had brick end walls and an entrance porch containing a cubicle for the chemical toilet. Remains of the aerial feeder cable still adhere to a nearby tree. *(East Ridings Secret Resistance, page 96)*

Major Jones' map shows that four OUT Stations served the South Dalton IN Station. One was situated in a <u>warehouse in Hull</u> and Stanley Judson remembers that the wireless set was concealed behind a pile of sacks on the top floor, but he was unable to recall where exactly in Hull this warehouse stood.

More details are known about the <u>Rudston</u> OUT Station which is described in some detail in Alan Williamson's book *East Ridings Secret Resistance* (page 104). The dugout was built into the side of a small chalk pit located within a wood. Built from breezeblocks, with a curved corrugated iron roof, its design and layout resemble the South Dalton IN Station apart from the escape tunnel being considerably shorter. Of particular interest is the ventilation system, which was made from square wooden trunking instead of the more commonly used concrete or ceramic pipes. Similar ventilation pipes are known to also have been used at the Goathland OUT Station. The wireless operators were Bill Galenby and Dr Leonard Watson, a doctor from Bridlington. The aerial tree still stands nearby.

Christian Smith, the farmer on whose land the station was situated, operated the <u>Sigglesthorne</u> OUT Station, located near the village of Hornsea. Peter Dunne is known to have assisted him. The site is located within a strip of woodland bounded by fields and a track currently leads right over the entrance. George Dawes, a volunteer of the DoB project, and his friend Mark Bond in 1966 were the first to visit and survey the site, which they found partially flooded. The dugout still contained the shelf unit concealing the door into the main chamber, which was still furnished with a wooden bench with a writing slope and a wooden table with two shelves. A chemical toilet was found in one corner. A number of glazed ceramic pipes provided ventilation. Two trees with the aerial feeder cables still in place were also found and recorded. (George Dawes & Mark Bond, DoB)

No information is to date known about the <u>Ottringham</u> OUT Station.

The <u>Scotch Corner</u> IN Station was situated in the vicinity of the Scotch Corner Hotel near Darlington, where 10th (X) Corps HQ was based. The Durham & North Riding Division HQ was stationed at Hollyhurst, Woodland Road, Darlington, and from September 1941 onwards the 9th (IX) Corps District HQ was also in Darlington. A crew of ATS officers operated the IN Station, which was served by three OUT Stations. It was also linked with an as yet unknown AU Signals-crewed IN Station near Hexham to the west of Newcastle upon Tyne in Northumberland (which operated on a different frequency) and with the Danby Lodge IN Station in the North Riding district of Yorkshire.

The exact locations of the "Met" hut and dugout (provided there was one) have as yet to be found. Interestingly, the Second World War Experience Centre based at Walton in West Yorkshire holds a record pertaining to an Army Intelligence officer called Gordon Fraser, who was attached to 10th Corps HQ and billeted on the Pallister family. (Reference: HF/LEEWW:2000.277.1)

Another snippet of information comes from an article titled "A Motor Trip around Swaledale and Wensleydale", published in the Reeth & District Gazette (Issue 35, 2 June 1998). The author, who is only referred to by the initials F.T.C.W., recalls that there used to be a Signals Office in the area which is currently taken up by the A1 – Barracks Bank (A6108) roundabout. 1940s maps of the area however suggest that this would not have been a suitable spot for an IN Station.

Another elusive station, presumably crewed by AU Signals, was located on the outskirts of the small village of Danby in North Yorkshire. Major Jones' map shows the <u>Danby</u> IN Station with a network of four OUT Stations and linked with the Scotch Corner IN Station. The station is believed to have been located at, or in the vicinity of Danby Lodge, which at the time was a shooting lodge used by Captain Anthony Quayle, the IO for the South Eastern district, as his HQ. No details are known about this IN Station and Beatrice Temple does not mention it in her diary. Since 1976 Danby Lodge has been the home of The Moors National Park Centre.

Based on his own research of Auxiliary Units, Dennis Walker has created a map showing the Danby IN Station as having been served by five OUT Stations and linked with a site at High Coniscliffe near Darlington in County Durham, as Mr Walker believes the wireless stations in North Yorkshire to have been linked "with the command bunker at Coniscliffe, which was in turn linked with the Army barracks at Richmond and Catterick".

Said map places the OUT Stations at Skelton, Glaisdale, Robin Hoods Bay, Cloughton and Goathland. A sixth wireless path links with the Danby Beacon RAF Radar Station which during WW2 was located on Beacon Hill, to the south-east of the village of Danby near Houlsyke. An intriguing idea, certainly, but all information available to date suggests that SD IN Stations would not have been linked with stations outwith the SD network, as indeed none are shown on Major Jones' map.

The Cloughton OUT Station was situated at Hulleys Farm, also referred to as "The Hulleys". It was a dugout accessed through a vertical shaft with breezeblock walls, and it consisted of two rooms. It did not appear to have had an escape tunnel. (*Defence of the UK – Whitby*, page 29) The OUT Station at "Seven Hills" cottage in the hamlet of Lindhead Gorse was only three kilometres (two miles) distant.

There was also an OUT Station in the cellar beneath the Post Office at 7 High Street in Castleton. The wireless set is reported to have been kept on a specially made shelf that also provided room for the batteries. The operator was the postmaster. (*Defence of the UK – Whitby*, page 47)

The SUBOUT Station at Redcar is said to have been in the attic of a house at 55 Coast Road, operated by Mr Harrison, who was also a local postmaster. (Stephen Lewins, pers comm)

The picturesque village of Goathland is situated in the North Yorkshire Moors national park, 150 metres (500 feet) above sea level. To the wider public it is probably best known for having been the setting of the fictional village of Aidensfield in the "Heartbeat" television series set in the 1960s, and to railway buffs for its station on the North Yorkshire Moors Railway line - a heritage railway providing about 30 kilometres of track and a variety of preserved steam and diesel locomotives. The only military relics still in existence, and from the Cold War at that, would seem to be two ROC (Royal Observer Corps) monitoring posts, one located to the south-east of the railway station on the edge of Mill Moor, the other to the east of the main road through the village. Not many people will know about the clandestine activities of a Goathland farmer during the WW2.

The OUT Station is intact and in good condition. It is a dugout, concealed beneath the floor of a shed which has since been converted into a summerhouse, in the garden of Partridge Hill Farm. Sadly, the owners have only on very rare occasions permitted access, and the few photographs of the interior, taken on the occasion of one of these visits, can not be made public. Alan Williamson's book contains a description of the site which is also mentioned, albeit briefly, in *Defence of the UK (Whitby)* by John Middleton Harwood and Stuart McMillan, who, after submitting their text to the owners for editing were unfortunately restricted to mentioning the bare essentials only.

One of the photographs (on page 92) in A Williamson's book shows the exterior of a somewhat ramshackle wooden outbuilding, and another shows the opening in its floor and steep wooden steps (these would appear to be original) leading down into the dugout, which is an elephant shelter consisting of three rooms divided by breezeblock walls. Interior pictures show that the walls would seem to have been whitewashed; the floors look concreted over or paved. There seem to be no remains of any wiring or shelves; the dugout looks dry and in good condition. Like at the Rudston OUT Station, the internal ventilation ducts were made from square wooden trunking, in a style similar to the wooden pipes commonly seen in old coal mines, where they too served the purpose of ventilation. Both pipes have large rectangular openings, with the sheet metal screens for closing these still in situ.

Main chamber (left) and the wooden ventilation ducts in generator room at Goathland. The sheet metal covers used for sealing the rectangular openings are also still in place. *(The drawings are based on original photographs taken in summer 2010)*

Harwood & McMillan give the dimensions of the entrance shaft as measuring 3 x 3 feet (0.90 x 0.90 metres); the dimensions of the lobby as 9 x 5 feet (2.75 x 1.50 metres) and the dimensions of the wireless room as 9 x 7 feet (2.75 x 2.10 metres), with the total floor space (including the end room) measuring 20 x 10 feet (6.10 x 3.05 metres). There does not appear to be an emergency escape exit. The remains of an aerial feeder cable are apparently still embedded in the trunk of an ancient beech tree growing beside the shed and a few insulators appear to also still be in place.

Whereas Williamson refers to the structure as an OUT Station, Harwood & McMillan suggest that is was an IN Station, basing their conclusion on the 'relative sophistication' of the dugout. Certainly, its layout and construction, to some extent at least, follow the standard IN Station dugout design, but so do a number of OUT Station dugouts. Bearing in mind the generous size and sophisticated design of some of the known OUT Station dugouts, and also the fact that the wireless operator would seem to have been a relative of the present owner, was living at the property in the 1940s and was known to have been a civilian, suggestions of the dugout having been anything else but an OUT Station are without merit. Major Jones' map shows that Goathland was one of the stations serving the Danby IN Station.

> The <u>Guisborough</u> OUT Station was a dugout in a disused quarry on the edge of Guisborough Plantation. It served the Danby IN Station.

> The <u>Eston</u> OUT Station near Middlesbrough is reported to have been a dugout in Rye Hill Wood. It served the Scotch Corner IN Station.

Scotland

Scotland had four IN Stations: one in the Borders, one in Elgin (Morayshire), one at Ladybank (Fife) and one in Edinburgh. The Borders IN Station was located on the site of the ruins of the medieval <u>Hume Castle</u>, often described as one of the most formidable defensive castles in the Scottish Borders. The station used the call-sign "Gilpin" (a river in Cumbria) and was linked with the Edinburgh IN Station. Beatrice Temple never visited this location nor did she mention it in her diary, suggesting that AU Signals for the whole duration of its existence operated this station. After the Area HQ had moved from Duns Castle to Edinburgh it would seem to have served the Borders Sub Area HQ based at St Boswells.

One of the AU Signals officers based in the area was Frank Hewitt, who was moved from Norwich to Hume Castle at some time in 1942.

> "I well remember the incident that took place when we all went swimming. Several of us were posted along the river in pairs, one in the water and one on the bank. I was the one on the bank when chaps in the water found the poor lad *(a drowning accident?)*. I also remember once trying to get the Army Chevrolet up to the Castle door – didn't quite make it!" (Letter to Stan Judson, dated March 1944; BROM Archive)

Les Parnell also remembers the location:

> "My late wife and I visited Hume Castle ruins in 1986. All traces of the hut had been removed. I left there in 1943 and have often wondered if the boxed in aerial is still in situ on top of the ruins. If it is I wonder what any future historian would think if it ever comes to light, a 52 mcs wire dipole, inside a wooden box, buried in the wall of a very old castle ruin." (Letter to Dr Will Ward, dated 28 March 1999; BROM Archive)

> The concealment of the box housing the aerial was documented, albeit unknowingly, when the local community raised complaints and objections (apparently published in the local newspaper) to the deployment of troops for 'repair' work at the castle at such a critical time. The official explanation was that engineers had to be trained in many skills, and where better to

practice for the benefit of a community than on an important historical feature such as Hume Castle. (*With Britain in Mortal Danger,* page 166)

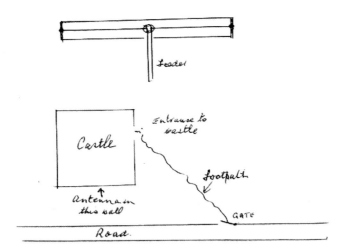

Drawing by L Parnell (in letter to Dr W Ward, 3 March 1999, BROM Archive)

Stanley Judson's recollections add a few more interesting details:

"The dugout at Hume Castle was of particular interest as it was buried within the castle itself. Actually the castle is a small area of land enclosed by high walls and the station was buried beneath the soil, and the aerial feeder cable was fed into the wall and the dipole aerial concealed beneath the parapet. The transmissions were usually carried out from a Nissen hut also situated within the castle walls. A path from the hut led to an outside toilet hut which in fact disguised the entrance to a tunnel leading to the dugout. (Undated letter to Arthur Gabbitas; BROM Archive)

The Signals crew based at the Hume Castle IN Station would seem to have posed as observers, and convincingly maintained this role throughout the war. On the website of the Clan Home Association the vice president, Dr Ian Maitland Hume (the owners of the castle, the Home family, changed their name to Hume in the 16th century), states that "the small level piece of ground in the north-west corner was where the Observer Corps had a post during WW2 and underneath was a small enclosed space designed to accommodate a few key resistance fighters." The description of the site by the Royal Commission on the Ancient and Historical Monuments of Scotland (RCAHMS) also contains the information that in WW2 an observation post was located within the ruined castle (site reference number: NT745W 3).

Three OUT Stations served the Hume Castle IN Station; their locations are known to have been in the vicinity of the village of Ramrig ("Gilpin 2"), where Major Askew of Ladykirk reported that he found a unit of REs digging on his land without his permission; at Stoneshiel Farm (to the south-west of Reston in the parish of Coldingham), where the operator was Jim Darling, the farmer; and near the town of <u>Coldstream</u> to the south-west of Berwick upon Tweed. Aux researcher Phil Rowett also mentions an OUT Station near Blackadder Mains, to the south-east of Duns, where Walter Davidson might have been involved.

The Advanced HQ of Scottish Command was based at Riccarton House, Edinburgh, which was located where the library of the Heriot Watt University now stands. The Rear HQ was at John Watson's School in Belford Road. Following the creation of new sub areas by the Gale Commission in September 1941 the North Highland District HQ was based in Inverness and the South Highland Area HQ was at Craigie, Perth. Sub-Area HQs were established in Elgin (Morayshire), Huntly (Aberdeenshire), Thurso (Caithness) and Alness (Cromarty). According to Frank Hewitt the first Area HQ was at Duns Castle, where he stayed when he first arrived. (Undated letter from Phil Rowett to A Gabbitas, BROM Archive)

Stanley Judson, who was stationed in Edinburgh as an Area Sergeant under the command of Captain (later Major) Peter Forbes recalls that the members of his crew had a flat with sleeping accommodation in Rutland Square which doubled as an office. Because of accommodation and travelling allowances he was able to cater for himself very well, as a three-course meal at the Overseas League Club or one of the various canteens cost very little in those days. In his time there were only two AU Signals maintenance sections operating in his area, one based at Broughty Ferry and the other at Hume Castle in Berwickshire. (Undated letter, BROM Archive)

The <u>Edinburgh</u> network used the call-sign "Barnack" – a village near Peterborough in Cambridgeshire. (Others have suggested that the call-sign was "Bannock"). The IN Station was located on Braid Hills – then and now a golf course – on the south-eastern fringe of Edinburgh. Frank Hewitt recalls the day he turned over his scout car on the golf links and losing his driving licence because of it. Thanks to the help of the SD IO it was soon reinstated. The station was served by eight OUT Stations and was linked with the IN Station at Hume Castle in Berwickshire. Beatrice Temple last visited in September 1942 and it would seem that an AU Signals crew then took over, because the station is shown on Major Jones' map as having been operational until closedown.

Another IN Station, presumably an outpost of Edinburgh, would appear to have been located in the grounds of Melville House near <u>Ladybank</u> in Fife, the HQ of the Scottish Auxiliary Units, where experts from the Argyll & Sutherland Highlanders and the Scots Guards instructed auxiliers in sabotage techniques and the use of explosives. The station was operational until closedown.

Les Parnell recalls how his crew encountered a serious problem during his time in Scotland:

> "In England our frequency was 56 megacycles and we used that at the start of our Scottish operations. Three of us sat on the highest point of the golf course using the 'call' Station A, whilst our signal officer travelled round

finding suitable sites. After two hours or so we found ourselves arrested by an armed patrol from the nearby AA Battery. Every time we spoke on air we apparently jammed the entire Firth of Forth defence network. We called in our officer as we had a 'problem' and he came along with the result that our frequency in Scotland was moved to 52 mcs forthwith." (According to Major Jones, the frequencies used by the wireless networks were 48, 52, 60 and 65 mcs. His map shows that by June 1944 all the Scottish networks operated on 60 mcs.) My own stay in the Scottish area was only from May 1942 to February 1943 when I was moved to Southern Area. This means I never saw Hume Castle fully operational though Braid Hills was, for the last few months of my being there. I never met any of the OUT Station operators." (Letter to Phil Rowett, dated 8 June 1999; BROM Archive)

The East Lothian OUT Station was located in <u>Smeaton Wood</u> ("Barnack 3") near East Linton. The wireless set is said to have been operated by Mr Niven, who farmed at Law Head, assisted by Mr Grieve, the head teacher at East Linton School. The Reverend James Tindall Souter, Minister at Whitekirk, was the runner. The Reverend mysteriously disappeared from his Edinburgh home on 8 August 1959 and was never seen again. Frank Hewitt recalled the station many years later in a letter to his colleague Stanley Judson.

Four OUT Stations were located in Fife: at <u>Linwood Hall</u> (now a boarding school) near Leven to the north-east of Kirkcaldy; at <u>Balmullo Farm</u> on the southern edge of the village of Balmullo south of Lucklawhill; and at <u>Fothringham Hill</u> to the south of Forfar. Apart from the locations no further details are known about these stations and their civilian operators. The OUT Station near <u>Stravithie</u> was operated by Major RW Travis who lived at Gilmerton House and Miss HWM Purvis (later the Dowager Lady, Wilhelmina Morrison-Law). Lady Morrison-Law recalls that the wireless set was kept in a 2.80 metres (8 feet) deep dugout in a wood near Kinaldy Farm, about 800 yards to the south of Gilmerton House. Access was through a vertical shaft, covered by a trapdoor hidden under leaves. The catch was released by a concealed wire which was about 10 yards long. The dugout was divided into three small rooms containing two bunks and iron rations in the main chamber. Lady Morrison-Law said that the wireless set was kept in the third room and she thought they used it only once a week. A Royal Signals officer occasionally came to see them at Gilmerton if there was anything to discuss. (Letter to Arthur Gabbitas, December 1996; BROM Archive). There was also an OUT Station at West Fenton (East Lothian).

The three OUT Stations located in Angus were near Camus' Cross on <u>Camustane Hill</u> to the south-east of the village of Craigton; at <u>West Woods of Ethie</u>, between the A92 road and Mains of Auchmithie to the south of Inverkeilor, and at <u>Hillside</u>, a small village to the north-west of Montrose. There is no information pertaining to the operators.

The Morayshire IN Station was located in or near <u>Elgin</u>, which from September 1941 onwards was the base of the North Highland District Sub-Area HQ. No details are known about the IN Station - which, according to Beatrice Temple's diary, was planned by Major Jones to be completed by 15 August 1943. She visited the station for the first time in mid-July and by September Winifrede "Nina" Gregory, Olga Jensen and Joan Pratten, the station's AU ATS wireless operators, appear to have been well settled in and organised. Beatrice Temple visited the station for the last time in December 1943, suggesting that an AU Signals crew took over operations. The station is shown as having been operational in 1944 on Major Jones' map. It served the Moray Sub-Area HQ based in Elgin.

The Elgin IN Station was served by four OUT Stations: one in the West Clyne/Gordonbush area, north-west of Brora and one near Torrish on the A897, south-west of Helmsdale, both in Sutherland, and at John O'Groats and in the Smerral/Latheronwheel area north-east of Dunbeath – a local man told Geoff Leet ("The Caithness Secret Army in WW2" published in Caithness Field Club Bulletin, 2005) that his father and the schoolmaster walked out at night for intelligence gathering, very secret, and that after the war had ended everything was burned. Arthur Gabbitas also mentions a station at Aultibea by Langwell Water.

> Stanley Judson has described the most northerly OUT Station, which was situated at John O'Groats:
>
>> "In John O'Groats, in a crofter's cottage, we had a bit of trouble with the set and we were sitting in this chicken house operating this set, with a row of chickens perched above us." (Interview by J Warwicker, IWM ref: 29468)

Wales

A "MOST SECRET" memorandum records the date – the 30th of March 1942 - when it was decided by the authorities to extend the wireless networks further north and westwards:

> "The C-in-C has decided that the organisation of the wireless installations for the Intelligence side of Auxiliary Units should be expanded to, inclusive, Montrose, and should also include the South Wales and North Somerset areas." (TNA, WO 199/1194)

There were two IN Stations in South Wales. One was built on the Blorenge mountain near Abergavenny in Monmouthshire; the other was located above the village of Crwbin in Carmarthenshire. The South Wales Area HQ of South-Western Command was based at St Ronans in Abergavenny. The Blorenge IN Station is situated on the Blorenge (near the memorial to the racehorse "Foxhunter") and it served the South Wales Area HQ based at Abergavenny. Bert Davis, who was involved, recalls that the dugout was created by enlarging an existing rock cave, using explosives (*The Mercian Maquis*, page 125). The station used the call-sign "Harcourt" (a coastal settlement in Cornwall) and was built to the same standards as almost all other IN Stations, with a vertical entrance shaft and three rooms divided by breezeblock walls. The structure has collapsed quite some time ago but some of its features are still in place. The short escape tunnel had a flat roof of concrete slabs, similar to the also very short escape tunnel at Halstead IN Station. The tunnel is described as having led into a hut, which would appear to have been the everyday workstation. This hut, which adjoined the dugout, no longer exists but its base is still in place. As the whole area is without trees, the aerial was fixed on a mast that was nine metres (30 feet) high and constructed from telegraph poles. The Signals crew consisted of Lance Corporal Greening and the signalmen Harvey, Baker and Larkin. (Jack Millie, letter to A Gabbitas, 22 March 1996; BROM Archive). A detailed description of the construction of one such mast comes from the then SD IO Captain David Wemyss (undated letter to Arthur Gabbitas):

> "I remember that to get the aerials high enough we made a tower out of eight new telegraph poles, each leg (of four) being two telegraph poles bolted together by the holes already in them for the cross arms. The aerials were then housed in the cross rails. I have a slight feeling that the poles were uplifted at night from a roadside dump."

Jack Millie, who was in Wales from June 1942 until April 1944, adds some more substance to this story:

> "There was the time I borrowed from a local D.L.I company a Bren gun carrier that I used to 'tow' four 30' G.P.O. poles across several fields to the station at Carmarthen (this was actually 6 miles south-east of Carmarthen)." (Letter to A Gabbitas, 9 January 1996; BROM Archive)

Major Jones' map shows that the station had five OUT Stations and that it was linked with the IN Station at Crwbin, further to the west, and with another station further to the east, near the border of Wiltshire and Berkshire. This station would seem to have been situated at, or in the vicinity of Coleshill House where the Auxiliary Units HQ was based.

A detailed description of the Rudry OUT Station is published on the BR Archive/CART website. The dugout, the roof of which has collapsed, is located on Forestry Commission land and the site has been fenced off. The dugout is not accessible although it is possible to get a good view down the entrance shaft and also through the partially collapsed roof. It has the size of an Anderson shelter and glazed ceramic pipes provided ventilation. The interior appears to be in good condition. (Dr Will Ward, BR Archive)

The location of another station was St Teilio's church at Llantilio Crossenny where the wireless set is said to have been hidden under the altar and the aerial clipped to the side of the church tower. Reverend Sluman operated the set, assisted by Reverends V Evans and Gower Rees. Messages would seem to have been left underneath a loose stone in the churchyard wall at St David's church in Llanddewi Rhydderch near Abergavenny. (Bernard Lowry & Mick Wilks, David Evans). The location is not marked on Major Jones' map and would hence seem to have been a SUBOUT Station.

The Langstone OUT Station was situated on Coed Y Careau Common. It was accessed through a vertical shaft leading into a Nissen hut-type shelter with end walls built from red brick. One of the operators was Arthur Allsop of Langstone Farm. Another OUT Station was hidden in a locker at <u>Newport</u> golf club.

> "I only remember constructing two OUT Stations. One was in a golf club locker at (I think) Newport golf club where the back of the locker consisted of a second (secret) door, with the batteries under the wooden floorboards in front of the locker. The <u>Bridgend</u> OUT Station was an old red GPO van situated in the middle of a large wire netting cage which housed masses of chickens. The wireless was under the floor in the back of the van, which had neither engine nor axles. I seem to remember that the old scrap van was uplifted during the night from a dump! The name of the operator was Johnson." (David Wemyss, undated letter to Arthur Gabbitas; BROM Archive)

The second IN Station in South Wales was located near the village of <u>Crwbin</u> in Carmarthenshire. Jack Millie's crew included Lance Corporal Jack Hemstock and the signalmen Dudding, Sims and Bob Cain. The station used the call-sign "Bramley" (a village in Derbyshire, Hampshire, Surrey or near Rotherham in South Yorkshire) and had six OUT Stations. No details are known about this station, which in all probability served the Carmarthen Sub-Area HQ based at Bron-y-Dre, Penllwyn Park. One of its OUT Stations is believed to have been at the boatyard in Haverfordwest in Pembrokeshire and another on the Gower peninsula in Glamorganshire.

> "The nature of hilly Wales proved a huge headache for our small power VHF static network. One day in December 1942 an OUT Station was reported flooded. Cold steady rain and east wind enough to cut you in half, when Lt *(sic)* Wemyss and myself, Jack Hemstock and DVR Murrow at the wheel set out to the station on an isolated farm on the Gemmer Pen (Gower peninsula) about 10 miles west of Swansea. I would have commandeered a two-man hand pump from the local Fire Brigade but this would have meant carrying up nearly half a mile. Wemyss said 'we will have to rescue the equipment' and it was agreed that Hemyock should go down and locate the two pegs to allow the false door to open. I would then go down to disconnect batteries and set and bring them out. 'Wait', said Wemyss, 'you can't go under there fully clothed'. It was 10' deep. 'You will have to undress', he said. We were all very cold already. Murrow was holding our clothes, down went Hemyock, I could see him fumbling and the door open.
>
> Down I went into the opening and in no time at all I had the batteries and set and gasping for air I made the trap door and up the ladder. What we didn't foresee, we had nothing to dry ourselves. 'Jump up and down', shouted Wemyss, full of ideas he was. We dressed as best we could and hurried back to the car, and the best suggestion of the day from Wemyss: 'Find the nearest pub, Murrow.' The set dried out and having been cleaned up continued to function. Wemyss must have made a report of this; less than two months later he is RTU" (returned to unit). (Letter from Jack Millie to Arthur Gabbitas, 9 January 1996; BROM Archive)

The D-Day Deception Campaign – Operation Fortitude

Throughout the war, the Allies focused much of their war effort on Operation Fortitude, a campaign which aimed at misinforming the Axis Powers. One extensive use of misinformation came before and after the assault on Normandy in June 1944, more popularly known as D-Day. The goal was to make the Germans believe that the attack would be coming at Pas de Calais, much further east and closer to England. A number of different strategies were devised to accomplish this, including extensively bombing the Calais area, using General George Patton as a commander 'decoy', and even creating a fake invasion force. There has been some speculation as to whether the Special Duties Branch was involved.

In his memoirs, Arthur Gabbitas writes that his crew (based at Lincoln at the time) were involved in what would seem to have been a spoofing exercise leading up to D-Day.

> "At the end of May 1944 we received instructions to broadcast dummy messages in code for 24 hours/day. Along with routine maintenance our group of three managed only snatched meals and short periods of sleep. After a fortnight the night of 5 June provided the climax, the air filled with the constant roar of aircraft engines. It was D-Day, June 6." (BROM Archive)

In his own memoirs, titled "Adventures of Roy Russell during World War II in the Royal Corps of Signals", the spoofing is also mentioned:

> "The time came that there was much speculation that we must soon be mounting a joint invasion of Northern France with the American forces, now building in Southern England. There was a much larger concentration in places like Salisbury Plain and the South Coast. Our tiny contribution, although I only guessed at the time, was to step up our on-air traffic. We made up hundreds of meaningless five-letter-coded group messages and transmitted them to our OUT Stations for their "dummy traffic" responses; round the clock. It was the first intimation I had that the enemy could pick up our very-high frequency; although maybe they couldn't, we'll never know. If they could it would tell them that our invasion would start from the Dover coastline. In support, their recce aircraft could have seen a concentration of tanks, landing craft and military vehicles in our area. It caused them to leave troops in the Pas de Calais that were not facing ours when D-Day came. But they were life-size blow-up dummies, even realistic when I saw them at ground level; as bogus as our surge in radio traffic." (BROM Archive)

In his book *FORTITUDE – The D-day Deception Campaign*, Roger Hesketh, who was one of the masterminds of 'Operation Fortitude', wrote:

> "By the spring of 1944 there were in the United Kingdom four separate signals organisations available to carry out the wireless deception programme of Fortitude: 'No 5 Wireless Group' to represent British land forces - '3103 Signals

Service Battalion' for American land forces - 'Fourth Army' for British formations taking part in Fortitude North and the 'CLH' units - an improvised force, later designated the 12th Reserve Unit.

"Throughout Fortitude the use of dummy traffic was forbidden on the ground that the German cryptographers might deduce from the general pattern of the groups that behind the cipher there lay nothing but a random series of letters" (page 38).

"Other plans had been laid with the sole object of lowering German vigilance during the last critical days. The periods of wireless silence and of intense wireless activity which had been instituted at the end of 1943 were intended to prevent the enemy from discovering the date of the invasion through his reading of the wireless traffic. On reflection, however, it was felt that these measures, far from confusing the enemy, might be of direct assistance to him, since a period of wireless silence would denote a period of danger. If the networks to which the enemy had become accustomed could be simulated by artificial means at a time when the real formations were embarking under a wireless silence, the chances of putting the Germans off their guard would be greatly increased.

During the month of May operators were accordingly infiltrated into the networks of all three Services in such a way that it was possible to simulate amphibious exercises in which the real assault divisions would appear to be engaged when they were, in fact, about to leave for France... Although such exercises were prepared ... it was felt when the time came ... that such exercises might encourage German air observation at the very moment when it was least wanted. The exercises were therefore cancelled" (page 122).

Guy Liddell (MI5 Deputy-Director-General under Percy Sillitoe), in his *War Diaries*, has recorded a meeting held on 13 July 1944, where a shortage of staff at the Radio Security Service had been discussed and where it had been concluded that "some of the stay-behind agents at present engaged in practice traffic may be instructed soon to begin operational traffic, the intercepting and reading of which may be of tactical or even strategic importance". A few weeks earlier, on 24 June, MI5 was involved in discussions over the deception planning but the discussion would seem to have been about the participation of some of their own agents and not of Royal Signals soldiers - the seven-day event described by Arthur Gabbitas had in any case already ended by then and D-Day too was history.

In his book *With Britain in Mortal Danger* (page 170), John Warwicker suggests that the standard Army No.17 sets which AU Signals had been issued with, were likely to be identified by the enemy, and that this would seem to have been deliberately useful in the final SD role as part of the successful deception campaign aimed to convince the German High Command of the presence in East Anglia of an (in reality entirely fictional) American Army. In *Churchill's Secret Army* (page 202), a whole chapter - titled "An Inside Story" - is devoted to detailing Roy Russell's activities during this time. There also is a reference to the deception programme orchestrated by the London Controlling Section, and of AU Signals in the south-east of England playing their small part by stepping up the volume of on-air traffic: "less sophisticated War Department

No.17 sets were also issued to selected SD networks, their traffic being deliberately intended to be detectable by the enemy". Lincolnshire however, where Arthur Gabbitas was based at this time, is not in the south-east of England and neither is it part of East Anglia.

According to Captain Ken Ward, the WS17 set was never used for this kind of communication: "the WS17 was used for communicating from the "Met" huts back to Army/Divisional HQ when it was realised that the static Divisional HQ might move away, and that was when the WS17 set came in". (John Warwicker interview dated 10 August 1999, audio tape 29472; IWM)

Apart from Arthur Gabbitas's and Roy Russells' recollections, no other historical sources mention anything other than the Home Forces exercise which involved standard Army units – not the Special Duties Branch. No information was found which would substantiate suggestions that the SD had indeed been involved in the D-Day deception plans. Neither Arthur Gabbitas nor Roy Russell mention WS17 sets nor do they say which sets they used. Be that as it may, it would seem to have been established that at least some of the Army units participating in the deception campaign used a special version of the WS19 set, known as the WS19 SPF.

In his book *Deception in World War 2* (1979) Charles G Cruickshank writes:

> "The enemy listened to every message passed on the air and knew quite well that there was the possibility that he was being taken for a ride. Security therefore had to be perfect. Therefore, the messages sent were constructed with considerable attention to detail and contained information expected from such an operation. A single careless mistake in operation, or careless talk with those who were not in on the secret, could give away the whole deception".

If the AU Signals crews had indeed made up and transmitted "hundreds of meaningless five-letter-coded group messages", as Roy Russell said they did, their messages would appear to have been literally meaningless and certainly did not fit in with the overall scheme. It is perhaps also worth noting that none of the veterans knew of or reported subsequently that what they remember doing was part of any spoofing operation to do with D-Day. Because Army wireless operators are trained in 'voice procedure' which takes a lot of practice to get it right and where the use of specific key words and a certain word order are mandatory, it can reasonably be assumed, at least, that neither the AU ATS nor the civilian OUT Station operators ever had any part in the spoofing exercise, as their wireless traffic would immediately have been recognised as non-Army. In this context, it is interesting to note that the Germans not only knew about the WS17, but, not surprisingly, that they had captured some, presumably from Searchlight batteries in overseas territories, and they also knew what they were used for, ie for linking searchlight batteries with individual searchlight sites. It would for this reason seem unlikely for them to be fooled into thinking that extra WS17 traffic would imply an Army build-up in some part of the UK.

The British Resistance Organisation Museum at Parham

Colonel JW Stuart Edmondson formally opened the BRO Museum on 30 August 1997, which to date is the only museum in Britain dedicated to the men and women who served in the various sections of the Auxiliary Units. It is situated on the now disused Parham airfield at Silverlace Green, approximately two kilometres to the east of the village of Parham, adjoining the 390th Bombardment Group Memorial Museum housed in the airfield's control tower. The museum is sign-posted "Air Museum" from the A12 road to the north of Woodbridge, after passing through Little Glemham.

The museum is housed in Nissen huts and includes a unique and rare collection of exhibits ranging from Auxiliary Units' weapons and original examples of time pencils, fuses to the crimping mechanism of explosives with which the men were familiar. The collection also includes uniforms, photographs of patrols and their officers, examples of dead-letter boxes, intelligence instruction dossiers as well as many other Auxiliary Units-related items that have over time been donated by former patrol members or their families. Pride of place is taken by a reconstructed TRD wireless set. Practical details of the wireless communications network installed by the Auxiliary Units Signals can also be seen.

A reconstructed operational base - based upon the nearby OB once used by Stratford St Andrew Patrol, which has long since become inaccessible - was opened in 2004. Visitors are able to tour this exhibit and hence able to experience for themselves the cramped conditions that the Auxiliers had to work in.

If you have skills or interests which you think could help the museum and can spare a few hours a week, please contact them.

390th Bomb Group Memorial Air Museum & The Museum of the British Resistance Organisation

Parham Airfield
Parham
Framlingham
IP13 9AF
Suffolk
England

Phone - 01728 621373

Museum buildings and the former control tower,
which houses the 390th Bomb Group Memorial Air Museum

Appendix A

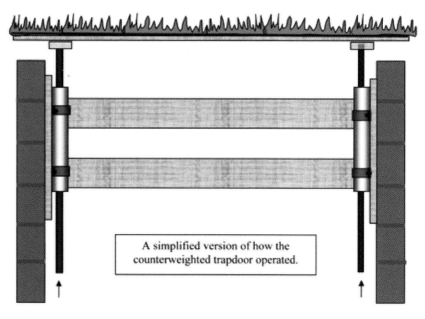

A simplified version of how the counterweighted trapdoor operated.

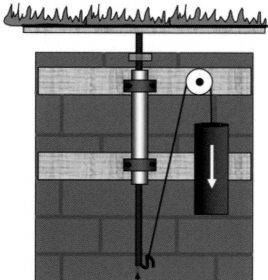

Side View

Appendix B

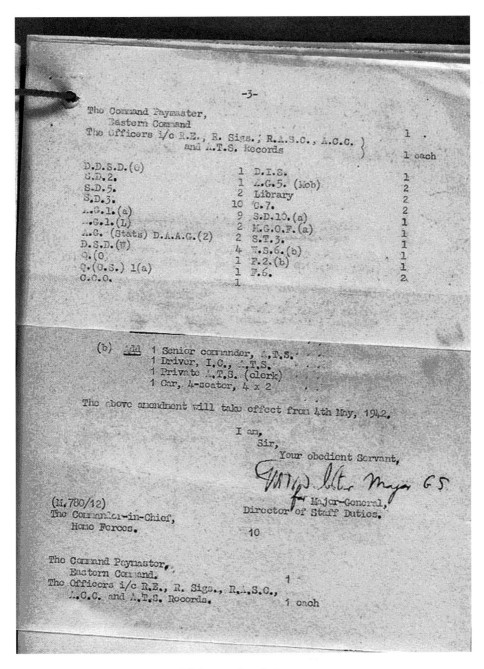

-3-

The Command Paymaster,
   Eastern Command
The Officers i/c R.E., R. Sigs.; R.A.S.C., A.C.C. }   1
         and A.T.S. Records   }   1 each

D.D.S.D.(0)	1	D.I.S.	1
S.D.2.	1	A.G.5. (Mob)	2
S.D.5.	2	Library	2
S.D.3.	10	C.7.	2
A.G.1.(a)	9	S.D.10.(a)	1
A.G.1.(L)	2	M.G.O.F.(a)	1
A.G. (Stats) D.A.A.G.(2)	2	S.T.3.	1
D.S.D.(W)	4	T.S.6.(b)	1
Q.(O	1	F.2.(b)	1
Q.(O.S.) 1(a)	1	F.6.	2
C.C.O.	1		

(b) <u>Add</u> 1 Senior commander, A.T.S.
        1 Driver, I.C., A.T.S.
        1 Private A.T.S. (clerk)
        1 Car, 4-seater, 4 x 2

The above amendment will take effect from 4th May, 1942.

            I am,
               Sir,
                   Your obedient Servant,

                                Major-General,
(M.780/12)   Director of Staff Duties.
The Commander-in-Chief,
    Home Forces.   10

The Command Paymaster,
    Eastern Command.   1
The Officers i/c R.E., R. Sigs., R.A.S.C.,
    A.C.C. and A.T.S. Records.   1 each

Amendment to the SD War Establishment dated May 1942

Appendix C

collected at IN Stations (manned by R. Sigs or by ATS offrs), and is passed from there to mil fmn.

For training and administrative purposes, the Sigs organisation in the country is divided into areas which closely correspond to existing Command areas. In each area there is a Sigs offr in charge, with a small headquarters of 1 Sgt, 1 Instrument Mechanic and 1 Driver. In the area there are a varying number of maintenance parties (3 men each); total maintenance strength in areas varying from 6 to 9 men. These maintenance parties are responsible for manning an IN Station, and for maintaining all OUT and SUBOUT Stations in their own areas.

The Signals HQ is at COLESHILL, where there is a small adm staff (CQMS, etc.) and a small workshops where major repairs and special work is done.

(c) Sites

All OUT Stations and SUBOUT Stations (i.e., those manned by civilians) and nearly all IN Stations are concealed, so that they could continue to function even though the area in which they were situated was occupied by the enemy.

OUT and SUBOUT Stations are either concealed in hidden dugouts, or in dummy walls of houses, sheds, etc.

IN Stations have concealed dugouts in which station crew can, if necessary, live without coming above ground at all for three weeks at a time. This includes provision for battery charging, feeding, etc.

3. ESTABLISHMENTS

		Offrs	O.R's					
			CQMS	Sgts	Cpls	Sgmn	Dvrs or Ptes	Total O.R's
(a) MALE	R. Sigs	7	1	7	20	41	-	69
	RASC						10	10
(b) FEMALE	ATS	57					3	3

4. STRENGTHS

		Offrs	O.R's					
			CQMS	Sgts	Cpls	Sgmn	Dvrs or Ptes	Total O.R's
(a) MALE	R. Sigs	8	1	6	18	43	-	68
	RASC						10	10
(b) FEMALE	ATS	55					3	3

Copy of latest Strength Return at Appx 'B'
Nominal Roll of R. Sigs by trades at Appx 'C'

5. EQUIPMENT

(a) Wireless   250 TRD sets)   Specially built, either in the HQ
             28 TRM sets)   workshop, or by contract. See Appx
             36 TRF sets)   'D' for general description
            200 No.17 sets

     Total   514

Excerpt from Major RMA Jones' report dated 28 June 1944. The complete document is held by the National Archives, ref: WO 199/1194)

Appendix D

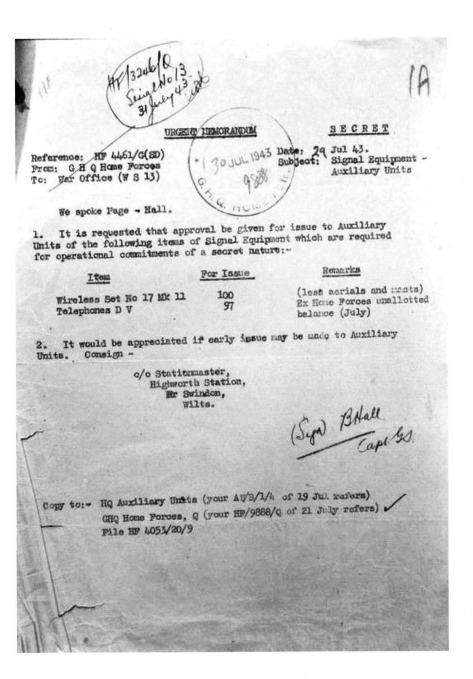

URGENT MEMORANDUM

Reference: HF 4461/G(SD)
From: G H Q Home Forces
To: War Office (W S 13)

Date: 29 Jul 43.
Subject: Signal Equipment –
Auxiliary Units

We spoke Page – Hall.

1. It is requested that approval be given for issue to Auxiliary Units of the following items of Signal Equipment which are required for operational commitments of a secret nature:-

Item	For Issue	Remarks
Wireless Set No 17 Mk 11	100	(less aerials and masts)
Telephones D V	97	Ex Home Forces unallotted balance (July)

2. It would be appreciated if early issue may be made to Auxiliary Units. Consign –

> c/o Stationmaster,
> Highworth Station,
> Nr Swindon,
> Wilts.

(Sgd) B Hall
Capt GS.

Copy to:- HQ Auxiliary Units (your AU/B/1/4 of 19 Jul refers)
GHQ Home Forces, Q (your HF/9888/Q of 21 July refers)
File HF 4053/20/9

More than 200 WS17 sets were requested by AU HQ during 1943 (TNA, WO 199/936)

Index of Wireless Stations used by the Special Duties Branch

(The place names printed in capital letters refer to IN Stations)

In his report dated 28 June 1944, Major Jones states that the wireless network at that time consisted of 30 IN, 125 OUT and 78 SUBOUT Stations. The above list contains the names of 176 known locations of SD wireless stations - the remaining 56, mainly SUBOUT stations, have as yet to be found.

Bibliography

Field Marshal Lord Alanbrooke, *War Diaries 1939-1945* (Phoenix 2002)

Stewart Angell: *The Secret Sussex Resistance* (Middleton Press 1996)

Colin Burbidge: *Preserving the Flame* (YouWriteOn.com 2008)

Charles G Cruickshank: *Deception in World War 2* (Oxford University Press UK 1979)

Peter Fleming: *Invasion 1940* (Panther Books Ltd 1959)

Donald Hamilton Hill: *SOE Assignment* (New English Library 1975)

John Middleton Harwood & Stuart McMillan: *Defence of the UK – Whitby* (Momentous Books 2008)

Roger Hesketh: *The D-Day Deception Campaign* (St Ermine's Press 1999)

David Lampe: *The Last Ditch* (Cassell and Co 1968)

Bernard Lowry & Mick Wilks: *The Mercian Macquis* (Logaston Press 2002)

Major N.V. Oxenden MC: *Auxiliary Units History and Achievement 1940-1944* (Reproduction of an original document published by the Parham Air Museum)

Roy Pryce: *Heathfield Park – a Private Estate and a Wealden Town* (Roy Pryce 1996)

Anthony Quayle: *A Time to Speak* (Berrie & Jenkins 1990)

Nicholas Rankin: *Ian Fleming's Commandos* (Faber and Faber Ltd 2011)

Evelyn Simak & Adrian Pye: *Churchill's Secret Army in Norfolk and Suffolk, Including Special Duties Branch* (aspye 2013)

Derek Warren: *Now You See It – Then You Didn't* (Somerset Industrial Archaeology Society 2000)

John W Warwicker: *Churchill's Underground Army* (Frontline Books 2008)

John W Warwicker: *With Britain in Mortal Danger* (Cerberus Publishing Ltd 2002)

Peter Wilkinson & Joan Bright Astley: *Gubbins & SOE* (Pen & Sword Paperback 1997)

Alan Williamson: *East Ridings Secret Resistance* (Middleton Press 2004)

Peter Wright: *Spycatcher* (Viking Penguin 1987)